BUILDING STRONG BRANDS

David A. Aaker

BUILDING STRONG BRANDS

FREE PRESS
BUSINESS

This paperback edition first published by
Simon & Schuster UK Ltd, 2002
A CBS COMPANY

7 9 10 8 6

Simon & Schuster UK Ltd
Africa House
Kingsway
London WC3B 6AH

www.simonsays.co.uk

Simon & Schuster Australia
Sydney

A CIP catalogue record for this book
is available from the British Library

ISBN 0–7432–3213–5

Printed and bound in Great Britain by
CPI Bath Press, Bath

CONTENTS

PREFACE

My book *Managing Brand Equity*, also published by The Free Press, set forth the perspective that a brand is a strategic asset that is key to long-term performance and should be so managed. That book helped to explain what brand equity is and how it contributes value. A brand equity structure was developed that included the four dimensions of awareness, perceived quality, loyalty, and associations. That book also discussed the role of the brand name and its symbols, explored issues surrounding brand extension decisions, and reviewed global brand strategies.

Since the time that *Managing Brand Equity* appeared, I have been involved, through my research and consulting, in several areas that were not addressed in any detail in that book. With the encouragement of Bob Wallace, my Free Press publisher, it seemed that a sequel was in order to explore these new issues.

There are five major themes to *Building Strong Brands*. First, the book delves into what *brand identity* is and how it can be developed. While a brand image is how a brand is perceived, a brand identity is aspirational—how the brand would like to be perceived. A common pitfall when creating brand identities is to focus on product-related brand characteristics. In this book, brand strategists are encouraged to break out of that box by considering emotional and self-expressive benefits, organizational attributes, brand personality, and brand symbols as well. In taking the broader view of the brand, the likelihood of creating real differentiating value is enhanced.

The second theme, *managing the brand identity*, involves developing a brand position (that part of the identity which is to be actively communicated) and an execution program. It also involves balancing the need to adapt to a changing environment with the power of consistent messages and symbols. There are powerful forces for change that sometimes should be resisted.

The third theme, centered around the concept of a *brand system*, adds a new dimension to the management of brands. A brand system—consisting of intertwined and overlapping brands and sub-brands—can create clarity and synergies, or it can generate confusion and inconsistency. The brand system view leads to an analysis of the different roles that a brand can play. In particular, a brand or sub-brand, in addition to driving a business area, can also play a role in supporting other brands or in providing clarity to customers. Another set of systems issues involves leveraging the brand via vertical or horizontal brand extensions, creating brands that range over product classes, and co-branding. The brand systems audit is introduced as a way to start managing brands as a system.

Fourth, an approach to *brand equity measurement* across products and segments is presented. Measurement is of practical interest to most managers attempting to build and manage multiple markets and brands, and it also provides a quantitative discipline to the conceptual branding models.

Fifth, *brand-nurturing organizational forms* are discussed. Brand building now needs to deal with brand systems issues and with problems of coordinating a brand across markets, products, roles and contexts. These challenges strain conventional organizations, and new approaches are often needed.

In addition, the *Saturn brand-building story* illustrates many of the issues and approaches raised in the book. I have become close to the Saturn project and have grown to believe that it is one of the most impressive examples of brand building in recent years.

As in *Managing Brand Equity*, conceptual models and issues in this book are illustrated with case studies and examples. I believe abstract models need to be placed in illustrative contexts in order to provide clarity and to stimulate new ways of looking at brands and their management. Further, where possible, academic research is drawn on to support hypotheses of how the process being discussed or modeled really works. Because I do not presume that all readers have read

Managing Brand Equity, some key concepts from that work are repeated, but the overlap involves considerably less than 5 percent of this book. References are occasionally made to material covered in detail in *Managing Brand Equity*.

ACKNOWLEDGMENTS

There are many who contributed to this book. I owe special thanks to Kent Grayson of the London Business School, who read the first draft and made numerous detailed comments and suggestions. I have benefited from stimulating conversations with Scott Talgo of the St. James Group, who contributed substantially to the core model developed in Chapter 3. My able assistant and editor extraordinaire, Carol Chapman, patiently helped provide extra polish. At the Free Press, Catherine Wayland cheerfully helped in a multitude of ways, and Celia Knight kept the book moving along.

My thoughts and the book have also benefited from sometimes intense discussion with some very insightful people in academia and industry that I respect, such as Kevin Lane Keller of North Carolina, Jennifer Aaker of UCLA, Roberto Alvarez of ESADE and the Haas School of Business, Bob Ellis at Hal Riney, Peter Sealey, now associated with Sony and the Haas School of Business, Steve Weisz of Marriott, Duane Knapp of Brand Strategies, Jeff Sinclair of the St. James Group, Rick Lightburn of McDonald's, Andrew Stodart of IDV, Janet Brady of Clorox, Bruce Jeffries-Fox at AT&T, Peter Georgescu and Stuart Agres at Young and Rubicam, Alexander Biel of Alexander Biel Associates, and my colleagues at the Haas School.

I had help on the manuscript from some outstanding students including Diane Gabianelli, Joan Kauffman, John Somerville, John Friedman, Beth Ulman, Vincent Weller, Jeff Yin, Tim Teirry, Ross van Woert, Satoshi Akutsu, Nicholas Lurie, Jane Liou, and Marcy Porus, and from a superb copyeditor, Chris Kelly.

Finally, I want to thank Bob Wallace of The Free Press for his encouragement and his positive attitude about me and my projects. And I especially want to thank my family, who supported yet another writing project.

1
WHAT IS A STRONG BRAND?

What do you need to be the best?
Concentration. Discipline. A dream.
  —Florence Griffith Joyner, Olympic gold medalist

An orange . . . is an orange . . . is an orange. Unless, or course, that orange happens to be a Sunkist, a name eighty percent of consumers know and trust.
  —Russell L. Hanlin, CEO, Sunkist Growers

THE KODAK STORY

In the 1870s, a photographer's outfit included not only a large camera but also a sturdy tripod, glass plates, a big plate holder, a dark tent, a nitrate bath, and a water container.[1] You did not bring just a camera to take a picture; you brought the whole lab.

All this was to change, thanks to George Eastman. Eastman founded a company that has had major worldwide influence almost since its inception. To initiate and maintain an organization with such clout, Eastman required a variety of resources, including the intelligence to develop new processes, a good business sense, and a willingness to take risks. But it is unlikely that Eastman's success could have been achieved without his strong brand: Kodak.

Kodak, with its block letters and bright yellow background, has been used for over a hundred years to crystallize and communicate the essence of Eastman's products and organization. The brand (and the company it represents) survives today primarily because of four factors: a commitment to quality, the generation of awareness, the fostering of loyalty, and—most important—the development of a strong and clear brand identity.

Eastman's commitment to quality was evident even in his first product introduction. In the late 1870s, he developed a patent for a "dry" plate that promised to greatly simplify the photographic process. The Eastman plates soon became known for superior results, particularly in weak light and with long exposures. A year after their introduction, however, trouble with a component caused some plates to lose sensitivity. Eastman's financially risky insistence on recalling the plates reflected his understanding that product quality was the fastest route to customer satisfaction. It also helped to initiate customer associations between the Kodak brand and quality, associations that persist today.

For Eastman's company, quality also meant ease of use. Over the years Kodak was associated repeatedly with photography products that produced reliable results without much effort on the consumer's part. In 1888, Eastman began marketing a camera that made photography accessible to all, not just to the committed artist. The camera, which sold for twenty-five dollars, had none of the laboratory accessories usually associated with photography of the day: The novice had only to "pull the cord, turn the key, and press the button." For another ten dollars the pictures would be developed and new film reloaded at a "modern," efficient facility in Rochester, New York.

One of Kodak's first ads, run in 1888, served to position the firm for the next century. It showed a picture of a hand holding a camera, with a headline written by Eastman: "You press the button, we do the rest" (see Figure 1–1). The camera delivered on the promise—and many Kodak products since have carried on in its spirit. The folding Kodak, introduced in 1890, was easier to carry and preceded the Kodak Brownie, a simple camera launched at the turn of the century that became the company's staple product for almost eighty years. More recently, the tradition has continued with the Instamatic (an easy-to-load camera with flash cubes), introduced in 1963, and the disposable Kodak FunSaver (which is returned to photofinishers, who process the film and recycle the camera), introduced in 1988.

One by-product of such consistent long-term quality and innovation was increased awareness of the Kodak name. Promotions, advertising, and a ubiquitous logo also did their part to build awareness for Kodak. In 1897, Kodak sponsored an amateur photographic competition in which twenty-five thousand people participated. In 1904, the company sponsored the Traveling Grand Kodak Exhibition of forty-one photographs. In 1920, it found scenic spots along highways and erected small "Picture Ahead!" road signs to alert motorists. The result of such efforts plus ongoing advertising campaigns has been to increase consumers' familiarity with the Kodak name and its yellow signature logo. Few people can see the Kodak symbols without the positive feelings that accompany the familiar, and one of the first things that come to mind when the subject of cameras, film, or family photos is raised is the word *Kodak*.

Kodak's strong awareness and presence worldwide can also be attributed to an early decision to distribute its products outside the United States. Only five years after the Kodak camera was introduced in the United States, a sales office was opened in London, and it was quickly followed by offices throughout Europe. In 1930, Kodak had 75 percent of the world market for photographic equipment and about 90 percent of the profit. This dominance has decreased very little over the years.

FIGURE 1–1
An 1888 Kodak Advertisement

The Kodak Camera

"You press the button, -
- - - we do the rest."

The only camera that anybody can use without instructions.   Send for the Primer free.

A Transparent Film

For Roll Holders.

The announcement is hereby made that the undersigned have perfected a process for making transparent flexible films for use in roll holders and Kodak Cameras.

The new film is as thin, light and flexible as paper and as transparent as glass.   It requires *no stripping*, and it is wound on spools for roll holders.

It will be known as *Eastman's Transparent Film*.   Circulars and samples will be sent to any address on receipt of 4 cents in stamps.

Price $25.00—Loaded for 100 Pictures.

The Eastman Dry Plate and Film Co.

ROCHESTER, N. Y.

Reprinted courtesy Eastman Kodak Company.

Kodak has a set of associations that provides a distinct image and the basis for a loyal relationship. The strong Kodak identity, backed by decades of products and marketing, can be summed up with two words: simplicity (supported primarily by product features) and family (supported primarily by marketing communications and visual imagery).

Around the turn of the century, Kodak introduced two characters—the Brownie boy and the Kodak girl—to represent its products. They created not only a sense that the camera was easy to operate (because even a child could use it), but also an association with children and family. Kodak's early advertisements showed settings that could be easily recorded on film, especially family scenes with children, dogs, and friends (see the 1922 advertisement in Figure 1–2). During the Kodak hour heard on radio in the 1930s, listeners might hear family photo albums described. A 1967 award-winning Kodak commercial featured a couple in their sixties cleaning the attic. They find a carton of old snapshots showing them in their twenties and in the years that followed—getting married, enjoying their honeymoon, having their first child, and attending the graduation of their son. The commercial ends with the woman, now a grandmother, running to grab an Instamatic to take a picture of her new grandchild.

Because of repeated marketing efforts like these—supported by an unmatchable set of quality products—consumers have come to view Kodak as a family friend who is always around to help enjoy the good times. This image has been a key factor in cementing customer loyalty for Kodak.

An indication of Kodak customer loyalty is the brand's resilience in the face of misfortune. For example, the Kodak Instant Camera (introduced in 1976 to compete with Polaroid) had captured one-third of the instant camera market after one year. However, the company was forced to discontinue the product in 1986 after a successful patent encroachment suit by Polaroid. Kodak's forced withdrawal of a product from a market it virtually owned is about as bad as it gets. Many brands would have been irrevocably tainted by such a calamity. The fact that Kodak survived this debacle is a tribute to its innate brand strength and to its handling of a painful situation. Every camera owner was invited to return their Kodak Instant Camera in exchange for either a Kodak Disk Camera and film, fifty dollars' worth of other Kodak products, or a share of Kodak stock. Kodak thus used the incident and the surrounding communication opportunities to reinforce Kodak associations and to support the Disk Camera.

Contexts change, though, even for Kodak. Its challenge for the next century is to stretch the Kodak brand name, known for traditional

FIGURE 1–2
Kodak 1922 Ad

Keep the story with a KODAK

Today it's a picture of Grandmother reading to the children. Tomorrow it may be Bobbie playing traffic policeman or Aunt Edna at the wheel of her new car or Brother Bill back from college for the week-end or—

There's always another story waiting for your Kodak.

Free at your dealer's or from us—"At Home with the Kodak," a well illustrated little book that will help in picture-making at your house.

Autographic Kodaks *$6.50 up*

Eastman Kodak Company, Rochester, N. Y. *The Kodak City* cameras and films, into the world of digital imagery, which is expected to become the company's prime business area. The Kodak name, with its tradition and connection with special times and family scenes, will need to adapt to an innovative, high-tech image to support products such as the Photo CD (which will store photographic images digitally and play them back on a computer) and the CopyPrint (which will instantly provide large copies from a print without a negative). This need to adapt, faced by a host of strong brands in different markets, is discussed in detail in Chapter 7.

Another problem faced by Kodak is aggressive price competition in the film business, coming in part from private-label (or "retail") brands. One Kodak response has been to offer three versions of its film: Royal Gold, a premium film for special events; GoldPlus, the everyday Kodak film; and FunTime, a lower-priced, seasonal brand targeted at bargain shoppers. The efforts of Kodak and other firms to move brands both up and down to react to deteriorating markets will be covered in Chapter 9.

Today, several studies suggest that Kodak is one of the world's strongest brands. In the film category, where the bulk of Kodak's sales and profits reside, the brand enjoys both a U.S. market share of around 60 percent and a substantial price premium over Fuji, its principal rival. In addition, Kodak is aggressively expanding its presence in the worldwide market, in which it holds a 40 percent share.

The Kodak story shows how brand equity can be created and managed. This chapter provides an overview of brand equity and, in so doing, expands on the conceptualization that was first offered in my book *Managing Brand Equity*. Although the conceptualization is the same, new research, case studies, and perspectives have been added. Chapter 1 also sets the stage for the key points that will be made in this book about building strong brands. The chapter's final section includes some observations about why it is so difficult to build strong brands in today's dynamic, competitive marketplaces.

WHAT IS BRAND EQUITY?

Brand equity is a set of assets (and liabilities) linked to a brand's name and symbol that adds to (or subtracts from) the value provided by a product or service to a firm and/or that firm's customers. The major asset categories are:

1. *Brand name awareness*
2. *Brand loyalty*
3. *Perceived quality*
4. *Brand associations*

Several aspects of the definition deserve elaboration. First, brand equity is a set of assets. Thus, the management of brand equity involves investment to create and enhance these assets. Figure 1–3, drawn from and discussed in *Managing Brand Equity*, provides a compact overview of how brand equity generates value. (Note that a fifth category of assets, other proprietary assets, is included for completeness in Figure 1–3. This category is meant to cover assets such as channel relationships and patents that are attached to the brand.)

Second, each brand equity asset creates value in a variety of very different ways (seventeen are actually listed in the figure). In order to manage brand equity effectively and to make informed decisions about brand-building activities, it is important to be sensitive to the ways in which strong brands create value.

Third, brand equity creates value for the customer as well as the firm. The word customer refers to both end users and those at the infrastructure level. Thus, Hilton needs to be concerned with its image among not only consumers who travel, but also travel agents. And Coke's image among retailers—particularly its perceived customer acceptance—can be critical to market success.

Finally, for assets or liabilities to underlie brand equity, they must be linked to the name and symbol of the brand. If the brand's name or symbols should change, some or all of the assets or liabilities could be affected and even lost, although some might be shifted to the new name and symbol.

Several observations will be made below about each of the four principal brand asset categories that will serve to recap, extend, and update the extensive discussion that appeared in *Managing Brand Equity*. The intent is to provide an understanding about exactly how each category underlies brand equity.

FIGURE 1-3
How Brand Equity Generates Value

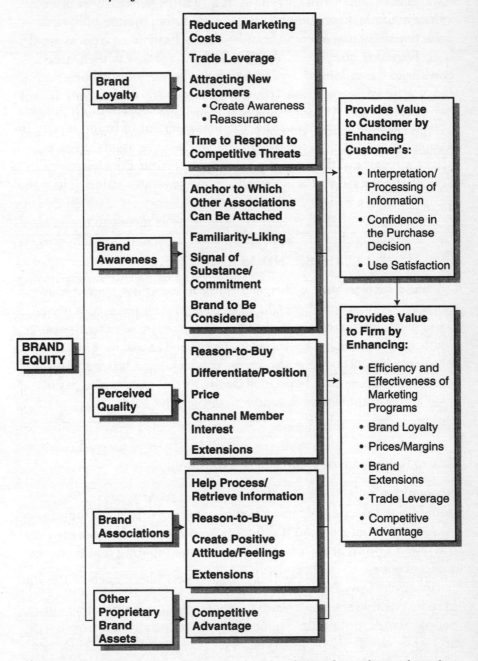

From *Managing Brand Equity: Capitalizing on the Value of a Brand Name* by David A. Aaker.
Copyright © 1991 by David A. Aaker. Reprinted with permission of The Free Press, a Division of
Simon & Schuster Inc.

BRAND AWARENESS

Awareness refers to the strength of a brand's presence in the consumer's mind. If consumers' minds were full of mental billboards—each one depicting a single brand—then a brand's awareness would be reflected in the size of its billboard. Awareness is measured according to the different ways in which consumers remember a brand, ranging from recognition (Have you been exposed to this brand before?) to recall (What brands of this product class can you recall?) to "top of mind" (the first brand recalled) to dominant (the only brand recalled). As psychologists and economists have long understood, however, recognition and recall are signals of much more than just remembering a brand.

THE BRAND AS A MENTAL BOX

A brand such as Mr. Goodwrench is much like a "box" in someone's head. As information about GM service programs is received, a person will file it away in the box labeled Mr. Goodwrench. After time passes, little in the box might be retrievable. The person knows, however, if it is heavy or light. He or she also knows in which room it is stored—the room with the positive boxes (that is, objects that have earned positive feelings and attitudes) or the one with the negative boxes.

BRAND RECOGNITION: FAMILIARITY AND LIKING

Recognition reflects familiarity gained from past exposure. Recognition does not necessarily involve remembering *where* the brand was encountered before, *why* it differs from other brands, or even *what* the brand's product class is. It is simply remembering that there was a past exposure to the brand.

Research in psychology has shown that recognition alone can result in more positive feelings toward nearly anything, whether it be music, people, words, or brands. Studies have demonstrated that, even with nonsense words (like "postryna" vs. "potastin" for example), consumers instinctively prefer an item they have previously seen to one that is new to them. Thus, when a brand choice is made—even when the decision involves products like computers or advertising agencies—the familiar brand will have an edge.

In a study that dramatically demonstrated the power of a recognized brand name, respondents were asked to taste each of three samples of peanut butter.[2] One of these samples contained an unnamed superior (preferred in blind taste tests 70 percent of the time) peanut butter. Another contained an inferior (*not* preferred in taste tests) peanut butter labeled with a brand name known to the respondents but neither purchased nor used by them before. Remarkably, 73 percent of the respondents selected the brand-name (inferior) option as being the best-tasting peanut butter. Thus the fact that a name was recognized affected what should have been a very objective taste test, making the peanut butter with a known brand name seem to taste better.

Economists tell us that consumer affinity for the familiar brand is not just an instinctive response. When consumers see a brand and remember that they have seen it before (perhaps even several times), they realize that the company is spending money to support the brand. Since it is generally believed that companies will not spend money on bad products, consumers take their recognition as a "signal" that the brand is good. How a company can use such signaling to its advantage is illustrated by the "Intel Inside" program described in the boxed insert.

The familiarity factor can be especially important to the brand that has a familiarity handicap with respect to more visible and established competitors. In such a case, awareness-building may be necessary to reduce this liability.

BRAND RECALL AND THE GRAVEYARD

A brand (for example, MetLife) is said to have recall if it comes to consumers' minds when its product class (for example, life insurance companies) is mentioned. Whether or not a customer recalls your brand can be the deciding factor in getting on a shopping list or receiving a chance to bid on a contract.

The relative power of recall (versus recognition) is shown in Figure 1–5, which depicts the "graveyard model" developed by Young and Rubicam Europe under the guidance of Jim Williams. In this model, brands in a product class are plotted on a recognition versus recall

INTEL INSIDE

Intel makes microprocessors, which are the heart of personal computers. Their successive product generations were called the 8086, 286, 386, and 486 microprocessors. Unfortunately, Intel did not obtain trademark protection on its numbering system, and thus the 386 and 486 names were available to competitors such as AMD, Chips and Technologies, and Cyrix who made their own chips and applied the X86 name to them.

Intel responded in 1991 by encouraging computer firms like IBM, Compaq, Gateway, and Dell to put the "Intel Inside" logo in their ads and on their packages. The enticement was a cooperative advertising allowance from Intel amounting to 3 percent of the companies' Intel purchases (5 percent if they used the logo on packaging). An Intel Inside ad is shown in Figure 1–4.

The campaign, which was initially budgeted at $100 million per year, worked on several levels. It generated more than ninety thousand pages of ads in an eighteen-month period, which translated to a potential 10 billion exposures. During that period, the recognition of Intel among business end users increased from 46 percent to 80 percent, the same level that Nutrasweet enjoyed among consumers after years of exposure of the Nutrasweet logo. The brand equity of Intel, as measured by the price discount needed to get a customer to accept a computer without an Intel microprocessor, appeared to be positively affected. During 1992, the first full year of the Intel Inside campaign, Intel's worldwide sales rose 63 percent.

Why should the Intel Inside program make a difference to consumers? No reason was provided as to why an Intel microprocessor was

graph. For example, the recall and recognition of each of twenty automobile brands could be measured, and these measurements could be used to position each brand on the graph. One finding consistent across dozens of product classes is that brands tend to follow the curved line shown in the figure. There are two exceptions, each of which reveals the importance of recall.

One exception is healthy niche brands, which fall below the line because they are not known to a substantial group of consumers, and therefore have relatively low overall recognition. But because they do better. In fact, it is likely that many customers did not even know what a microprocessor was.

A customer's logic might have been something like this: Computer makers, including industry leaders like IBM and Compaq, are expending a lot of money and effort to tell me that Intel makes a part of this computer. These people are not dumb. Therefore the component must be an important one, and Intel must be a good supplier. I could do some research to determine what a microprocessor is and how much better Intel is than its competitors, or I could just pay a little more and get Intel. An easy decision—I will simply rely on the reassurance of the Intel brand name.

Interestingly, the Intel Inside campaign actually originated in Japan, where Matsushita used it as a way to build high-tech credibility for its computers. Japan is a country in which the prestige and visibility of corporate names is extremely important. By building up the Intel corporate name, Matsushita created credibility for itself.

(A postscript: The Pentium chip, which succeeded the 486 in late 1994, was found to make some arithmetic errors under certain conditions. Instead of immediately acknowledging the error and offering to replace the involved products—few customers may have actually gone through the bother—Intel claimed the problem was rare and could be ignored. Intel belatedly did adopt a customer-oriented return policy, but only after a storm of damaging protest from the press and the public. Because Intel's equity was based on awareness and the presumption that a customer did not have to know what happens "inside," the incident had considerable potential for damage. Although initial sales were not affected, recovering from the incident presents a challenge for Intel.)

have high recall among their respective loyal customer groups, their low recognition is not necessarily an indication of poor performance. And healthy niche players sometimes have the potential to expand recognition and thus the scope of their customer base.

The second exception is the graveyard, an area in the upper-left-hand corner populated by brands with high recognition but low recall. Being in the graveyard can be deadly: Customers know about the brand, but it will not come to mind when considering a purchase. Breaking out of the graveyard can actually be hindered by high recog-

FIGURE 1-4
Intel Inside Ad

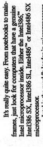

How to spot the very best computers.

It's really quite easy. From notebooks to main-frames, just look for computers that have a genuine Intel microprocessor inside. Either the Intel386,™ Intel386 SX, Intel386 SL, Intel486™ or Intel486 SX microprocessor.

Intel is the world's leader in microprocessor design and development. And no other microprocessors have a larger installed base of software. Plus, every chip is literally put through millions of tests. So with Intel inside, you know you've got unquestioned com-

patibility and unparalleled quality. Or simply put, the very best computer technology.

So look for the Intel Inside symbol on ads for leading computers. Or call 800-548-4725. It'll show you've got an eye for spotting the best.

intel.

The Computer Inside.™

Reproduced with permission of Intel Corporation.

FIGURE 1–5

Recognition Versus Recall: The Graveyard Model

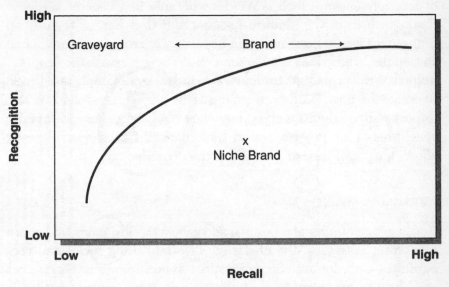

nition, because there is little reason for people to listen to a story (however new) about a familiar brand. One point of the graveyard model is that high recognition is not necessarily the mark of a strong brand—it is associated with weak ones as well.

The dynamics of brands located in the upper-middle or upper-right part of the figure can be important predictors of future brand health. Movement toward the graveyard is associated with sliding sales and market share. If, however, the brand is moving away from the graveyard, sales and market share can be expected to increase. Thus the graveyard model provides evidence that recall is as important as recognition.

BRAND NAME DOMINANCE

The ultimate awareness level is brand name dominance where, in a recall task, most customers can only provide the name of a single brand—e.g., A-1 Steak Sauce, Kleenex, Xerox, Jell-O. Ironically, this ultimate success can be tragic if the brand name becomes such a common label for the product that it is not legally protectable and is lost. Such a fate occurred with Aspirin, Cellophane, Escalator, and Windsurfer.

In order to avoid losing a trademark, a firm should begin protecting it early in its life, starting with the selection of the name itself. Beware of descriptive names such as Windows because they become harder to distinguish from the generic product and thus harder to protect. Sometimes it is helpful and even necessary to create a generic name so that the brand does not become one. The generic name "copier" helped Xerox protect its trademark. Windsurfer belatedly attempted to create the term "sailboard" to mean the generic product. It is also important to be rigorous about how the brand name is used. Chrysler states that "Jeep is a registered trademark of Chrysler" and never allows the use of Jeep to describe a type of product.

CREATING AWARENESS

Because consumers are bombarded every day by more and more marketing messages, the challenge of establishing recall and rec-ognition—and doing so economically—is considerable. Two factors are likely to be increasingly important as firms struggle with this challenge.

First, given the resources required to create healthy awareness levels, a broad sales base is usually an enormous asset. It is expensive and often impossible to support brands with relatively small unit sales and a life measured in years instead of decades. For this reason, cor-porate brands such as General Electric, Hewlett-Packard, Honda, or Siemens have an advantage when it comes to building presence and awareness, because multiple businesses support the brand name. Firms are thus attempting to reduce the number of their brands in order to provide focus to brand-building efforts. (More on this subject and on the value of spreading brands over different businesses follows in Chapters 8 and 9.)

Second, in the coming decades, the firms that become skilled at operating outside the normal media channels—by using event promotions, sponsorships, publicity, sampling, and other attention-getting approaches—will be the most successful in building brand awareness. For example, WordPerfect created instant visibility and credibility in Europe for its word processing software by sponsoring one of the top three bicycle racing teams. Media coverage of the team, both during and outside the races, established WordPerfect as a recognized brand. A yellow race car sponsored by Kodak similarly created over a billion individual impressions in 1993.[3]

Getting consumers to recognize and recall your brand thus can considerably enhance brand equity. As will be emphasized throughout this book, however, simple recall, recognition, and familiarity are only part of the awareness challenge. "Just spell the name right," the classic dictum of old-time PR firms, will not suffice as a brand-building strategy. The strongest brands are managed not for general awareness, but for *strategic* awareness. It is one thing to be remembered; it is quite another to be remembered for the right reasons (and to avoid being remembered for the wrong reasons).

PERCEIVED QUALITY

Perceived quality is a brand association that is elevated to the status of a brand asset for several reasons:

- among all brand associations, only perceived quality has been shown to drive financial performance.
- perceived quality is often a major (if not the principal) strategic thrust of a business.
- perceived quality is linked to and often drives other aspects of how a brand is perceived.

PERCEIVED QUALITY DRIVES FINANCIAL PERFORMANCE

There is a pervasive thirst to show that investments in brand equity will pay off. Although linking financial performance to any intangible asset (whether it is people, information technology, or brand equity) is difficult, three studies have demonstrated that perceived quality does drive financial performance:

- Studies using the PIMS data base (annual data measuring more than one hundred variables for over 3,000 business units) have shown that perceived quality is the single most important contributor to a company's return on investment (ROI), having more impact than market share, R&D, or marketing expenditures.[4] Perceived quality contributes to profitability in part by enhancing prices and market share. The relationship holds for Kmart as well as Tiffany: Improve perceived quality, and ROI will improve.
- A five-year study of 77 firms in Sweden, conducted by Claes Fornell and his colleagues at the National Quality Research Center at the University of Michigan, revealed that perceived quality was a

major driver of customer satisfaction, which in turn had a major impact on ROI.[5]

- A study of 33 publicly traded firms over a four-year period showed that perceived quality (as measured by the EquiTrend method, which is described in Chapter 9) had an impact on stock return, the ultimate financial measure.[6] The study looked at American Express, AT&T, Avon, Citicorp, Coke, Kodak, Ford, Goodyear, IBM, Kellogg's, and 23 other firms for which the corporate brand drove a substantial amount of sales and profits. Figure 1–6 portrays the relative impact of changes in perceived quality and ROI on stock return. Remarkably, the impact of perceived quality was nearly as great as that of ROI (an acknowledged influence on stock return), even when the researchers controlled for advertising expenditures and awareness levels.

FIGURE 1–6
Stock Market Reaction to Changes in ROI and Perceived Quality

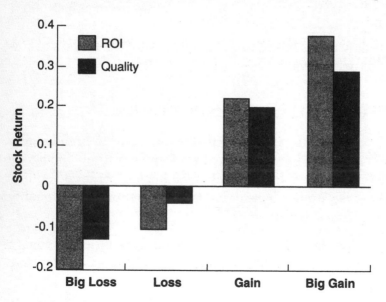

PERCEIVED QUALITY AS A STRATEGIC THRUST

Perceived quality is a key strategic variable for many firms. Total quality management (TQM) or one of its relatives has been central to many firms for the past decade, and perceived quality is usually the end goal of TQM programs.

Many firms explicitly consider quality to be one of their primary values and include it in their mission statement. For example, one of the guiding principles put forth by IBM's president, Lou Gerstner, is an "overriding commitment to quality." In one study in which 250 business managers were asked to identify the sustainable competitive advantage of their firms, perceived quality was the most frequently named asset.[7]

Perceived quality is often the key positioning dimension for corporate brands (such as Toshiba or Ford) and other brands that range over product classes (such as Weight Watchers, Kraft, and store brands such as Safeway Select). Because these brands span product classes, they are less likely to be driven by functional benefits, and perceived quality is likely to play a larger role.

Further, for many brands perceived quality defines the competitive milieu and their own position within that milieu. Some brands are price brands, and others are prestige or premium brands. Within those categories, the perceived quality position is often the defining point of differentiation.

PERCEIVED QUALITY AS A MEASURE OF "BRAND GOODNESS"

Perceived quality is usually at the heart of what customers are buying, and in that sense, it is a bottom-line measure of the impact of a brand identity. More interesting, though, perceived quality reflects a measure of "goodness" that spreads over all elements of the brand like a thick syrup. Even when the brand identity is defined by functional benefits, most studies will show that perceptions about those benefits are closely related to perceived quality. When perceived quality improves, so generally do other elements of customers' perception of the brand.

CREATING PERCEPTIONS OF QUALITY

Achieving perceptions of quality is usually impossible unless the quality claim has substance. Generating high quality requires an understanding of what quality means to customer segments, as well as a supportive culture and a quality improvement process that will enable the organization to deliver quality products and services. Creating a quality product or service, however, is only a partial victory; perceptions must be created as well.

Perceived quality may differ from actual quality for a variety of reasons. First, consumers may be overly influenced by a previous image of poor quality. Because of this, they may not believe new claims, or they may not be willing to take the time to verify them. Suntory Old Whiskey, Audi automobiles, and Schlitz beer all found that making excellent products was not enough to erase consumer doubts raised by previously tarnished quality.[8] Thus it is critical to protect a brand from gaining a reputation for shoddy quality from which recovery is difficult and sometimes impossible.

Second, a company may be achieving quality on a dimension that consumers do not consider important. When Citibank dramatically increased back-office efficiency by automating its processing activities, the expected impact on customer evaluations was disappointing. Customers, it turned out, either did not notice the changes or did not recognize any benefit from them. There is a need to make sure that investments in quality occur in areas that will resonate with customers.

Third, consumers rarely have all the information necessary to make a rational and objective judgment on quality—and even if they do have the information, they may lack the time and motivation to process it. As a result, they rely on one or two cues that they associate with quality; the key to influencing perceived quality is understanding and managing these cues properly. Thus, it is important to understand the little things that consumers use as the basis for making a judgment of quality. If consumers kick a car's tires to judge its sturdiness, then the tires had better be sturdy.

Fourth, because consumers may not know how best to judge quality, they may be looking at the wrong cues. For example, jewelry stores that cater to first-time diamond buyers must educate consumers that quality is not necessarily reflected in price tags or carat claims. A metaphor or visual image can help consumers see the context in the right way.

THE BRAND AS A SHIP

A brand can be likened to a ship in a fleet facing an upcoming battle. This metaphor provides some insight into the brand management problem and the cast of characters. The brand manager is the captain of the ship, who must know where his or her ship is going and keep it on course. The other brands in the firm, like other ships in a fleet, need to be coordinated to achieve the maximum effectiveness. Competitors correspond to enemy ships; knowing their location, direction, and strength is critical to achieving strategic and tactical success. The perceptions and motivations of customers are like the winds: It is important to know their direction, their strength, and possible changes.

BRAND LOYALTY

Brand loyalty, the third brand asset category, is excluded from many conceptualizations of brand equity.[9] There are at least two reasons, however, why it is appropriate and useful to include it. First, a brand's value to a firm is largely created by the customer loyalty it commands. Second, considering loyalty as an asset encourages and justifies loyalty-building programs which then help create and enhance brand equity.

LOYALTY AND BRAND VALUE

Brand loyalty is a key consideration when placing a value on a brand that is to be bought or sold, because a highly loyal customer base can be expected to generate a very predictable sales and profit stream. In fact, a brand without a loyal customer base usually is vulnerable or has value only in its potential to create loyal customers.

Further, the impact of brand loyalty on marketing costs is often substantial: It is simply much less costly to retain customers than to attract new ones. A common and expensive mistake is to seek growth by enticing new customers to the brand while neglecting existing ones. The loyalty of existing customers also represents a substantial entry barrier to competitors in part because the cost of enticing customers to change loyalties is often prohibitively expensive.

All organizations should estimate the value of their existing customers. The results are usually surprising and instructive. Reducing defections by just 5 percent generated 85 percent more profits in one bank's branch system, 50 percent more in an insurance brokerage, and 30 percent more in an auto-service chain.[10] At MBNA, a financial services company, it was estimated that a 5 percent increase in customer retention increased the company's profits by 60 percent by the fifth year.[11] At Club Med, one lost customer costs the company at least $2,400 in lost future business.[12] Credit card companies have found that newly acquired customers use the card slowly at first, but that in the second year the usage grows and the card becomes more profitable. A similar trend was found in more than one hundred companies in two dozen industries.[13] For one industrial distributor, net sales per account continue to rise into the nineteenth year of the relationship.

LOYALTY SEGMENTATION

A focus on loyalty segmentation provides strategic and tactical insights that will assist in building strong brands. A market can usually be divided into the following groups: noncustomers (those who buy competitor brands or are not product class users), price switchers (those who are price-sensitive), the passively loyal (those who buy out of habit rather than reason), fence sitters (those who are indifferent between two or more brands), and the committed. The challenge is to improve the brand's loyalty profile: to increase the number of customers who are not price switchers, to strengthen the fence sitters' and committed's ties to the brand, and to increase the number who would pay more (or endure some inconvenience) to use the brand or service. Two segments in which firms often underinvest are the passively loyals and the committed customers.

The passively loyal customer is often neglected or taken for granted. Active management of this segment does not really involve identity building; rather, it requires efforts to avoid distribution gaps or out-of-stocks that might precipitate a decision to switch brands. It also means having the sizes, colors, or flavors that might be desired, even though providing a wide line may seem economically unattractive. The appropriate analysis of line breadth needs to include the impact upon the habitual behavior of the passively loyal segment.

At the other extreme are the committed or highly loyal customers. Firms also tend to take this group for granted. Yet there may be a significant potential to increase business from the very loyal. For example, the loyal Marriott customer might be encouraged to select Marriott even more often with an improved portfolio of business support services such as fax machines in rooms. Further, there is a risk that loyal customers can be enticed away by a competitor if the performance of the product or service is not improved. For these reasons, firms should avoid diverting resources from the loyal core to the noncustomers and price switchers.

ENHANCING LOYALTY

One approach to enhancing the loyalty of fence sitters and the committed is to develop or strengthen their relationship with the brand. Brand awareness, perceived quality, and an effective, clear brand identity can contribute to this goal. Increasingly, however, programs that can build loyalty more directly are becoming important and even critical in many product classes. Included among these are frequent-buyer programs and customer clubs.

Frequent-Buyer Programs

Frequent-buyer programs, which were pioneered by airlines (United Airlines' Mileage Plus, American Airlines' Advantage, and British Airways' Frequent Traveler programs) are now being adapted by a host of brands in a variety of product classes, including books (Waldenbooks Preferred Reader), hotels (Hilton Senior Honors Frequent Traveler Program), fast food (Burger King Frequent Customers Club), parking (Park-n-Fly Reward) and even cars. The GM MasterCard, launched in 1992, provides customers with a rebate on the purchase of a GM car or truck (excluding Saturn) equal to 5 percent of their credit card purchases. After the first year and a half, GM had sold 140,000 cars and trucks to these buyers and had issued more than 12 million cards.

A frequent-buyer program provides direct and tangible reinforcement for loyal behavior. Not only do such programs enhance the value proposition of a brand and often its point of differentiation as well, they also affirm the commitment that the firm is making to loyal customers. It is clear that their loyalty is not taken for granted.

Customer Clubs

A potentially more intense loyalty level can be precipitated by customer clubs. Kids who joined the Nintendo Fun Club (and received newsletters and access to on-call advisers), for example, were rabid Nintendo users and the heart of the firm's early success. Claridge Hotel and Casino has without question increased the intensity of customer loyalty with its 350,000-member Claridge CompCard Gold club. The club's members receive discounts, news of upcoming events, and special offers ranging from monogrammed bathrobes to door-to-door limo service. Apple Computer users groups provide support and assistance, as well as the chance for customers to express their interest in computers and their loyalty to Apple.

The Casa Buitoni Club played a key role in establishing Nestlé's Buitoni brand of Italian food in the United Kingdom. Members received a regular full-color newsletter with editorials about Tuscany and Italy, information about the lifestyle of Italians, pasta recipes, and discount vouchers. Membership benefits also included a toll-free line for cooking advice, chances to win an invitation to visit the original Casa Buitoni villa in Tuscany, cookery weekends, opportunities to sample new products, and numerous suggestions as to how members could create their own events.

Like the frequent-buyer programs, a customer club provides visible evidence that the firm really cares about its clientele. While the frequent-buyer program is somewhat passive and inclusive, however, a customer club is potentially more involving. The customer club provides a vehicle by which the customer can identify with the brand, express his or her brand perceptions and attitude, and experience the sharing of a brand relationship with like-minded people.

Database Marketing

A by-product of frequent-buyer programs and clubs, customer data can be used for database marketing targeted at narrow, focused segments. News about new products and special promotions can be tailored to those segments most likely to respond. Targeted customers will feel the firm is connecting with them individually, and the brand-customer relationship will become stronger.

For example, Beverages & More! is a retail chain that offers a huge selection of wines, beers, liquors, and drink complements. Each customer is invited to be a member of "Club Bev" and is given a card that is used to track all purchases. In addition to a newsletter and a frequent-buyer program, customers receive personal notification of special purchases, products, or events that are relevant to people with their purchase profile. In addition to matching products to customers, the interaction pattern shows that the store is involved enough to care about the interests of each individual customer.

BRAND ASSOCIATIONS

Managing Brand Equity emphasized that brand equity is supported in great part by the associations that consumers make with a brand. These associations might include product attributes, a celebrity spokesperson, or a particular symbol. Brand associations are driven by the brand identity—what the organization wants the brand to stand for in the customer's mind. A key to building strong brands, then, is to develop and implement a brand identity.

One of the goals of this book is to expand the concept of brand identity. A common pitfall is to focus on the product attributes and tangible functional benefits of a brand. Chapter 3, in which brand identity is formally defined and discussed, encourages strategists to expand their concept of brand identity by (1) considering emotional and self-expressive benefits as well as functional benefits, and (2) employing four brand identity perspectives: the brand-as-product, the brand-as-organization (covered in detail in Chapter 4), the brand-as-person (the subject of chapter 5), and the brand-as-symbol. Chapter 6 covers the brand identity implementation process and introduces strategic brand analysis and brand positioning. Chapter 7 discusses the delicate problems of managing brand associations over time.

OBJECTIVES OF THE BOOK

There are several objectives motivating this book. One, just discussed, is to develop the concept of brand identity: How can you create an identity that is clear, connects with the customer, can be implemented so that its potential is realized, and is rich enough to provide guidance to those implementing it? How do you manage it over time in the face of a shifting environment and changing competitors and customers? Chapters 3, 4, 5, 6, and 7 will address these questions.

A second objective is to move beyond the management of a brand to the management of brand systems. Most organizations need to manage not only multiple brands but also large varieties of sub-brands, ingredient brands, brand extensions, co-brands, and branded services. Further, each brand can take on different roles, which vary from simply being an endorser (such as Marriott's role in "Fairfield by Marriott") to playing a driver role (that is, being the brand that will drive the purchase decision). Management of brand systems involves determining the roles that brands play and understanding how they relate to and impact each other. Chapters 8 and 9 will sort out these issues.

A third objective of the book is to address the critical measurement issue. How do you measure brand equity, especially across product classes and markets? Several major efforts to do just that will be described in Chapter 10.

A fourth objective is to consider how to develop organizational forms and structures that will be effective at building brands. A variety of approaches will be discussed in Chapter 11.

The overall goal of this book is to help managers build strong brands. Because knowing the terrain is indispensable to traversing it successfully, it is useful to understand why this task is hard and what pressures the brand builder must face. Therefore, I now turn to a general discussion of why it is hard to build brands.

BUILDING STRONG BRANDS: WHY IS IT HARD?

It is not easy to build brands in today's environment. The brand builder who attempts to develop a strong brand is like a golfer playing on a course with heavy roughs, deep sandtraps, sharp doglegs, and vast water barriers. It is difficult to score well in such conditions. The brand builder can be inhibited by substantial pressures and barriers, both internal and external. To be able to develop effective brand strategies, it is useful to understand these pressures and barriers.

Toward that end, eight different factors (shown in Figure 1–7) that make it difficult to build brands will be discussed. The first, pressure to compete on price, directly affects the motivation to build brands. The second reason, the proliferation of competitors, reduces the positioning options available and makes implementation less effective. The third and fourth reasons, the fragmentation in media and markets and the involvement of multiple brands and products, describe the context of building brands today, a context that involves a growing level of complexity.

The remaining reasons reflect internal pressures that inhibit brand building. The fifth reason, the temptation to change a sound brand strategy, is particularly insidious because it is the management equivalent of shooting yourself in the foot. The sixth and seventh reasons, the organizational bias against innovation and the pressure to invest elsewhere, are special problems facing strong brands. They can be caused by arrogance but are more often caused by complacency coupled with pride and/or greed. The final reason is the pressure for short-term results that pervades organizations. The irony is that many of the formidable problems facing brand builders today are

FIGURE 1–7
Why Is It Hard to Build Brands?

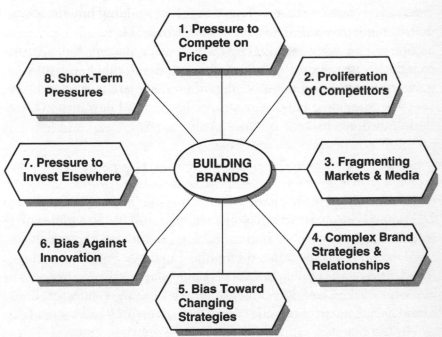

caused by internal forces and biases that are under the control of the organization.

The fact that many brands fail to reach their potential or maintain their equity is neither surprising nor puzzling when the various pressures against building strong brands are examined. The real curiosity may be that strong brands exist at all in the face of these pressures.

1. PRESSURE TO COMPETE ON PRICE

There are enormous pressures on nearly all firms to engage in price competition. In industry after industry—from computers to cars to frozen dinners to airlines to soft drinks—the picture in today's market is the same: Price competition is at center stage, driven by the power of strong retailers, value-sensitive customers, reduced category growth, and overcapacity (often caused by new entrants and by old competitors hanging on, sometimes via bankruptcy).

In presentations on brand equity, I often ask executives to raise their hand if their industry is one in which brutal price competition is not the norm or becoming the norm. Of the thousands of executives who have attended these presentations, only one person has ever held up his hand—the director of the Panama Canal!

Retailers have become stronger year by year, and they have used that strength to put pressure on prices. Whereas a decade ago, information was largely controlled by the manufacturer, retailers are now collecting vast amounts of information and developing models to use it. As a result, there is an increasing focus on margins and efficient use of space. Suppliers, particularly those in the third or fourth market-share position with only modest loyalty levels, are exposed to harsh pressure to provide price concessions.

A decade ago, private-label brands were largely limited to low-quality, low-price products unsupported by effective packaging or marketing. Given these characteristics, they enjoyed only temporary sales spurts during recessionary times. No more. While still offering so-called price brands, retailers are also increasingly offering private-label brands at the high end of the business. Such brands are competitive with national brands in quality and marketing support but have substantial cost advantages—in part because the cost of the brand management team, sales force, and advertising is lower and can be spread over hundreds of product classes and in part because of logistical advantages. The result is more price pressure.

Sales promotion is both a driver and an indicator of the price focus. In the 1950s, about 10 percent of the communication mix was devoted to price promotions. Those were the days: Distribution was simple, retailers were concerned with building new stores rather than squeezing margins, and markets were growing. Today, more than 75 percent of the advertising/promotion dollars in the United States are going to promotion.

These market realities imply that *the* key success factor is low cost. Organizations must reduce overhead, trim staff, downsize, and cut all unnecessary expenditures. What, then, happens to the people who support the brand with market research or other brand-building activities? They are vulnerable to the organization's new cost culture. Also vulnerable are investments in brand equity, which come out of precious margin dollars.

2. PROLIFERATION OF COMPETITORS

New, vigorous competitors come from a variety of sources. A host of food categories have watched Weight Watchers and Healthy Choice enter their markets through brand extension strategies. In the snack category, Frito-Lay has seen regional brands expand and Budweiser's Eagle brand break out of its niche to become a major competitor. The soft drink market has been encroached on by new product forms that provide real alternatives for the customer: bottled water, carbonated water, fruit-based drinks, and "new age" drinks, among others.

Additional competitors not only contribute to price pressure and brand complexity, but also make it much harder to gain and hold a position. They leave fewer holes in the market to exploit and fewer implementation vehicles to own. Each brand tends to be positioned more narrowly, the target markets become smaller, and the nontarget market becomes larger. Efforts to market to a broad segment thus become more difficult in the face of the complex "brandscape." Further, some new or desperate competitors may be motivated to take risks or attempt unusual approaches. The result can be destabilization of the competitive dynamics. There is also an enhanced motivation to copy anything that is successful, in part because the risks of copying are offset by the difficulty of coming up with brilliant new alternatives.

3. FRAGMENTING MARKETS AND MEDIA

At one time, being consistent across media and markets was easy. There were a limited number of media options and only a few national media vehicles. Mass markets were the norm, and microsegmentation did not exist. Brand managers now face a very different environment, one in which it is difficult to achieve the consistency that is needed to build and maintain strong brands.

The bewildering array of media options today includes interactive television, advertising on the Internet, direct marketing, and event sponsorship, and more are being invented daily. Coordinating messages across these media without weakening the brand is a real challenge, especially when promotional vehicles are included in the mix. A promotion involving a giveaway or a price reduction that "rings the bell" (that is, results in a noticeable sales spike), for example, may be inconsistent with a brand identity based upon quality because it signals that the brand needs to lower price to gain sales. Pressure to include promotions (such as the couponing used by packaged-goods brands or the cash rebates used by automobile firms) makes it difficult to keep the brand-building effort on track.

Coordination is all the more difficult because different brand-support activities are often handled by different organizations and individuals with varying perspectives and goals. When advertising, public relations, event sponsorship, promotions, trade shows, event stores,[14] direct marketing, package design, corporate identity, and direct mail for a single brand are handled by separate organizations, each with direct influence on the brand—and even worse, when the firm's internal organization mirrors this diversity in order to interface with these various players—conflict and lack of coordination must be anticipated.

In addition, companies are dividing the population into smaller and more refined target markets, often reaching them with specialized media and distribution channels. It is temptating to develop different brand identities for some or all of these new target segments. Developing and managing multiple identities for the same brand, however, presents problems for both the brand and the customer. Since media audiences invariably overlap, customers are likely to be exposed to more than one identity relating to the same brand.

Consider the problem of a mature Dewar's Scotch consumer, accustomed to the brand's traditional advertising, who encounters the firm's advertisements geared for younger Scotch drinkers. Or think of the potential confusion of a prestige-oriented shopper, accustomed to seeing Saks Fifth Avenue advertisements in fine fashion magazines, who one day sees a newspaper advertisement for a Saks discount outlet. The more numerous and diverse a brand's images are, the more difficult it is to coordinate them in support of a strong brand.

4. COMPLEX BRAND STRATEGIES AND RELATIONSHIPS

There was a time, not too long ago, when a brand was a clear, singular entity. Kraft and Oscar Mayer, for example, were brand names that simply needed to be defined, established, and nurtured. Today, the situation is far different. There are subbrands (such as Kraft Free Singles and Oscar Mayer Zappetites) and brand extensions (such as Kraft Miracle Whip). There are ingredient brands (such as Hershey's chocolate syrup in Pillsbury's Deluxe Chocolate Brownies), endorser brands (such as the role of Kellogg's in Kellogg's Rice Krispies), and corporate brands (such as General Electric). The Coke logo can be found on a dozen products, including Diet Cherry Coke, Caffeine Free Diet Coke, and Coke Classic—and it doesn't stop there. In the grocery store, Coke is a product brand; at sporting events, it's a sponsoring brand; and in the communities where its bottling plants operate, Coke is a corporate brand.

This complexity makes building and managing brands difficult. In addition to knowing its identity, each brand needs to understand its role in each context in which it is involved. Further, the relationships between brands (and subbrands) must be clarified both strategically and with respect to customer perceptions. Chapters 8 and 9 delve into these murky issues.

Why is this brand complexity emerging? The market fragmentation and brand proliferation mentioned above have occurred because a new market or product often leads to a new brand or subbrand. Another driving force is cost: There is a tendency to use established brands in different contexts and roles because establishing a totally new brand is now so expensive. The resulting new levels of complexity often are not anticipated or even acknowledged until there is a substantial problem.

5. BIAS TOWARD CHANGING STRATEGIES

There are sometimes overwhelming internal pressures to change a brand identity and/or its execution while it is still effective, or even before it achieves its potential. The resulting changes can undercut brand equity or prevent it from being established. Most strong brands, such as Marlboro, Volvo, and Motel 6, have one characteristic in common: Each developed a clear identity that went virtually unchanged for a very long time. The norm is to change, however, and thus powerful identities supported by clear visual imagery never get developed. Chapter 7 discusses the benefits of consistency over time and why it is difficult to achieve.

6. BIAS AGAINST INNOVATION

While there may be a bias toward changing a brand identity or its execution, a psychic and capital investment in the status quo often prevents true innovation in products or services. There is an incentive to keep the competitive battleground static; any change not only would be costly and risky but could cause prior investment to have a much reduced return (or even make it obsolete). The result is a vulnerability to aggressive competitors that may come from outside the industry with little to lose and none of the inhibitions with which industry participants are burdened.

Companies managing an established brand can be so pleased by past and current success, and so preoccupied with day-to-day problems, that they become blind to changes in the competitive situation. By ignoring or minimizing fundamental changes in the market or potential technological breakthroughs, managers leave their brands vulnerable and risk missing opportunities. A new competitor thus is often the source and the beneficiary of true innovation.

Consider Weight Watchers, one of the great brand success stories of the 1980s. Building on its association with professional weight control, Weight Watchers created a $1.5 billion business by investing in products, packaging, and advertising with a single-minded vision. But in the late 1980s, consumer interest in weight control was eclipsed by a broader concern about a healthy diet. Along came Healthy Choice (whose story is told in Chapter 9), a brand designed to address this new market paradigm. Why didn't this health-oriented innovation come from Weight Watchers, a company with many resources and a better knowledge of the market? A major reason was that the Weight Watchers brand was already a money machine, and the company didn't want to dilute it by investing in a new and different market position.

There are countless examples of strong brands that neither saw nor responded to opportunities, then watched competitors innovate and attack the core of their equity. In Japan, Kirin beer saw four decades of 60 percent share fall abruptly to below 50 percent when Asahi Dry became a hit product. Why wasn't Kirin the innovator instead of Asahi? It is likely that Kirin, being pleased with the status quo, saw no reason to look for major disruptive changes in the beer category.

7. PRESSURE TO INVEST ELSEWHERE: THE SINS OF COMPLACENCY AND GREED

A position of great brand strength is also a potential strategic problem, because it attracts both complacency and greed. When a brand is strong, there is a temptation to reduce investment in the core business area in order to improve short-term performance or to fund a new business diversification. There is an often-mistaken belief that the brand will not be damaged by sharp reductions in support, and that the other investment opportunities are more attractive. Ironically, the diversification that attracts these resources is often flawed because an acquired business was overvalued, or because the organization's ability to manage a different business area was overestimated.

Xerox may be the prototypical example of a dominant brand that lost its position because of an inadequate commitment to the core business. In the 1960s, Xerox virtually owned the copier industry; its market share was literally 100 percent. Barriers to entry included a dominant brand name, a strong set of patents, and a huge customer base committed to a leasing program and service organization. Instead of sticking with its strengths and defending either the low end by attacking costs or the high end by developing new technologies,

Xerox diverted resources into an "office of the future" concept. As a result, the company was blindsided by Savin, Kodak, and Canon, who entered the industry with innovative, superior, and often less expensive products. While there are many reasons why Xerox lost position in the 1970s, one key explanation is the brand's strong equity, which engendered complacency and a temptation to look for greener pastures.

8. SHORT-TERM PRESSURES

Pressures for short-term results undermine investments in brands, especially in the United States. Sony founder Akio Morita has opined that most U.S. corporate managers unduly emphasize quick profits rather than try to make products competitive over the long haul. And the MIT Commission on Productivity, after studying firms in eight major industrial sectors (including textiles, steel, consumer electronics, aircraft, and automobiles), concluded that an excessive preoccupation with immediate profit at the expense of longer-term opportunities is a major factor responsible for the declining competitiveness of American businesses relative to Japanese and European firms.[15]

There are several reasons why a short-term focus might persist among U.S. executives. First, there is wide acceptance in the United States that maximization of stockholder value should be the overriding objective of the firm. This acceptance is coupled with a perception that shareholders are inordinately influenced by quarterly earnings—partly because they lack the information and insight to understand the firm's strategic vision, and partly because they cannot evaluate intangible assets. As a result, managers are motivated to make current performance look good.

Second, management style itself is dominated by a short-term orientation. Annual budgeting systems usually emphasize short-term sales, costs, and profits. As a result, brand-building programs are often sacrificed in order to meet these targets. Planning is too often an exercise in spreadsheet manipulation of short-term financial data rather than strategic thinking. In addition, because U.S. firms tend to rotate managers through the organization, the long term becomes much less important than current results to career paths. Managers feel pressure to perform—to "turn it around" quickly and visibly.

Third, a short-term focus is created by the performance measures available. Measurements of intangible assets such as brand equity, information technology, or people are elusive at best. The long-term value of activities that will enhance or erode brand equity, for example, is difficult to convincingly demonstrate, in part because the marketplace is "noisy" and in part because experiments covering multiple years are very expensive. In sharp contrast, short-term performance measurements are ever more refined, timely, and detailed. The short-term impact of promotions, for example, can be demonstrated with scanner data. The resulting situation is a bit like the drunk who looks for his or her car keys under a street light because the light is better there than where the keys were lost.

The net outcome is a sometimes debilitating bias toward short-term results. This bias translates into a need to demonstrate with hard sales, share, or cost numbers that expenditures pay off. In that context, it becomes difficult to justify investments in intangible assets (like brands, people, or information technology) which lack a demonstrable short-term payoff. As a result, these investments are often forgone and the organization becomes weak at the core, lacking such assets when they are needed.

BUILDING BRANDS: DIFFICULT, FEASIBLE, AND NECESSARY

It is true that building brands is difficult. But it is doable, as is evidenced by those who have done so. The next chapter, which is about Saturn, describes a brand-building success story in one of the most hostile contexts that exists: the U.S. automobile market, with excess capacity, many competitors, a fragmented market, and an increasingly strong price focus. This story demonstrates that it is possible to build, maintain, and manage the four assets that underlie brand equity—awareness, perceived quality, brand loyalty, and brand association.

One key to successful brand-building is to understand how to develop a brand identity—to know what the brand stands for and to effectively express that identity. The five chapters that follow the Saturn story discuss brand identity and its management over time. The book then moves to consider a brand systems perspective—how to manage a set of brands to generate synergy instead of destructive confusion.

Another key to brand-building success is to manage internal forces and pressures. The need is to recognize organizational biases against true innovation and toward diversification, short-term results, and frequent changes in brand identity/execution and then to counter those pressures by developing conceptual models and measurements that support a brand-building culture and policies. Chapter 10 will cover measurement, and Chapter 11 will directly address how an organization can be structured to deal with the problems and pressures facing those who would build and maintain brands.

QUESTIONS TO CONSIDER

1. What is the level of recognition and recall for your brand? Is it moving toward or away from the graveyard? What can be done to improve awareness? What are others doing?
2. Evaluate the perceived quality for your brand and for its major competitor brands. Are you satisfied with the actual quality levels? What are the important quality cues? How could the quality message be better communicated?
3. What are the brand loyalty levels of your customers by segment? How could loyalty be enhanced? What are competitors doing to improve loyalty?
4. How are the major competitors perceived by customers? What associations is each trying to create? What is the desired image of your brand? Is the brand and the communication effort consistent with that image?
5. Are there internal pressures that work against brand building— pressures against true innovation and toward short-term results, diversification, and frequent changes in brand identity/execution? Assess each. What organizational device can combat those pressures? Is the brand environment hostile? How can brand building proceed in such a context?

2

BUILDING A BRAND— THE SATURN STORY[1]

Saturn is more than a car. It's an idea. It's a whole new way of doing things, of working with our customers and with one another. It's more of a cultural revolution than a product revolution.

—Richard "Skip" LeFauve, Saturn CEO

We came here to create something that had never been built before. And it was harder than we ever could have suspected. We've been through some tough times together. These days, I feel as if there's nothing this team couldn't take on.

—Bob Downs, Saturn transmission engineer

The American auto industry was under attack from all directions. That's why I came here. It was a chance to turn things around. A chance to help build a car that would go up against the imports—and best of all, to have a say in the way it was done. . . . One day . . . there was the president of our union, standing right next to me, putting bolts in and whistling. . . . In the old days, those guys made the rules but never came near the production line.

—Steve Halloway, Saturn technician, Spring Hill

We knew from the beginning that if Saturn was to succeed, we'd have to do more than just sell a good car. We'd also have to change the way cars are sold, the way the people who sell them are perceived, and the way customers feel about the experience of shopping for a car.

—Stuart Lasser, Saturn dealer

I can't say it was patriotism, really, that made me go to see a Saturn that day. . . .
I just wanted to find out what these cars were like. . . . The car was great, but
what really impressed me was the people. They didn't pressure you, but they
were glad to talk, if you wanted to. It was like going to a museum, and they were
docents.

—Steve Schaefer, Saturn owner[2]

On January 7, 1985, the General Motors chairman Roger Smith
announced the creation of the Saturn Corporation, calling it "the
key to GM's long-term competitiveness, survival, and success as a do-
mestic producer."[3] The new company's mission, in part, was to market
compact vehicles "developed and manufactured in the U.S. that are
world leaders in quality, cost, and customer satisfaction."[4] Saturn was
an ambitious undertaking for General Motors, but a critical one given
the ominous inroads that imports had made, especially in the compact
arena. The Saturn project was pursued at a time when many felt that
U.S. manufacturers lacked the ability to make world-class compact
cars, and GM itself had aborted several efforts to do so.

After four years on the market, the verdict was in: Saturn had succeeded in building from scratch one of the strongest brands in the
United States, suggesting comparisons with the Ford Mustang of the
1960s, the Ford Pinto of the 1970s, and the Ford Taurus of the 1980s.
The first section of this chapter will discuss and support that assertion. What exactly is a strong brand? Did Saturn earn that distinction
during its early years? Second, the creation of Saturn's brand equity
will be analyzed. What decisions paved the way? What strategies and
programs were behind the brand? Third, the challenges that Saturn
and GM now face will be considered. Building a brand may not be
as difficult as maintaining its momentum tactically and managing it
strategically; in Saturn's case, success created its own problems and
options.

SATURN: A STRONG BRAND?

A bottom-line measure of the success of the Saturn brand-building
effort is its sales performance. Saturn sold 74,000 cars in 1991,
196,000 cars during 1992, 229,000 in 1993, and 286,000 in 1994, a
result that made it the eighth highest-selling brand out of some two-

hundred-plus brand names. Only Ford Escort had higher sales among brands in Saturn's class. Further, sales would have been substantially higher had they not been inhibited by production capacity limitations. Saturn was frequently short of product during this period.

Because Saturn sold substantially more cars per dealer than did its competitors—Saturn had 335 dealers in 1994 versus approximately 800 for Honda, 1,000 for Toyota, and many more for Ford and Chevrolet—it can be argued that Saturn was the leading brand in regional and local markets.

Another bottom-line indicator of the strength of the Saturn brand is the fact that with a sticker price comparable to the competition, it successfully eliminated price haggling, dealing, discounts, and rebates—an incredible achievement given the times. To appreciate this achievement, it is useful to provide perspective. In virtually every industry from airlines to pet food to computers to diapers to hotels, even strong brands with few competitors (for example, Coke and Pepsi) have been unable to break out of a price environment characterized by promotions and deals. The automobile industry has long suffered from pervasive price haggling in the dealership, which has focused attention on price at the point of decision. Since the mid-1980s, debilitating, company-sponsored price discounts and rebates have worsened this situation. In 1992, for example, more than 60 percent of Ford Taurus sales were made with a cash discount or involved heavily discounted fleet sales. Only a few years earlier, nobody would have predicted that a major automobile brand could have stepped away from this practice. Further, the brand that did was not European or even an upscale brand—not Lexus, BMW, Acura, Lincoln, or Cadillac—but a General Motors compact.

Another indicator of the strength of the price and margins associated with Saturn comes from the attitude of Saturn dealers. Two studies found that Saturn was either the most valued franchise in the industry or second only to Lexus.[5] This appraisal by dealers would have been unlikely if Saturn had not achieved above-average margins.

As discussed in Chapter 1 and in *Managing Brand Equity*, there are four principal dimensions to brand equity: perceived quality, brand loyalty, brand awareness, and brand associations. In the sections below, Saturn's performance on each of these dimensions will be considered.

PERCEIVED QUALITY

The J. D. Power measures of customers' response to their new car purchase reflect perceived quality. Saturn was fourth (behind Lexus, Infiniti, and Cadillac) in the 1992 J. D. Power Sales Satisfaction Index (SSI), which measures reactions to the salesperson, delivery activities, and initial product condition. Further, Saturn was third in the 1992 J. D. Power Customer Satisfaction Index (CSI), which examines product quality and dealer service after one year of ownership. The two brands that exceeded Saturn on the 1992 CSI, Lexus and Infiniti, had sticker prices substantially higher than that of Saturn.[6] Notably, Saturn's performance on both of these J. D. Power measures was maintained in 1993, 1994, and 1995, and, in fact, Saturn moved to third position on the SSI in 1994 and, remarkably, to first position in 1995.

Another measure of perceived quality comes from the resale market. In 1993, the suggested retail price of a 1991 Saturn averaged 5 percent above the original list price, whereas those of the Honda Civic averaged 5 percent below the original list price. The resale prices of 1991 Toyota and Nissan models reflected substantially more depreciation.[7]

Market research has demonstrated that Saturns are favorably perceived by car shoppers. During the brand's first year, showroom visitors intercepted before they saw the sticker price estimated the Saturn price would be three to five thousand dollars more than it actually was.[8] The car itself implies high quality.

LOYALTY

In-house customer surveys provide direct measures of loyalty. During 1994, 87 percent of Saturn buyers said they would definitely recommend the retailer, a percentage that had steadily climbed from 80 percent after year one.[9] The J. D. Power CSI and SSI indices also reflect loyalty as well as perceived quality.

A series of anecdotes suggests that some Saturn owners feel intense loyalty toward their cars. When one dealer attached Polaroid pictures of buyers to the showroom wall, customers who bought Saturns before the picture program began insisted that their snapshot be added to the others. One couple got married in their Saturn. Some owners have volunteered to display their Saturns at car shows. There is a "Saturn groupies" interest group on the Prodigy on-line computer network. Such anecdotes are reminiscent of the Volkswagen Beetle phenomenon of the 1960s.

AWARENESS

Saturn was successful at building awareness. Recognition among the target segment started at under 1 percent, went to 40 percent a few months after launch, reached 79 percent a year later, and was nearly 100 percent in the fourth year. Recall had reached 14 percent at the end of 1992 (just behind Dodge and Pontiac and ahead of Mazda, Mitsubishi, and Geo), and grew to 17 percent in 1994, approximately the same as competitor brands, most of which had been supported by advertising for decades.

ASSOCIATIONS

Saturn was even better at creating associations. After one year, the percentage among the target segment (those intending to buy a smaller car) reporting agreement that Saturn had five key associations ranged from 30 to 40 percent, and in mid-1993, Saturn exceeded all Japanese brands on the "friendly" dimension.

By early 1995, the percentage of respondents who agreed that Saturn cared about its customers and was friendly exceeded 60 percent and was twice that of the average of six competitors in its class (such as the Honda Civic). Saturn was also strong in having very good dealers, being a company you like, having safe cars, providing good value and offering an intelligent approach.

Thus a wide range of perspectives and measures support the proposition that Saturn succeeded in creating a strong brand during its initial two years and beyond. It should be noted that Saturn was not profitable during those first two years and only modestly so thereafter. It can be argued, however, that the indicators discussed above reflect brand strength better than does profitability, which is influenced by product design, manufacturing, and production capacity. In particular, expanding Saturn's capacity and product line might dramatically increase profitability (more on this later).

HOW SATURN BUILT A BRAND

How did Saturn become a strong brand in only a few years? What were the key decisions, policies, and programs? Below is a description of seven areas of strategy that were potential contributors. The goal is not only to describe what was done but also to suggest the logic behind the strategies: why they were pursued, and how they were intended to contribute to the brand. Although certainly some elements of the Saturn strategy may have been critical, it was the synergy of the total program—rather than the power of any single element—that led to its success.

THE MISSION: A WORLD-CLASS PRODUCT

From the beginning, the driving concept behind Saturn was to create a world-class compact car that could match or exceed such Japanese imports as the Honda Civic and the Toyota Corolla in quality. The car needed to have the reliability, safety, feel, appearance, and overall excellence that people expected in the top imports while remaining competitive in price. This quality imperative was one of the defining dimensions of Saturn's corporate culture and brand identity.

Too often there is a delusion that brands can be created by advertising without a product or service that really delivers quality and value—in short, that image is a "problem" of advertising. In reality, the product drives the image. The Edsel of the 1950s would have been a symbol of quality today if it had been an excellent product in that key first year; some very good Edsel advertising and marketing was wasted because of a shoddy product. The Volkswagen Beetle phenomenon of the 1960s very likely could have been transferred to the Rabbit in the mid-1970s if it were not for the initial mechanical problems that plagued the Rabbit during its early years. These problems doomed the effort to use advertising and the rabbit symbolism to transform the Beetle equity to the Rabbit. In fact, VW has lived in the shadow of those days ever since.

Saturn did not make the mistake of the Edsel or the Rabbit; its product was good from the outset. Reviews in car magazines provided objective judgments that the car was designed and built well, and that there was substance behind the positive feedback from the customer surveys. The 1991 Saturn was called "a major step forward" by *Road and Track*, and the 1992 Saturn SL was called the "best value" of any 1992 small car in its price range. The already cited J. D. Power indices delivered even more persuasive evidence that Saturn had pulled it off.

One visible example of the Saturn quality emphasis has been the decision to offer a money-back guarantee. Within the first thirty days or 1,500 miles, whichever comes first, an original purchaser may return his or her Saturn for a full refund or for a replacement car. The guarantee not only reassures the buyer about the purchase decision but also (because of the substantial economic penalty for poor quality) provides an internal signal about the quality level that is needed and expected.

Recalls have given Saturn numerous opportunities to graphically demonstrate its quality culture. When it was found during one recall that defective coolant (antifreeze) might have caused some unrepairable damage, the 1,836 involved cars were never resold. During another recall, a Saturn engineer personally delivered a seat to a customer who lived on a remote Alaskan island.

THE TEAM APPROACH: "A DIFFERENT KIND OF COMPANY"

GM's basic premise was that a world-class compact car and a strong quality culture could not be created within the confines of an existing General Motors division. A new company was therefore formed and given the freedom to create not only a product but a whole new organization—free from the restrictive UAW contract and the historically confrontational relationship between labor and GM management, free from the constraints caused by an existing brand family, and free from the inhibitions of an existing way of doing business. People who joined Saturn broke ties with their prior GM unit and often moved to Spring Hill, Tennessee, where a "green field" manufacturing facility was built. This new organization was integral not only to creating the product but also to the broader challenge of creating a brand and communicating its identity. The initial Saturn ad, shown in Figure 2–1, illustrates the commitment of the first people to sign on.

FIGURE 2–1
The First Saturn Ad—Going Home

**EFX: MUSIC UNDER THROUGHOUT
NARRATOR:** There was Barney, Billy, Scooter, and me.

We grew up on the corner of Jefferson and Palmer. And if you lived there then, you lived, breathed, swore at, and by, cars.

The more buck toothed and hole riddled the better. We grew up some. Went away. But we came back to build Mustangs, Corvettes, and GTO's. Among other things.

It was the '60s. And of all the things we could be thinking about, we still mostly just thought about cars.

Life was good. Work was good. But then, the oil dried up.

And it seemed like overnight somethin' happened to the way people thought about cars. It got frustrating.

Then I decided to go to work for a company called Saturn, and build cars again. But in a brand new way.

There were some things I knew I'd miss. . . But there were certain things I wanted to remember.
EFX: MUSIC OUT

Reprinted with permission of Saturn.

A group of ninety-nine people drawn from the ranks of labor and management throughout GM—now reverently called the "99 club"—was charged with deciding what type of organization was needed. After visiting sixty benchmark companies to see how successful organizations operated, they developed a team/partnering approach, very unlike anything at General Motors, to design and manufacture Saturns. This partnering concept was ultimately extended to all elements of the business, from engineering to marketing, dealers, suppliers, and the advertising agency.

THE 1993 RECALL

In June 1993, Saturn decided that a recall was needed on all 350,000 cars made before April 1993 to ensure that a wire was properly grounded. The initial negative publicity was gradually replaced by more positive reports. Why? First, the recall was voluntary, not mandated by the government. Second, it was handled expeditiously: After two weeks 50 percent of the cars had been repaired, in part because of the contact that retailers had with their car owners. (In contrast, a major recall by a competitor—mandated by the government—was only 33 percent complete after twelve months.) Third, retailers handled the event positively. One chartered a bus to a baseball game; when the bus returned, the cars had been repaired and washed. Another had a barbecue that customers could attend while their car was being fixed. A third offered theater tickets.

In all, Saturn's strong customer relationship was reflected in the way that the recall was handled. Tracking studies indicated that the Saturn image on the "takes care of customers" dimension was not affected, and that the brand had actually improved on the "good dealer" dimension.

There are now cross-functional teams of people assigned to modules within Saturn that stimulate change, maintain standards, and provide the basic organizational structure. A team focus pervades the organization and provides a sense of empowerment. It is behind the partnering relationship with the UAW, which is unique within GM. The extensive training effort (5 percent of all work time) contains a heavy dose of team-building exercises. Objectives and rewards are based upon team and organizational goals. For example, manufacturing people have 20 percent of their compensation based upon the quality and productivity of the plant. This team orientation is part of the "different kind of company" that emerged at Saturn.

CREATING PERCEPTIONS BY SELLING THE COMPANY, NOT THE CAR

Having a world-class car was not enough to create a strong brand. Customer perceptions are what matter, and perceptions do not automatically follow reality. Audi, for example, found that spending a billion dollars to create what may have been the best car in its class was not enough to attract buyers who were skeptical of the Audi name. The VW Rabbit was a quality car one or two years too late; the perception of low quality caused by the model's early problems could not be overcome.

So, given that Saturn had created a world-class car, how could it convince people of that fact? The obvious tactic, essentially used by all car makers, would be simply to tell audiences why the car was so good, using phrases like "the relentless pursuit of perfection" or "as finely tuned under the roof as it is under the hood." The story would build upon specifics: safety features, exterior design and finish, fuel economy, acceleration performance, comfort, road tests, endorsements by car magazines, guarantees, nimble and quick handling, and so forth. The focus would be on the car, using unrelenting logic and mind-numbing facts. Saturn certainly would have had plenty of facts to use if that option had been exercised.

A logical, product-oriented approach would have been almost surely doomed to fail, in part because others had already been there. Ford's motto had been "Quality is Job 1" for over a decade. Buick was the "symbol of quality." Honda seemed to own the J. D. Power index. For at least half a decade, Lee Iacocca, former chairman of Chrysler Corporation, had been saying that Chrysler cars were just as good as Japanese cars. Saturn advertising along these lines would surely look like that of a dozen others brands and thus might not be noticed or believed. Further, an emphasis on attributes would tend to make price a focus, given the similarity of the quality claims.

The solution was to sell the company—its values and culture, its employees, and its customers—rather than the car. The initial advertising showed Saturn employees as people with personalities and a deep emotional commitment to both quality and the teamwork

FIGURE 2–2
Saturn LAUNCH Day

EFX: MUSIC UP & UNDER THROUGHOUT
EFX: (TV SET) 78 degrees today. In other news, the first Saturn car will be rolling off the line in Spring Hill.

NARRATOR: It used to be, I saw the product that I was making, but that was just one part of a thousand parts that went into the makeup of a car.

"It's gonna be some day, I guess." There was no way I would ever see the cars that it went into. The way things were done, I wasn't involved.

No one would ever ask me what I thought. Then I heard about Saturn building a whole new car plant to build a new car. And they figured out a new way of running things too.

No one else in the world had done all this, not that I know of, not since the Model T anyway. Raw material comes in the back door and a car comes out at the other end.

Seems to me, that when you see where your part fits into the big picture, it means a lot more. It's my perception anyway.

Now we got people watching us, some are for us, some against.

But I'll tell you, when I go to the end of this building and I see that car sitting there, I'm gonna feel alright.

Gonna be a great feelin' to know that I was a small part of history.
EFX: MUSIC OUT

approach. The commercial in Figure 2–1, for example, had workers describing the role of cars in their childhood. Another showed the sacrifice and risk of moving to a new area and beginning with a new company; a third, shown in Figure 2–2, portrayed workers' pride in seeing the first car come off the line.

A print ad telling the story of a powertrain technician at Saturn began with a scene of a Spring Hill farmhouse on a misty morning and the line, "I remember standing here in the middle of nowhere, no sign of an automobile plant in sight and thinking, 'What the heck am I doing here?'" During year two, much of the advertising focused upon customers and their experience with the car and the Saturn retailer—still a departure from product-oriented advertising. In 1995, when Saturn told the story of a redesigned car, it was again through the eyes of employees and other members of the Saturn family.

In early ads, prospective car buyers were made to feel that Saturn and its employees would not design, build, or sell anything less than a world-class car, simply because of who the people were. The believability of the ads undoubtedly was transferred to the implicit product claims. In contrast, a prime problem of most product-oriented car advertising is the credibility gap spawned by conflicting claims, all of which cannot be true. The resulting judgment that some ads must be false or exaggerated casts a shadow over all. Further, the simple fact that Saturn chose a very different tack was helpful in breaking through the clutter of automobile advertising.

The visual imagery of the Spring Hill plant helped to support the whole concept of a new kind of American company. As a new plant in the middle of a border state not associated with automobile manufacturing, the Spring Hill facility had the clear potential to start from scratch and to do things the right way. The "middle of nowhere" of the early print ad subtly implied a breath of fresh air. The employees also provided strong imagery. Think of Pontiac and your mind might visualize a car; mention Saturn, however, and the picture is more likely to be one of people.

Two important name decisions are noteworthy. First, Saturn distanced itself from GM. Early concept research had made it clear that cueing the GM name resulted in a substantially lower quality perception and credibility, whereas cueing a Japanese name (such as Sony) did the reverse. Further, the whole concept of Saturn involved a fresh start at building an organization and a car; linking the effort to GM would have undercut that concept.

Second, the option of naming models (like the Honda Civic, Prelude, and Accord) was resisted. The focus was to be on Saturn the company and the product. A model can provide a useful subbrand when it distinguishes something very different from the rest of the brand, like the Mazda Miata or the Ford Taurus. In this case, however, models would have drawn attention away from the main story.

CREATING A RELATIONSHIP BETWEEN SATURN AND THE CUSTOMER

Most brands, particularly car brands, focus upon such attributes as safety, economy, handling, or comfort in developing a brand identity. Such positioning strategies are often relatively easy to copy or surpass and thus are weak bases for loyalty. Strong brands usually move beyond product attributes to a brand identity based upon a brand personality and a relationship with customers. For example, an important part of Saturn's brand identity is its commitment to treat customers with respect and as a friend. Properly implemented, this relationship and the brand personality that underlies it have the potential to create an intense, enduring brand loyalty.

Along with the quality imperative and the team orientation, the Saturn way of treating customers is a defining dimension of its corporate culture and the basis of many of its characteristics. The retail experience, for example, follows from this relationship concept. Haggling over price and playing negotiation games is not compatible with the Saturn–customer relationship. It seems incredible that nearly fifty years after the marketing concept appeared on the scene, treating the customer with respect and as a friend was a breakthrough in the automobile industry. But it was.

To understand the nature of a brand–customer relationship, it is useful to consider the metaphor of a brand as a person who has a personality and interpersonal relationships with customers. For example, Volvo personified might be dependable and reliable (with a European accent) but somewhat stodgy and lacking a sense of humor. The customer relationship might be characterized by feelings of being secure and comfortable. In sharp contrast, Mercedes as a person might be elegant, successful, and perhaps a bit stuffy and aloof. Its customer relationship might then be based on the customer aspiring to belong to the Mercedes group.

Saturn might be personified as young (at heart), genuine, honest, friendly, and down-to-earth, and as someone who cares about individuals (whether they are clients, patients, or customers) and treats them with respect and as a friend. This person would also be competent and reliable—a person you would respect and trust. The head of the Saturn engineering team talks of his company as a person who is "thoughtful and friendly" and who "won't let you down and won't outshine you."[10] The personified Saturn would not have a foreign accent, and would not speak to you condescendingly (as might, say, a personified Volkswagen who thinks you don't get the Fahrvergnügen concept), but would speak with respect and as a friend. The concept

---

THE SATURN "HOMECOMING"

Toward the end of June 1994 some 44,000 Saturn owners were invited to a "homecoming" at the Saturn plant in Spring Hill, Tennessee (see Figure 2–3). This "Saturnstock" event was modeled after a festival sponsored by Harley-Davidson that had drawn more than 100,000 Harley bikers to Milwaukee. As with the Harley-Davidson event, many Saturn owners traveled to Spring Hill in caravans organized by local retailers. In addition, over 100,000 other "Saturn-ites" attended picnics and parties organized by local dealers.

The "family get-together" participants at Spring Hill were treated to entertainment and activities. Six stages featured country music (with Wynonna Judd and others), rhythm and blues, gospel singers, mimes, clowns, and jugglers. The activities included line dancing, barbecues, craft fairs, mingling with celebrities (like Olympic gold medal skater Dan Jansen), and in the spirit of Harley-Davidson, a Saturn-logo "tattoo" parlor (the logo was removable). The centerpiece was the plant tour. In fact, the whole event was stimulated in part by the many requests from Saturn owners to visit the plant.

The event captured and reinforced the Saturn charisma. The focus was on Spring Hill, the plant, and the people; in fact, some 2,300 employees volunteered to be hosts for the event.

of Saturn as a person helps to give the brand–customer relationship more depth and texture.

According to Saturn retailers, another aspect of the firm's brand–customer relationship is a sense of customer pride in Saturn as a U.S. car that has beaten the Japanese firms at their own game, in the employees for their commitment and achievement, and in themselves for buying an American car. This is different from the product-centered pride felt by many new car buyers. The purchase and use of a Saturn goes beyond enjoying the functional characteristics to ex-pressing a customer's values and personality. Among the keys to this pride are the plant at Spring Hill, Tennessee, and the American employees' intense loyalty to Saturn. Ironically, Saturn never adopted a slogan like (Chevrolet's) "Heartbeat of America" or (Oldsmobile Aurora's) "An American Dream." If it had, the pride might not have been as strong, because it would have had less chance to be discov-ered by and to emanate from within Saturn owners.

Saturn has much in common with other charismatic brands (such as Apple, Harley, and the VW Beetle) that have developed intense and loyal relationship levels. Each is an underdog to a larger compet-itor, each has a strong user group with an identity of its own, and each has users who encourage others to buy.

THE RETAILER STRATEGY

The retailer organization both draws on and contributes to the Saturn culture and brand identity. In particular, retailers provide a very different buying experience that reflects the Saturn–customer re-lationship. Retailers also engage customers in activities which indicate that Saturn is interested in more than just selling a car.

Automobile customers are used to a high-pressure salesperson pouncing on them as they arrive at the showroom, and immediately pressuring them toward a test drive and a purchase decision. The classic line is, "If I can get this car to you for X dollars, would you buy?" Focus groups, a dealer-involved team, and simple logic told Saturn that customers intensely disliked this approach.

Saturn therefore has chosen to sell its product very differently. When the customer enters the showroom of the retailer (not a dealer), he or she is not pressured by a commissioned salesperson. Rather, the

FIGURE 2–3
Homecoming Ad

"Homecoming"

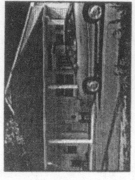

They came from Alaska and North Dakota.

From California and even farther West.

This summer we invited everyone who owns a Saturn to Tennessee. The place where their car was born.

We called it The Saturn Homecoming.

People could see where their cars had been built.

Spend some time with the men and women who built them.

Where the new idea for a car company had taken shape. Thank them for believing we could do it.

44,000 people gave up their usual summer vacations to spend them with us.

Pretty good turn out for our first big party.

Of course, not everything went exactly as we had planned. But, we were all in it together, the way we had always been.

Reprinted with permission of Saturn.

A Different Kind Of Company.
A Different Kind Of Car.

SATURN

salaried "sales consultant" is likely to wander over and ask if the browser has any questions. Further, the consultant is trained not only to answer questions but to explain in detail the design philosophy of the car and company, as well as point out features. Most important, the hated price haggling is eliminated; the retail price allows for a comfortable but not excessive margin (around $1,400 per car), the customer buys or does not buy, and that is that.

A key ingredient in making no-haggle pricing feasible was the market area retail network. Early in the development phase, Saturn retail team members pointed out that competing dealers in close proximity would have every incentive to reduce prices. Their suggestion—perhaps self-serving at the time, but brilliant in retrospect—was to find retailers who would take responsibility for a broad market area and to open as many as six dealerships in that area. Thus potential price competition among adjacent dealers, a driving force behind low profit margins, was nearly eliminated. The market area retail network, one of Saturn's most sustainable advantages, would be virtually impossible for competitors, locked into existing dealer agreements, to duplicate.

In addition to the market area concept, Saturn's system of low-pressure selling by salaried sales consultants is based upon the total organization. Its key components include a mix of sales consultants hired from outside the car industry, a compensation and incentive system based more on group efforts to satisfy customers than on individual sales results, a culture that emphasizes treating customers with respect and as friends, and structural links to the rest of the organization. At Ford, Chevrolet, and Toyota, in contrast, the whole organization is set up to push cars through the system. An effort by these firms to copy the Saturn selling system without overhauling their organization is unlikely to be successful. And changing the organization is most difficult.

Nordstrom is an example of a firm that has shaken up the retail environment in several major markets. Upscale department stores have attempted to respond by copying the "Nordstrom style" of doing business. They have been largely unsuccessful, however, because the elements of their organizations—especially employees used to another approach—are simply not capable of adapting. Competitors of Saturn would find similar problems if they tried to copy the Saturn retail style.

SATURN RETAILERS AS BRAND BUILDERS

Saturn retailers have played a key role in supporting the Saturn identity. Not only have they implemented a retail experience that leads to a relaxed, comfortable feeling rather than the tense, pressured and intimidating feeling associated with buying a car, but they have visibly communicated the fact that Saturn is about much more than making and selling cars.

Saturn retailers engage in a host of customer-involving activities that serve to connect customers to the brand. A monthly event such as a BBQ, ice cream social or outing is the norm at Saturn retailers. A Saturn Singles Social was organized for single Saturn owners by one retailer. "Local" homecomings were held by many retailers for those who could not make the Spring Hill event (see the Saturn Homecoming boxed description). A 100,000-mile club has been started by a Detroit retailer— any person whose Saturn has at least 100,000 miles on it becomes a member and receives a package of "Saturn stuff" and an official membership certificate.

Saturn retailers have been unusually active in local charities in part because charitable activities fit naturally with the Saturn way of thinking and relating to customers. Some of these projects are particularly visible because of their scope or continuity over time.

For example, the twelve Saturn retailers in the New York area have built twelve huge Saturn "Kid's Kingdoms," playgrounds that 150 kids can use. Each playground cost about $35,000 and involved many volunteers. This effort has been promoted by New York's Director of Parks and Recreation, the governor of New Jersey, and others as one of the best examples of a private-public sector partnership.

The Columbus Saturn dealer has links to the local zoo which include an annual "Saturn-day-at-the-zoo" party for Saturn owners (which attracts some five thousand people), the Saturn Safari which treats approximately thirty thousand children to a zoo experience, sponsorship of numerous fund-raising events for the zoo, and the use of zoo animals in ads and in the retail setting. (Live tigers have even visited the showrooms.)

A DIFFERENT KIND OF COMPANY, A DIFFERENT KIND OF CAR

A slogan can capture the essence of a brand and become an important part of the brand equity. If a brand is "packaged meaning," a slogan can be the ribbon that ties the package together and provides an extra touch. For example, the famous Avis slogan "We're number 2, we try harder" clearly positions the brand with respect to the competition (the leader, Hertz) and captures the thrust of the Avis strategy. Addressed to the employees as much as the customers, the slogan helps to crystallize the values and culture of the firm. Moreover, it provides an umbrella construct which organizes and communicates specific features and programs that otherwise would be disjoined and confused.

The slogan "A different kind of company, a different kind of car" provides the same kind of function for Saturn and is an important part of its brand equity. It suggests that unlike other Detroit cars, Saturn is a world-class product comparable to the best Japanese imports. The "different company" position captures the unique way in which Saturn operates and interacts with its customers. However, it also lends credence to the different-car position by implying that only a special car could be made by such a special company. If Saturn had claimed directly to be a world-class car, it is highly unlikely that it would have achieved the desired perceptions.

The slogan provides a core meaning, yet allows a host of specific features and programs to be introduced without confusion. A prospective customer may not recall exactly how the company and its car are different, but the impression of being different remains. The slogan also provides a center of gravity for the employees, suppliers, and retailers. An important part of the culture, it helps people enforce norms by saying, "That is not done here. We are different."

INTEGRATED COMMUNICATION

One practical problem in building and maintaining brand equity is the development of effective communication that is consistent over different media and over time. The automobile industry has been characterized by look-alike, product-focused Detroit advertising, a temptation to use price appeals, dealer advertising that is usually off strategy, and the involvement of a host of communication organizations. The result too often has been ineffective and inconsistent messages.

At Saturn, a very different approach was taken. A West Coast agency, Hal Riney, was selected as a "communications partner." In order to make sure the message was consistent across media and through time, Riney was charged with being involved in all the Saturn communication efforts, including brochures, retailer advertising, and the design of the retail showroom. The Riney shop was experienced with this broader scope: It had created the life-size story display for the Bartles & Jaymes wine cooler spokesmen Frank and Ed, a logo for Mirage Resorts, a package design for Stroh Brewery, and a seven-minute entertainment film for Alamo Rent-A-Car customers to watch while waiting in line.

Early on Riney produced "Spring in Spring Hill," a twenty-six-minute documentary in which Saturn team members explained the excitement and challenge of being part of their new company. The piece captured the emotion and feeling of Saturn. It was shown to employees, suppliers, the press, and eventually to the general public as an infomercial.

Illustrative of the integrated communication effort is the work that Riney did to ensure that the retailer effort was on strategy. The print ads designed for retailers were very different from local automobile newspaper advertising which usually emphasized price. With a large picture of the car, considerable white space, and witty headlines, the series of ads were compatible with the Saturn car and personality. One asked, "Gosh, what if we all came back as cars?" Riney had to resist the inclination of retailers to fill the white space with used-car prices or maps showing directions to the nearest showroom.

Perhaps the most telling example of enforced consistency occurred when a group of retailers considered a car giveaway to generate store traffic when awareness and interest was at a low point. Riney insisted that such a promotion would damage the huge investment in brand equity, especially among customers unfamiliar with the Saturn concept. When the retailers persisted, Riney designed a promotion that would enhance the equity rather than damage it: Winners would go to Spring Hill and participate in building their car. The focus was then on Spring Hill and the com-

FIGURE 2–4

Saturn Brand Equity Drivers and Challenges

PRIMARY DRIVERS OF BRAND EQUITY	BRAND EQUITY DIMENSIONS	CHALLENGES TO MAINTAIN EQUITY
• Advertising • Retail presence • Publicity • Word of mouth	Awareness	• Maintain awareness in the face of reduced news value and competitive clutter
• Advertising • Slogan/position • Spring Hill plant • Retail experience • Integrated communication • Relationship based on brand identity	Brand Associations: • Committed employees • Enthused customers • Spring Hill plant • Different company/car • Retail experience • Liking/friend • U.S. car in Honda Civic class • Treat customers with respect	• Need to communicate the Saturn message to those new to the brand in the face of pressures to talk product, not company
• Product design • Manufacturing commitment • New organization/ culture • Empathy with employees • Empathy with customers • Slogan/position • Money-back guarantee	Perceived Quality	• Maintaining actual quality after the initial excitement is over and in the face of competitors' efforts to improve their position
• Friendship relationship • Retail experience • Pride in U.S. company	Loyalty	• Keep relationship strong over time
• Market area concept • Corporate culture	Retail System	• Keep the retail culture in place in the face of slow sales and imitation

mitted employees building quality cars, not on mercenary appeals to entice people into a showroom.

CREATING BRAND EQUITY

Figure 2–4 summarizes how brand equity was created at Saturn. The figure shows five dimensions of brand equity (the retail system is added to the four conceptualized in Chapter 1); also shown are the principal drivers of each dimension. Note that some eighteen different decisions and programs are mentioned as drivers, and that the list is not meant to be comprehensive.

There was no primary driver of the Saturn results. Rather, it seems clear that the synergy and fit of the various pieces combined to create the brand equity. Four elements of the strategy, however, stand out as being especially crucial: the ability to design and build a quality car, the relationship-based brand identity, the decision to focus advertising on the company and its employees and customers (rather than the car), and the retail experience (based upon the Saturn culture and the market area concept). The last three represented a real difference in automobile brand management.

CHALLENGES FACING SATURN AND GENERAL MOTORS

A number of questions surface as Saturn moves from creating a brand to maintaining its strength and vitality. Can Saturn keep it going? What should General Motors do with its market success? It is a bit like the car-chasing dog who finally catches one: What does it do now? There are several issues and problems facing both General Motors and Saturn.

KEEPING IT GOING

One set of issues facing GM involves managing the beast. In some respects, it was actually easier to create Saturn than it will be to keep it going and maintain the intensity of its culture. The excitement of inventing an aggressive new strategy and pulling it off provides considerable motivation and momentum. But what happens when competitors copy or appear to copy some of the key customer relationship aspects, such as no price haggling? When the product gets old and the heady days of no backlog change? When the product quality gets surpassed by competitors taking dead aim at Saturn? When Saturn fails to get priority for GM resources? It will be a real management challenge to manage the norms of behavior, communicate values, and nurture symbols and role models when adversity sets in.

Figure 2–4 also summarizes some of the key operational problems facing Saturn. An important challenge will be to maintain awareness levels and associations as the brand matures. The introductory phase had inherent drama and interest, especially given the decision to talk about the company instead of the brand. The brand benefited from publicity, word-of-mouth support, and interest in the advertising message. As Saturn matures, there will be a tendency for it to fade into the clutter of the marketplace. Management will have to fight hard to keep the brand fresh, interesting, and visible.

Continuing to communicate the Saturn "different kind of company" message will be an important task. Unfortunately, the introductory phase lacked a strong visual image capturing the company spirit and commitment. There is no lingering image with the potential to be a Marlboro country, a lonesome Maytag repairman, a Michelin man, or even a funky Apple logo. (The Saturn logo and name, inspired by the Saturn rocket, is hardly helpful in this regard). In the absence of such a visual image, Saturn must find ways to communicate its philosophy to the market, particularly to newcomers who were not exposed to or have forgotten the early advertising.

Maintaining perceived quality is perhaps the most crucial chore facing Saturn. The excitement in the factory will fade, and the team concept will come under pressure as it has elsewhere. Keeping the faith either under prolonged success—where the risk of failure is less intense—or amid downturns and setbacks is not easy. In addition, quality signals (such as the J. D. Power indices that measure initial customer satisfaction with the car and the dealer experience) require constant focus. A host of competitors will be targeting Saturn's lofty Power index scores, and though it may be unrealistic to assume that they can be maintained, these high numbers are a vital quality cue.

Another challenge is to nurture the pride and the charismatic brand characteristics that drive the loyalty levels achieved by Saturn.

Nintendo, Harley-Davidson, Apple, and the fabled VW Beetle all sustained high loyalty levels over time by maintaining strong personalities and by providing a sense of group involvement. Some Saturn retailers have arranged group events for owners and have provided other mechanisms for involvement; however, the Saturn loyalty relies largely on the concept that the product and the organization are different. Maintaining this reality, as well as finding ways to express it, will be both difficult and crucial.

The Saturn retail experience involves a strong culture that will be challenged. A strong culture, though, works best when there is frequent success and reinforcement. When an organization inevitably goes through hard times, it is more difficult to sustain the culture. Further, there will be many competing auto dealers who will attempt to imitate Saturn. Some of these imitators will be Saturn retailers who own dealerships of other brands, and who will thus have firsthand experience with the Saturn approach. Even unsuccessful copycats will confuse the positioning of Saturn, making it harder for the brand to stand out.

THE SATURN RELATIONSHIP TO GM

A second set of tough issues involves the relationship of General Motors to Saturn. Should General Motors support Saturn by aggressively updating the design, expanding its production capacity (initially limited to 300,000 vehicles), and most critically, adding a midsize car to compete with the Honda Accord and Ford Taurus? Such investments could cost billions (the original Saturn plant and car were estimated to cost $5 billion), and GM is a firm with many demands on its resources.[11]

In many respects, such decisions seem like no-brainers. After all, with Saturn, General Motors took on Honda, Toyota, and Nissan and won. Surveys indicated that more than 70 percent of Saturn's sales came from buyers who otherwise would not have bought GM products, and more than half from customers who would have bought imports.[12] In the process, Saturn developed strengths that are likely to be sustainable with proper management and investment. The obvious course, then, is to back the winner and run with it.

The choice, however, is not so simple for General Motors. Saturn has been slow to turn the profit corner—in part because it is competing in an inherently low-margin business area, in part because its volume is still inadequate, and in part because it is still low on the experience curve. Although Saturn did enter the black in 1993, a satisfactory return on the total Saturn investment is still a long way off. With a relatively weak profit picture, it is difficult to fight for resources and new products within General Motors. In fact, Saturn sales suffered in 1993 when GM sharply curtailed advertising, cut plans to add dealers (at that time Saturn had only 285 outlets serving about 60 percent of the U.S. market), and delayed plans to provide a face-lift and add passenger air bags.

GM must also consider Chevrolet, which has long been positioned as the entry-level car for GM. With its car sales falling in the early 1990s, Chevrolet was desperate for new products and resentful of the investment that went into Saturn. Chevrolet management naturally believed that Saturn should have had a Chevrolet nameplate. Although the consensus of more objective observers is that the Saturn miracle simply would not have happened in that case, Chevrolet—which needs to be a healthy survivor, especially in the midsize car area—casts a shadow over Saturn.

Another GM strategy could be to exploit Saturn by transferring its trailblazing approach to other GM divisions, in keeping with its mission to "transfer knowledge, technology and experience throughout General Motors." Indeed, Oldsmobile's strategy is to "Saturnize" itself—in part through the Vision Center, a weeklong training program for the staff of Oldsmobile and its some 3,000 dealers which is largely staffed by Saturn employees. Including team-building exercises and customer-interaction classes, the course (which dealers were required to attend before they could sell the new Aurora) was designed to create a Saturn customer culture and teamwork atmosphere. "Oldsmobile Simplified Pricing," a practice in which dealers offer a no-haggle, no-rebate price for a car equipped with the most popular options, is an effort to incorporate one of the most visible aspects of Saturn.

Transferring the Saturn magic to Oldsmobile and other GM division will not be easy, though, because it is based not on programs but on the whole organization. The other divisions will have to struggle to change in the face of long-established systems, rigid and confrontational unions, an established dealer structure and culture, and significant internal resentment of Saturn's success.

ATTACHING THE GM NAME TO SATURN

An endorser such as GM can detract from a brand such as Saturn, inhibiting it from establishing the level of perceived quality and the identity crucial for its success. For that reason, it was wise to avoid initially associating Saturn with GM. Similarly, the Oldsmobile label is de-emphasized in the Aurora car and advertising so that the Aurora can establish its own identity free of the Oldsmobile baggage.

There will be a time when Saturn can lend its equity to GM, however, thereby becoming a vehicle to help revitalize the parent brand. Two conditions are necessary. First, Saturn needs to be firmly established in its own right as a distinct brand and organization, so that the negative impact on Saturn of adding GM as an endorser will be minimal. Second, the other divisions need to actually be truly capable of delivering Saturn-level quality and customer interaction. With GM quality improving and the Saturn brand established, that time may be close.

ASSESSING THE SATURN STORY

The Saturn story is about how a modest GM compact created a charisma and loyalty normally associated with brands like Harley-Davidson, the VW Beetle, or the Ford Mustang. Several lessons stand out. First, key elements of the Saturn brand (such as the retail buying experience) resonated with customers and were very different from those of competitors. There was no question that Saturn differentiated itself. Second, the Saturn identity was created from within the organization, by its people, culture, values, structure, and systems. These deep roots make it difficult for competitors to duplicate the Saturn programs. Third, the success of the Saturn brand was due not to any key programs or policies but rather to the total gestalt formed by a dozen Saturn decisions and practices. It is therefore unrealistic to measure quantitatively the role that any one element played in the ultimate performance.

The story is also not only about how GM has created a strong brand under adverse circumstances but, strangely, about how to handle success. How can Saturn keep maintaining the Saturn equity past the initial thrust, especially with the competing demands for GM resources? And hgw should GM manage the strategic fit of Saturn with the rest of the GM family? These tough questions have yet to be answered.

QUESTIONS TO CONSIDER

1. What elements of the Saturn brand-building effort would you classify as critical (if the part were missing, Saturn would not have pulled it off)? What was the single most important Saturn decision?
2. Develop a drivers-and-challenges model like that in Figure 2–4 for a key brand in your organization. Pick one or two or more of the challenges and develop a program to address it.

3

THE BRAND
IDENTITY SYSTEM[1]

Customers must recognize that you stand for something.
—Howard Schultz, Starbucks

They laughed when I sat down at the piano—but when I started to play . . .
—John Caples for International Correspondence School

WHAT IS BRAND IDENTITY?

A person's identity serves to provide direction, purpose, and meaning for that person. Consider how important the following questions are: What are my core values? What do I stand for? How do I want to be perceived? What personality traits do I want to project? What are the important relationships in my life?

A brand identity similarly provides direction, purpose and meaning for the brand. It is central to a brand's strategic vision and the driver of one of the four principal dimensions of brand equity: associations, which are the heart and soul of the brand. Nestlé uses the term *brand constitution* to reflect the importance and reverence with which a brand identity should be held. So, what exactly is brand identity?

> *Brand identity is a unique set of brand associations that the brand strategist aspires to create or maintain. These associations represent what the brand stands for and imply a promise to customers from the organization members.*

> *Brand identity should help establish a relationship between the brand and the customer by generating a value proposition involving functional, emotional or self-expressive benefits.*

> *Brand identity consists of twelve dimensions organized around four perspectives—the brand-as-product (product scope, product attributes, quality/value, uses, users, country of origin), brand-as-organization (organizational attributes, local versus global), brand-as-person (brand personality, brand–customer relationships), and brand-as-symbol (visual imagery/metaphors and brand heritage).*

> *Brand identity structure includes a core and extended identity. The core identity—the central, timeless essence of the brand—is most likely to remain constant as the brand travels to new markets and products. The extended identity includes*

brand identity elements, organized into cohesive and meaning-
ful groupings, that provide texture and completeness.

The purpose of this chapter is to elaborate the definition of brand identity and of related concepts, such as the value proposition and credibility, that a brand identity generates. A theme of the chapter is that *there is value in expanding the concept of a brand*. Too often a limited, tactical perspective inhibits strategists from building a strong brand even when the potential exists. To achieve maximum brand strength, the scope of a brand identity should be broad rather than narrow, the thrust should be strategic rather than tactical, and there should be an internal as well as external focus to brand creation.

BRAND IDENTITY TRAPS

An examination of four all-too-common identity traps (summarized in Figure 3–1) demonstrates the value of expanding the concept of a brand and provides substantial insight into what a brand identity is and is not. These four traps represent approaches to creating an identity that are excessively limiting or tactical and that can lead to ineffective and often dysfunctional brand strategies. After these traps have been analyzed, a broader identity concept will be developed, its scope and structure discussed, and the value proposition and credibility that flow from it examined.

THE BRAND IMAGE TRAP

Knowledge of the brand image (how customers and others perceive the brand) provides useful and even necessary background information when developing a brand identity. In the brand image trap, however, the patience, resources, or expertise to go beyond the brand image is lacking, and the brand image *becomes* the brand identity rather than just one input to be considered.

The brand image trap does not tend to occur when a brand image is obviously negative or inappropriate. When there are only subtle image inadequacies caused by customers' past brand experiences or by changes in their needs, however, the use of the brand image as an identity statement often goes unchallenged.

FIGURE 3–1
Brand Identity Traps

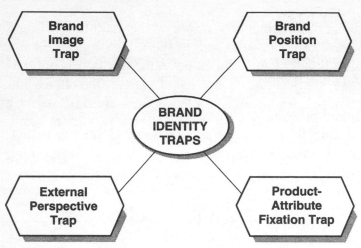

An insidious problem caused by the brand image trap is that it lets the customer dictate what you are. In short, it is a customer orientation gone amok, much like the Wiley cartoon where a market researcher arrives at a nearly finished Sistine Chapel to say, "Personally, I think it looks OK, Michelangelo, but the focus group says it needs more mauve."[2] Creating a brand identity is more than finding out what customers say they want. It must also reflect the soul and vision of the brand, what it hopes to achieve.

While brand image is usually passive and looks to the past, brand identity should be active and look to the future, reflecting the associations that are aspired for the brand. While brand image tends to be tactical, brand identity should be strategic, reflecting a business strategy that will lead to a sustainable advantage. The brand identity should also reflect the brand's enduring qualities, even if they are not salient in the brand image. Like any identity, it represents the basic characteristics that will persist over time.

A brand identity is to brand strategy what "strategic intent" is to a business strategy. Strategic intent involves an obsession with winning, real innovation, stretching the current strategy, and a forward-looking, dynamic perspective; it is very different from accepting or even refining past strategy. Similarly, a brand identity should not accept existing perceptions, but instead should be willing to consider creating changes.

THE BRAND POSITION TRAP

A brand position is the part of the brand identity and value proposition that is to be actively communicated to the target audience and that demonstrates an advantage over competing brands.

Thus the brand position guides the current communication programs and is distinct from the more general brand identity construct. Some elements of brand identity (such as cleanliness for a restaurant) may not be actively communicated, and other elements (such as a product class association) will recede in visibility as the brand matures. Thus there is a distinction between three related constructs:

BRAND IMAGE	BRAND IDENTITY	BRAND POSITION
How the brand is now perceived	How strategists want the brand to be perceived	The part of the brand identity and value proposition to be actively communicated to a target audience

The brand position trap occurs when the search for a brand identity becomes a search for a brand position, stimulated by a practical need to provide objectives to those developing the communication programs. The goal then becomes an advertising tag line rather than a brand identity.

This trap inhibits the evolution of a full-fledged brand identity, because strategists continuously weed out those aspects that they feel are not worth communicating. The tendency to focus on product attributes is intensified, and there is often no room to consider brand personality, organizational associations, or brand symbols because they simply do not make the cut when developing a three-word phrase.

Further, a compact phrase is unlikely to provide much guidance to brand-building activities. A brand position does not usually have the texture and depth needed to guide the brand-building effort—which event to sponsor, which package is superior, or what store display supports the brand. There is a need for a richer, more complete understanding of what the brand stands for.

THE EXTERNAL PERSPECTIVE TRAP

From the perspective of most brand strategists, particularly in the United States and Europe, a brand identity is something that gets customers to buy the product or service because of how they perceive the brand. The orientation is entirely external.

The external perspective trap occurs when firms fail to realize the role that a brand identity can play in helping an organization understand its basic values and purpose. Because an effective identity is based in part on a disciplined effort to specify the strengths, values, and vision of the brand, it can provide a vehicle to communicate internally what the brand is about. It is hard to expect employees to make a vision happen if they do not understand and buy into that vision.

In most organizations, employees have a difficult time answering the question, "What does your brand stand for?" "Achieving a 10 percent increase in sales" (or profitability)—an all-too-typical response—is hardly inspiring. In firms with strong brands, the response comes faster and with more substance from motivated, even inspired employees. Saturn executives, plant workers, retailers, and suppliers all know that Saturn stands for a world-class car and treating customers as respected friends. Employees in the Kao organization know that the Kao brand stands for innovation and leadership. Such employee response and buy-in comes from a strong brand identity.

THE PRODUCT-ATTRIBUTE FIXATION TRAP

The most common trap of all is the product-attribute fixation trap, in which the strategic and tactical management of the brand is focused solely on product attributes. Based in part on the erroneous assumption that those attributes are the only relevant bases for customer decisions and competitive dynamics, the product-attribute fixation trap usually leads to less than optimal strategies and sometimes to damaging blunders.

A Brand Is More Than a Product

The failure to distinguish between a product and a brand creates the product-attribute fixation trap. Consider Hobart, which is the premium, dominant brand in industrial-grade food preparation equipment (such as mixers, slicers, dishwashers, and refrigerators). Hobart bases its brand identity and strategy on its product attributes: high quality, durability, reliability, and a premium price. In reality, however, the brand also delivers the feeling of buying and using the best. A baker or cook who has a self-image of being the best wants first-class equipment in the kitchen. Buying Hobart is one way for these individuals to express their values, both to themselves and to others.

Understanding that Hobart is more than a product has significant implications for pricing, segmentation, and communication strategies. One is that it is unnecessary and probably undesirable for Hobart to compete in price-sensitive segments. Rather, the goal should be to seek out those customers that who are interested in having the best and to develop communication materials that associate the best with Hobart.

Figure 3–2 summarizes the distinction between a product and a brand. The product includes characteristics such as scope (Crest makes dental hygiene products), attributes (Volvo is safe), quality/value (Kraft delivers a quality product), and uses (Subaru is made for the snow). A brand includes these product characteristics and much more:

- Brand users (the Charlie woman)
- Country of origin (Audi has German craftsmanship)
- Organizational associations (3M is an innovative company)
- Brand personality (Bath and Body Works is a retail brand with energy and vitality)
- Symbols (The stagecoach represents Wells Fargo Bank)
- Brand–customer relationships (Gateway is a friend)
- Emotional benefits (Saturn users feel pride in driving a U.S. car)
- Self-expressive benefits (a Hobart user uses only the best)

Product-Attribute Research

The product-attribute fixation trap is often caused in part by a reliance on research focusing on attributes. Such research is popular for several reasons:

- It is often effective, because attributes are important to the purchase decision and the use experience.

FIGURE 3–2
A Brand Is More Than a Product

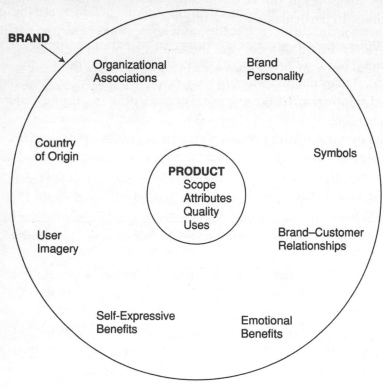

- It is relatively easy, since customers are more comfortable talking about attributes than about less tangible benefits (which might seem irrational).
- It reassures managers that customers evaluate brands using a logical model, which means that their decisions are easier to predict and understand.

With extensive data in hand, the firm may feel that a thorough job of gauging consumer needs has been done when its research has in fact been restricted to a list of product attributes. Such information, even when coupled with relative-importance weights and competitor positions, is likely to be incomplete and may therefore inhibit a brand from reaching its full potential. This problem is particularly severe in the worlds of high-tech, industrial products, and durable goods, where managers are especially fond of the rational customer model.

Limitations of Product-Attribute–Based Identities

Product attributes as the basis for a brand identity have important limitations. In particular, they too often:

Fail to Differentiate. A product attribute can be extremely important to customers, but if all brands are perceived to be adequate on this dimension, it does not differentiate the brand. When Procter & Gamble decided to position Jif peanut butter on a freshness dimension because customers said it was the most important attribute and because Jif had a manufacturing process (involving inert gas) that generated real freshness superiority, the effort bombed. Research revealed that customers simply believed all brands were the same on this dimension; Jif could not convince them that the other brands had a freshness liability.

Similarly, in the hotel business, cleanliness is always rated as one of the attributes most important to consumers. Thus it would be appropriate for cleanliness to be a part of the identity for Hilton. Because *all* hotels are expected to be clean, however, it will not be a differentiator.

Are Easy to Copy. Attribute-oriented benefits are relatively easy to copy. A brand that relies on the superior performance of a key attribute will eventually get beaten on that attribute, even if it is continuously improving the product, because the attribute is a fixed target for competitors. In the words of Regis McKenna, the Silicon Valley brand guru, you will eventually get "out-spec'd" (that is, a competitor will announce a product with superior technical specifications) when the focus is on a product attribute. The result can be a loss of differentiation or, worse, an inferior position on an attribute that is integrally associated with the brand. Consider Taster's Choice, which surpassed the freeze-dried coffee category innovator, Maxim, by being superior on the key dimension of taste.

Assume a Rational Customer. Product attribute research and the resulting strategies usually assume that customers obey a rational decision-making model. The rational model suggests that customers collect information about product attributes, adjust the information to reflect the relative importance of the attributes, and then make a reasoned judgment. The reality is that customers experience mistrust, confusion, or impatience in most contexts, and that they do not (or cannot) seek out and process objective information about the brands in the category. In addition, many customers do not care as much about function as they do about style, status, reassurance, and other less functional benefits.

Attribute research on trucks, for example, suggests that durability, safety features, options, and power are the most important attributes. Yet style, comfort, and being "fun" to drive are more likely to influence the decisions of consumers who often cannot or will not admit that such frills are really important to them. Of course, there are other more indirect research approaches available to explore these hidden motivations (see chapter 6 in *Managing Brand Equity*), but the basic problems with the rational model remain.

Limit Brand Extension Strategies. Strong product-attribute associations, while potentially providing a source of advantage, can be limiting with respect to brand extension strategies. The fact that Heinz means slow-pouring, rich ketchup may limit its role in extension strategies, whereas the association of Contadina with Italians provides more flexibility. An identity that is based upon intangible associations or brand personalities provides the brand with more strategic scope.

Reduce Strategic Flexibility. Finally, product-attribute associations reduce a brand's ability to respond to changing markets. If a brand becomes associated with a single product attribute, the ability of that brand to adjust when the attribute's relevance declines is inhibited. In this manner, Weight Watchers' emphasis on professional weight control limited its ability to respond when Healthy Choice entered its market with a "healthy eating" identity.

BROADENING THE CONCEPT OF A BRAND

The four identity traps suggest how a brand identity can become confining and ineffective. In particular, the focus of a brand is too often restricted to product attributes, existing brand images, brand position, and the brand's external role of influencing customers. A key to developing a strong brand identity is to broaden the brand concept to include other dimensions and perspectives.

The model in Figure 3–3 provides a broader perspective on brand identity planning that can help strategists avoid identity traps. The heart of the model is the brand identity system, where the brand identity provides a value proposition to customers or credibility to other brands. The ultimate goal of the system is a strong brand–customer relationship.

As shown in the model, brand identity does not have to be drawn entirely from the brand-as-product perspective. Three additional perspectives (brand-as-organization, brand-as-person, and brand-as-symbol) can enhance the understanding of and create bases of differentiation for the brand.

Figure 3–3 includes two other major components: the strategic brand analysis and the brand identity implementation system, both of which are discussed in Chapter 6. The implementation system includes the brand position (the statement of communication objectives drawn from the brand identity and value proposition) as well as an execution and tracking component. The strategic brand analysis, which involves analyses of the customers, competitors, and self, provides the necessary inputs to the planning model.

BREAKING OUT OF THE TRAPS

A primary point of this chapter—indeed, of this book—is that brand identity tends to be conceptualized too narrowly. A more complete view of brand identity can help strategists break out of the traps by considering the following:

- A brand-as-product perspective that includes user imagery and the country (or region) of origin
- A brand identity based on the perspectives of the brand as an organization, a person, and a symbol in addition to a product
- A value proposition that includes emotional and self-expressive benefits as well as functional benefits
- The ability of a brand to provide credibility as well as a value proposition
- The internal as well as external role of the brand identity
- Brand characteristics broader than a brand position (active communication objectives) or a core identity

Creating a Frame of Reference

One goal of the strategist should be to create a frame of reference to be used by the customer and others when they think of and evaluate the brand and its competitors.[3] For example, Wells Fargo uses a stagecoach, Marlboro promotes Marlboro country, and Saturn highlights the values of the Saturn employee team to create a context that helps customers understand what the brand stands for. One way to think about a brand identity system is to ask what frame of reference customers should use when recalling the brand, processing information about it, and evaluating it.

FOUR BRAND IDENTITY PERSPECTIVES

As suggested by Figure 3–3, to help ensure that the brand identity has texture and depth, a firm should consider its brand as: (1) a product, (2) an organization, (3) a person, and (4) a symbol. The perspectives are very different. Their goal is to help the strategist consider different brand elements and patterns that can help clarify, enrich, and differentiate an identity. A more detailed identity will also help guide implementation decisions.

Not every brand identity needs to employ all or even several of these perspectives. For some brands, only one will be viable and appropriate. Each brand should, however, consider all of the perspectives and use those that are helpful in articulating what the brand should stand for in the customer's mind.

The brand-as-product perspective will be described next. The brand-as-organization and the brand-as-person views, described in detail in Chapters 4 and 5, will then be previewed. An analysis of the brand-as-symbol perspective will follow. The chapter will then turn to the identity structure, the value proposition, the credibility role, the brand–customer relationship, and finally the case where a brand has multiple identities as it travels across products and markets.

THE BRAND AS A PRODUCT: PRODUCT-RELATED ASSOCIATIONS

Although strategists should avoid the product-attribute fixation trap, product-related associations will almost always be an important part of a brand identity because they are directly linked to brand choice decisions and the use experience.

The Product Scope: Associations with Product Class

A core element of a brand's identity is usually its product thrust, which will affect the type of associations that are desirable and feasible.

FIGURE 3–3
Brand Identity Planning Model

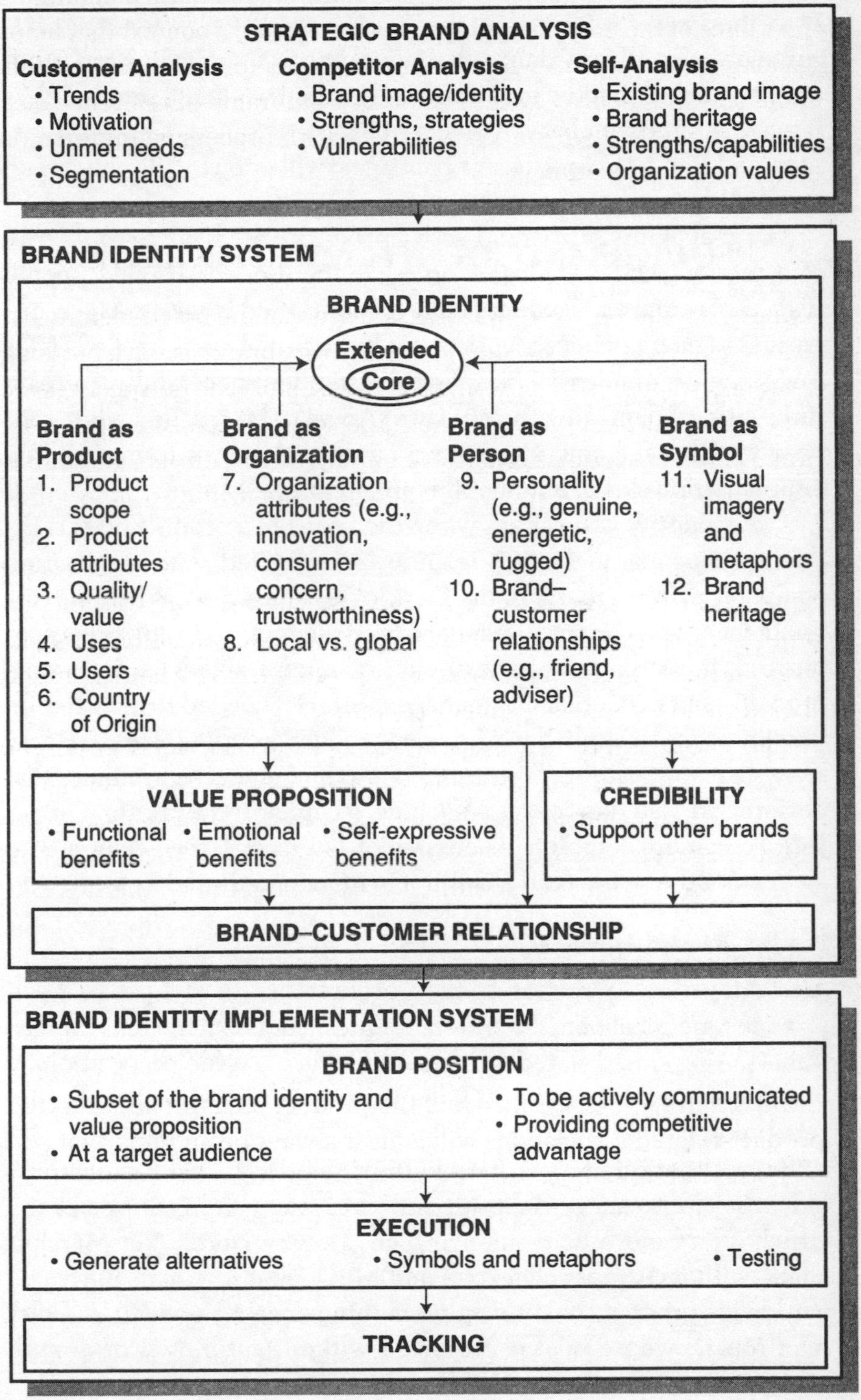

STRATEGIC BRAND ANALYSIS

Customer Analysis
- Trends
- Motivation
- Unmet needs
- Segmentation

Competitor Analysis
- Brand image/identity
- Strengths, strategies
- Vulnerabilities

Self-Analysis
- Existing brand image
- Brand heritage
- Strengths/capabilities
- Organization values

BRAND IDENTITY SYSTEM

BRAND IDENTITY

Extended
Core

Brand as Product
1. Product scope
2. Product attributes
3. Quality/ value
4. Uses
5. Users
6. Country of Origin

Brand as Organization
7. Organization attributes (e.g., innovation, consumer concern, trustworthiness)
8. Local vs. global

Brand as Person
9. Personality (e.g., genuine, energetic, rugged)
10. Brand–customer relationships (e.g., friend, adviser)

Brand as Symbol
11. Visual imagery and metaphors
12. Brand heritage

VALUE PROPOSITION
- Functional benefits
- Emotional benefits
- Self-expressive benefits

CREDIBILITY
- Support other brands

BRAND–CUSTOMER RELATIONSHIP

BRAND IDENTITY IMPLEMENTATION SYSTEM

BRAND POSITION
- Subset of the brand identity and value proposition
- At a target audience
- To be actively communicated
- Providing competitive advantage

EXECUTION
- Generate alternatives
- Symbols and metaphors
- Testing

TRACKING

With what product or products is the brand associated? For Häagen-Dazs the answer is ice cream, for Visa it is credit cards, for Buick it is automobiles, and for Compaq it is computers. A strong link to a product class means that the brand will be recalled when the product class is cued. A dominant brand (such as A1 in steak sauce, Kleenex in tissues, and Band-Aid in adhesive bandages) will often be the only brand recalled.

The goal of linking a brand with a product class is *not* to gain recall of a product class when the brand is mentioned. Having people respond "rental cars" when Hertz is mentioned is not nearly as important as having Hertz mentioned when a rental car is needed. Thus A&W, the venerable root beer brand, extended successfully to cream soda without damaging the ability of A&W to be recalled when root beer was the cue, and Honda is a name that comes to mind when either motorcycles or automobiles are mentioned.

A key identity issue arises when the scope of a product class is expanded. For many, the HP Jet line is associated with the leading computer printers (namely, the DeskJet and LaserJet). When the distinction between printers, scanners, fax machines, and copiers became blurred, the strong printer association, once a key asset, became a problem that needed active management. HP needed to alter the Jet identity so that it applied to a broader product grouping. Thus HP now has a scanner (ScanJet), fax machines (FaxJet), and even machines that perform the functions of a fax machine, a copier, and a printer (Office-Jet). For a more complete discussion of extensions, see Chapter 8 on leveraging the brand (and chapter 9 in *Managing Brand Equity*).

Product-Related Attributes

Attributes directly related to the purchase or use of a product can provide functional benefits and sometimes emotional benefits for customers. A product-related attribute can create a value proposition by offering something extra (like features or services) or by offering something better.

Brands that offer something better include Norelco, which provides the closest shave via its lift-and-cut system; the 7-Eleven chain, which offers more convenience than grocery stores; the Marriott chain, with its express checkout; and McDonald's, with its unrivaled worldwide product consistency. Something extra is provided by Coleman Meats, whose beef is produced without antibiotics or growth hormones, and by Virgin Airlines, which offers free limousine service with a business class ticket. As noted above, though, the problem is that product attributes tend to be the focus of identity efforts to the exclusion of other perspectives that can add value and distinctiveness to the brand.

Quality/Value

The quality element is one product-related attribute important enough to consider separately. Is the brand a Mercedes, a Buick, or a Ford? A Neiman Marcus, a Macy's, or a Kmart? For each competitive arena, perceived quality provides either the price of admission (you need to deliver a minimum level of quality to survive) or the linchpin of competition (the brand with the highest quality wins). Many brands use quality as a core identity element. Gillette, for example, is positioned in large part by "The Best a Man Can Get," and Gillette's Good News is the best of the disposable razor category. Starbucks' brand identity is based in large part on its reputation for providing the finest coffee in the world with integrity and consistency.

Value is closely related to quality; it enriches the concept by adding the price dimension. Rubbermaid, for example, strives to provide value by offering the highest-quality products at reasonable prices. Wal-Mart is also primarily positioned as a value retailer.

Associations with Use Occasion

Some brands successfully attempt to own a particular use or application, forcing competitors to work around this reality. Gatorade, for example, owns the use context of athletes looking to sustain a high level of performance. Clorox bleach has become strongly associated with the whitening of clothing, even though bleach can be used for cleaning and disinfecting a wide variety of things. Although Miracle Whip is a versatile salad dressing, its real strength is a close association with sandwich making. Starbucks coffeehouses provide a familiar, yet upscale place to relax staffed by friendly employees.

Associations with Users

Another tack is to position a brand by a type of user. Eddie Bauer, for example, offers contemporary fashions for the person with an outdoor lifestyle. Gerber focuses on babies, Weight Watchers is associated with those who are interested in weight control and nutrition, and

Friskies is the food for active cats. A strong user-type position can imply a value proposition and a brand personality. This dimension and its relationship to brand personality will be discussed further in Chapter 5.

Link to a Country or Region

One more strategic option is to associate one's brand with a country or region that will add credibility to it. For example, Chanel is seen as indelibly French, Swatch watches as Swiss, Beck's beer and Mercedes as German, Stolichnaya vodka as Russian, and Molson Ice beer as from Canada ("where ice was invented"). Champagne similarly means France, just as Bloomingdale's means New York. In each case, the brand's association with a country or region implies that the brand will provide higher quality, because that country or region has a heritage of making the best within that product class.

A host of studies have explored the country-of-origin effect. One study showed that the extent of the effect depends on the product class: For example, Japanese electronic goods are rated higher than Japanese food, and French fashions are more highly regarded than French electronic goods.[4] The country of origin, however, can impart attributes that travel across categories. Han and Terpstra, in comparing U.S. consumers' evaluations of automobiles and television sets, found that American products were considered high in serviceability, Japanese products were considered only moderate in prestige (despite their dominant ratings in other dimensions), and German products were high on prestige but low on economy.[5]

THE BRAND-AS-ORGANIZATION

The brand-as-organization perspective focuses on attributes of the organization rather than those of the product or service. Such organizational attributes as innovation, a drive for quality, and concern for the environment are created by the people, culture, values, and programs of the company. The Saturn brand is a good example of such an identity, tying together Saturn values (building a world-class economy car), programs (including the retailer system) and people (who visibly buy into the values).

Some brand aspects can be described as product attributes in some contexts and organizational attributes in others. Quality or innovation, for instance, could be a product-related attribute if it is based on the design and features of a specific product offering. If it is based on organizational culture, values, and programs (and thus transcends a particular product model context), however, it would then be an organizational-related attribute. In some cases there will be a combination of the two perspectives.

Organizational attributes are more enduring and more resistant to competitive claims than are product attributes. First, it is much easier to copy a product than to duplicate an organization with unique people, values, and programs. Second, organizational attributes usually apply to a set of product classes, and a competitor in only one product class may find it difficult to compete. Third, because organizational attributes such as being innovative are hard to evaluate and communicate, it is difficult for competitors to demonstrate that they have overcome any perceived gap. It is relatively easy to show that one's printer is faster than that of a competitor; it is hard to show that one's organization is more innovative.

Organizational attributes can contribute to a value proposition. Associations such as a customer focus, environmental concern, technological commitment, or a local orientation can involve emotional and self-expressive benefits based on admiration, respect, or simple liking. They can also provide credibility for the product claims of sub-brands, just as the Post-it products from 3M were undoubtedly helped by the 3M reputation for innovation.

In Chapter 4, the brand-as-organization will be considered in detail. Additional insight will be provided into what organizational attributes are and how they work to support a brand.

THE BRAND-AS-PERSON: BRAND PERSONALITY

The brand-as-person perspective suggests a brand identity that is richer and more interesting than one based on product attributes. Like a person, a brand can be perceived as being upscale, competent, impressive, trustworthy, fun, active, humorous, casual, formal, youthful, or intellectual. For example, Saturn has the personality of a reliable, down-to-earth friend.

A brand personality can create a stronger brand in several ways. First, it can help create a self-expressive benefit that becomes a vehicle for the customer to express his or her own personality. For example, an Apple user might identify himself or herself as casual, anti-corporate, and creative.

Second, just as human personalities affect relationships between people, brand personality can be the basis of a relationship between the customer and the brand. The friend relationship helps drive the Saturn identity and program. Similarly, Dell Computer might be a professional who helps with the tough jobs; Levi Strauss a rugged outdoor companion; Mercedes-Benz an upscale, admired person; WordPerfect a competent, caring professional; and Hallmark a warm, emotional relative.

Third, a brand personality may help communicate a product attribute and thus contribute to a functional benefit. For example, the Michelin man's strong, energetic personality suggests that Michelin tires are also strong and energetic. Chapter 5 will discuss the brand personality in more detail, including different personality types, how they work to link the brand to the customer, and how they are created.

THE BRAND-AS-SYMBOL

A strong symbol can provide cohesion and structure to an identity and make it much easier to gain recognition and recall. Its presence can be a key ingredient of brand development and its absence can be a substantial handicap. Elevating symbols to the status of being part of the identity reflects their potential power.

Anything that represents the brand can be a symbol, including programs such as the Ronald McDonald House for McDonald's or the no-haggle pricing policy for Saturn. In Figure 3–3, however, three types of symbols are highlighted: visual imagery, metaphors and the brand heritage.

Symbols involving visual imagery can be memorable and powerful. Consider the Transamerica pyramid, Nike's "swoosh," the McDonald's golden arches, the Kodak yellow, the Coke Classic can or bottle, the Mercedes-Benz emblem, and the Quaker Oats man. Each strong visual image captures much of its respective brand's identity because connections between the symbol and the identity elements have been built up over time. It just takes a glance to be reminded of the brand.

The Saturn brand, in contrast, is handicapped because it lacks a specific visual image. There is no single employee (like Bill Gates for Microsoft), user (like Shaquille O'Neal for Reebok), or product design (like the Ford Taurus or VW Beetle) that represents Saturn. Nor did Saturn use a visual of its Spring Hill plant to play such a role, much as Lynchburg, Tennessee, does for Jack Daniel's whiskey. The Saturn logo, developed early when the car's identity was unknown, is not now much of an asset.

Symbols are more meaningful if they involve a metaphor, with the symbol or a symbol characteristic representing a functional, emotional, or self-expressive benefit. For instance the Prudential rock is a metaphor for strength, Allstate's "Good Hands" logo for reliable, caring service, the Pillsbury Doughboy's soft tummy for freshness, Michael Jordan's leaping ability for the performance of a Nike, and the Energizer bunny for long battery life.

A strong symbol can be the cornerstone of a brand strategy. Kroeber-Riel, a German brand strategist, always starts a brand identity analysis by asking, "What visual image do you want people to have of your brand in five years?" The resulting image then drives everything—in some cases, even the product and the name. For the cookery line of one client, Kroeber-Riel came up with the "Black Steel" image/metaphor that was used as a basis for product design, packaging, and communication.

A vivid, meaningful heritage also can sometimes represent the essence of the brand. The U.S. Marines draw on a rich, storied legacy with the tag line "The few, the proud, the Marines." Amtrak relates its riders' experience to the heritage of first-class rail travel, reminding customers that "there's something about a train that's magic." Starbucks coffee has a link to the first coffeehouse in Seattle's Pike Place market.

THE IDENTITY STRUCTURE

Brand identity, as suggested by Figure 3–4, consists of a core identity and an extended identity. In addition the identity elements are organized into enduring patterns of meaning, often around the core identity elements. It is therefore important to understand core identity, extended identity and patterns of meaning.

THE CORE IDENTITY

The core identity represents the timeless essence of the brand. It is the center that remains after you peel away the layers of an onion or

FIGURE 3–4
The Identity Structure

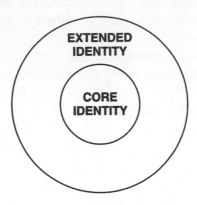

the leaves of an artichoke. The following are illustrations of core identities:

- Michelin—advanced-technology tires for the driver who is knowledgeable about tires
- Johnson & Johnson—trust and quality in over-the-counter medicines
- Rubbermaid—value and innovation, plus a heritage of making practical plastic products for the home
- Saturn—world-class quality; treating customers with respect and as a friend (see Figure 3–5)
- Black Velvet—soft and smooth; priced a cut above the popularly priced brands (see Figure 3–8)

The core identity, which is central to both the meaning and success of the brand, contains the associations that are most likely to remain constant as the brand travels to new markets and products. For example, when Black Velvet expands to new countries, it is always a value brand (as opposed to a price brand or a superpremium brand), and it always delivers the "soft and smooth" product and message. The rest of the Black Velvet identity, described in Figure 3–8, is less central.

The core identity for a strong brand should be more resistant to change than elements of the extended identity. Ivory's "99^{44}/100% pure" and "it floats" slogans reflect an identity that has lasted for more than one hundred years. The brand position and thus the communication strategies may change, and so might the extended identity, but the core identity is more timeless.

Ultimately, the core identity follows from the answers to some tough, introspective questions.

- What is the soul of the brand?
- What are the fundamental beliefs and values that drive the brand?
- What are the competencies of the organization behind the brand?
- What does the organization behind the brand stand for?

One brand strategist observed that if you get the values and culture of the organization right, the brand identity takes care of itself. For many brands, there should be a close correspondence between the values of the organization and the core identity.

The core identity should include elements that make the brand both unique and valuable. Thus the core identity should usually contribute to the value proposition and to the brand's basis for credibility. Sometimes a slogan can capture at least part of the core identity:

- "We're number two; we try harder" suggests that Avis is committed to delivering the best customer service.
- "The relentless pursuit of perfection" suggests that Lexus cars are built to the highest quality standards with respect to workmanship, handling, comfort, and features.
- "melt in your mouth, not in your hand" suggests the unique combination of flavor and convenience provided by M&M candies.

Even the core identity, however, is usually too multifaceted for a single slogan. The Saturn identity, for example, had a quality component (a world-class car) and a relationship component (treating customers with respect and as a friend). The slogan "A different kind of company, a different kind of car" provided an umbrella under which these two core elements of the identity could be sheltered. However, by no means did the slogan alone capture the Saturn core identity.

THE EXTENDED IDENTITY

The extended brand identity includes elements that provide texture and completeness. It fills in the picture, adding details that help portray what the brand stands for. Important elements of the brand's marketing program that have become or should become visible associations can be included. In the case of Saturn, the extended identity includes the product itself, the no-pressure feel of the retail experience, the no-haggle pricing, the "different company" slogan, and the brand personality. Each has a role to play as a driver of the brand identity, but none is as basic a foundation as the core identity.

The core identity usually does not possess enough detail to perform all of the functions of a brand identity. In particular, a brand identity should help a company decide which program or communication is effective and which might be damaging or off target. Even a well-thought-out and on-target core identity may ultimately be too ambiguous or incomplete for this task.

For example, the core identity of an insurance company—delivering "peace of mind"—resonated with the target segment and represented what the firm was and could provide. When developing communication objectives and executions, however, the company realized that any of three communication strategies could depict peace of mind—strength (which could describe either Prudential or Fortis), planning ahead for retirement or emergencies (Fireman's Fund), and personal caring and concern (Allstate, State Farm). An analysis of competitor profiles, the target market's needs, and the firm's heritage all led to the latter strategy, but only after the addition of a personality element—a concerned friend rather than a rugged protector or a successful planner—to the brand's extended identity helped crystallize the direction of the brand.

A brand personality does not often become a part of the core identity. However, it can be exactly the right vehicle to add needed texture and completeness by being part of the extended identity. The extended identity provides the strategist with the permission to add useful detail to complete the picture.

A reasonable hypothesis is that within a product class, a larger extended identity means a stronger brand—one that is more memorable, interesting, and connected to your life. A person whom you find uninteresting and bland and who plays only a small role in your life can be described in a few words. An interesting person with whom you are involved personally or professionally would usually require a much more complex description. The number of relevant brand identity elements will depend on the product class, of course. For instance, a strong candy or spirits brand will likely be less complex than that of a service company such as Bank of America, because the former is likely to have a simpler product attribute set and probably will not involve organizational attributes.

Figures 3–5, 3–6, 3–7, and 3–8 illustrate the above concepts by suggesting possible identities for four brands—Saturn, McDonald's, Nike, and Black Velvet.

FIGURE 3–5
A Saturn Brand Identity

Core Identity

Quality: A world-class car

Relationship: Treat customers with respect and as a friend

Extended Identity

Product Scope: U.S. subcompact

Retail Experience: No pressure; informative, friendly; no-haggle pricing

Slogan: "A different kind of company, a different kind of car"

Personality: Thoughtful and friendly, down-to-earth and reliable, but also
  youthful, humorous, and lively; thoroughly American

Committed employees

Loyal users

Spring Hill plant: A symbol of Saturn's U.S. workforce

Value Proposition

Functional benefits: A quality economy car; a pleasant buying experience;
  excellent, friendly service backup

Emotional benefits: Pride in a U.S.-made car; friend relationship with Saturn
  and dealers

Self-expressive benefits: Owning a Saturn identifies a person as frugal,
  down-to-earth, fun, and young at heart

Relationship

Customers are treated with respect and as a friend

FIGURE 3–6

A McDonald's Brand Identity

McDonald's, which does about $26 billion of business in seventy-nine countries, has one of the most successful global brands. The focus for McDonald's has been on value, in part because customers are value conscious and in part because it must compete with the aggressive value approach of Pepsico's Taco Bell. However, the brand as symbolized by the golden arches has a rich identity that provides several links to the customer.[6]

Core Identity

Value offering: McDonald's provides value as defined by the product, special offers, and the buying experience given the price

Food quality: Consistently hot, good-tasting at any McDonald's in the world

Service: Fast, accurate, friendly, and hassle free

Cleanliness: The operations are always spotless on both sides of the counter

User: Families and kids are a focus, but serves a wide clientele

Extended Identity

Convenience: McDonald's is the most convenient quick-service restaurant—it is located close to where people live, work, and gather; features efficient, time-saving service; and serves easy-to-eat food

Product scope: Fast food, hamburgers, children's entertainment

Subbrands: Big Mac, Egg McMuffin, Happy Meals, Extra Value Meals and others

Corporate citizenship: Ronald McDonald Children's Charities, Ronald McDonald House

Brand personality: Family oriented, all-American, genuine, wholesome, cheerful, fun

Relationship: The family/fun associations are inclusive, and McDonald's is part of the good times

Relationship: The Ronald McDonald Children's Charities engender respect, liking, and admiration

Logo: Golden arches

Characters: Ronald McDonald; McDonald's dolls and toys

Value Proposition

Functional benefits: Good-tasting hamburgers, fries, and drinks that provide value; extras such as playgrounds, prizes, premiums, and games

Emotional benefits: Kids—fun via excitement of birthday parties, relationship with Ronald McDonald and other characters, and feeling of special family times; adults—warmth via link to family events and experiences reinforced by the McDonald's emotional advertising

FIGURE 3–7
A Nike Brand Identity

Nike has been a dramatic success in the world of sports and fashion. Like many strong brands, it has identities that differ by segment: The identity for the fitness segment (including cross trainers, joggers, and hikers) is different, for example, than the identity for those in competitive sports like tennis and basketball. In fact, the Nike identity is modified for subbrands such as the Force basketball shoe or the Court Challenge tennis shoe. In most contexts, however, Nike still has an overriding identity, whose elements include the following:[7]

Core Identity

Product thrust: Sports and fitness

User profile: Top athletes, plus all those interested in fitness and health

Performance: Performance shoes based on technological superiority

Enhancing lives: Enhancing peoples' lives through athletics

Extended Identity

Brand personality: Exciting, provocative, spirited, cool, innovative, and aggressive; into health and fitness and the pursuit of excellence

Basis for relationship: Hanging out with a rugged, macho person who goes for the best in clothing, shoes, and everything else

Subbrands: Air Jordan and many others

Logo: "Swoosh" symbol

Slogan: "Just do it"

Organizational associations: Connected to and supportive of athletes and their sports; innovative

Endorsers: Top athletes, including Michael Jordan, Andre Agassi, Deion Sanders, Charles Barkley, and John McEnroe

Heritage: Developed track shoes in Oregon

Value Proposition

Functional benefits: High-technology shoe that will improve performance and provide comfort

Emotional benefits: The exhilaration of athletic performance excellence; feeling engaged, active, and healthy

Self-expressive symbolic benefits: Self-expression is generated by using a shoe with a strong personality associated with a visible athlete

Credibility

Makes performance shoes and clothing that are stylish

FIGURE 3–8
A Black Velvet Brand Identity

Black Velvet is a brand of Canadian whiskey. The Black Velvet lady, wearing a black velvet dress, first appeared in ads in the early 1970s, and she has since become a key symbol for the brand (see Chapter 7). The Black Velvet lady is credited by Heublein as being largely responsible for the brand's share growth in the United States from 3.6 % in 1971 to 8.9 % in 1980 (when the category doubled to 21 million cases) and to 10.3 % in 1993 (during a time when overall category volume dropped to 16 million cases). Black Velvet has a substantial presence in Sweden and Hungary and is on a sharp growth track in many other countries.

Core Identity

Product attribute: Soft and smooth

Price/quality: A cut above popular price (not among the highest-priced brands)

Extended Identity

Product scope: A spirits brand, not just a Canadian alternative

Local/Global: An imported brand

Symbol: The Black Velvet lady with the black velvet dress; also the bottle with its black label

Personality: Classy and elegant but friendly and approachable

Taste: Lacks the bite of Scotch and other spirit drinks

Users: A broad age spectrum (not restricted to older males)

Value Proposition

Functional benefits: Soft and smooth taste at a value price

Emotional benefits: Feeling relaxed, rewarded, and sensual

Self-Expressive benefits: Serving a brand with a touch of class

---

COHESIVE, MEANINGFUL IDENTITY ELEMENT GROUPINGS

Core and extended identities organize the identity elements as to their role in representing the essence of a brand. The brand identity elements can also be organized into cohesive and meaningful groupings (or mental networks), usually around the core identity components.

Strong, effective brands will have cohesive and interpretable groupings of identity elements. In contrast, weaker brands will have an
identity based on fewer elements, and those elements will appear dis-
jointed or even inconsistent.

An important aspect of brand identity structure, then, is how the
elements fit together. Are there meaningful patterns? Are the elements of the identity grouped cohesively? Or are the elements a set
of seemingly random associations that are possibly inconsistent?

Consider McDonald's for example. At least three such cohesive
groupings can be identified, each supported by a host of identity
elements. The kids/fun/family associations are supported by and consistent with Ronald McDonald, McDonald's birthday-party experiences, McDonaldland games, Happy Meals, and McDonald's dolls
and toys. A set of social involvement associations includes Ronald
MacDonald House. Finally, there is a set of functional associations organized around the concepts of service, value, and meals. The "golden
arches" provide a linking function as well as representing the whole
identity.

A useful exercise is to draw a *mental network* of identity elements
with links between them, perhaps using heavy lines for strong links
and light or dotted lines for weak links. The role of the core identity
and the pattern of linked elements then become apparent, as Figure
3–9 illustrates for the case of McDonald's.

Wells Fargo Bank could have a grouping around banking that would
include its automated tellers, high service level, reliability, and financial strength. Another grouping could be around the bank's stagecoach
symbol, which associates Wells Fargo with the old West, individual-
ism, courage, a commitment to deliver, and safekeeping of funds. The
stagecoach, by also representing reliability and service, would be
linked to the banking associations.

The concept of a whole, or gestalt, as developed by Gestalt psychologists (beginning with Max Wertheimer in 1912), can help illustrate the power of a meaningful pattern of associations. The gestaltists
emphasize that human beings do not usually perceive things in terms
of their separate attributes but, rather, look for an overall picture or
pattern. In Figure 3–10, the four separate lines in panel A become a
flag in panel B and a letter in panel C—images that have meaning and
are much easier to understand and recall than random lines.[8] In

FIGURE 3–9
A Mental Network

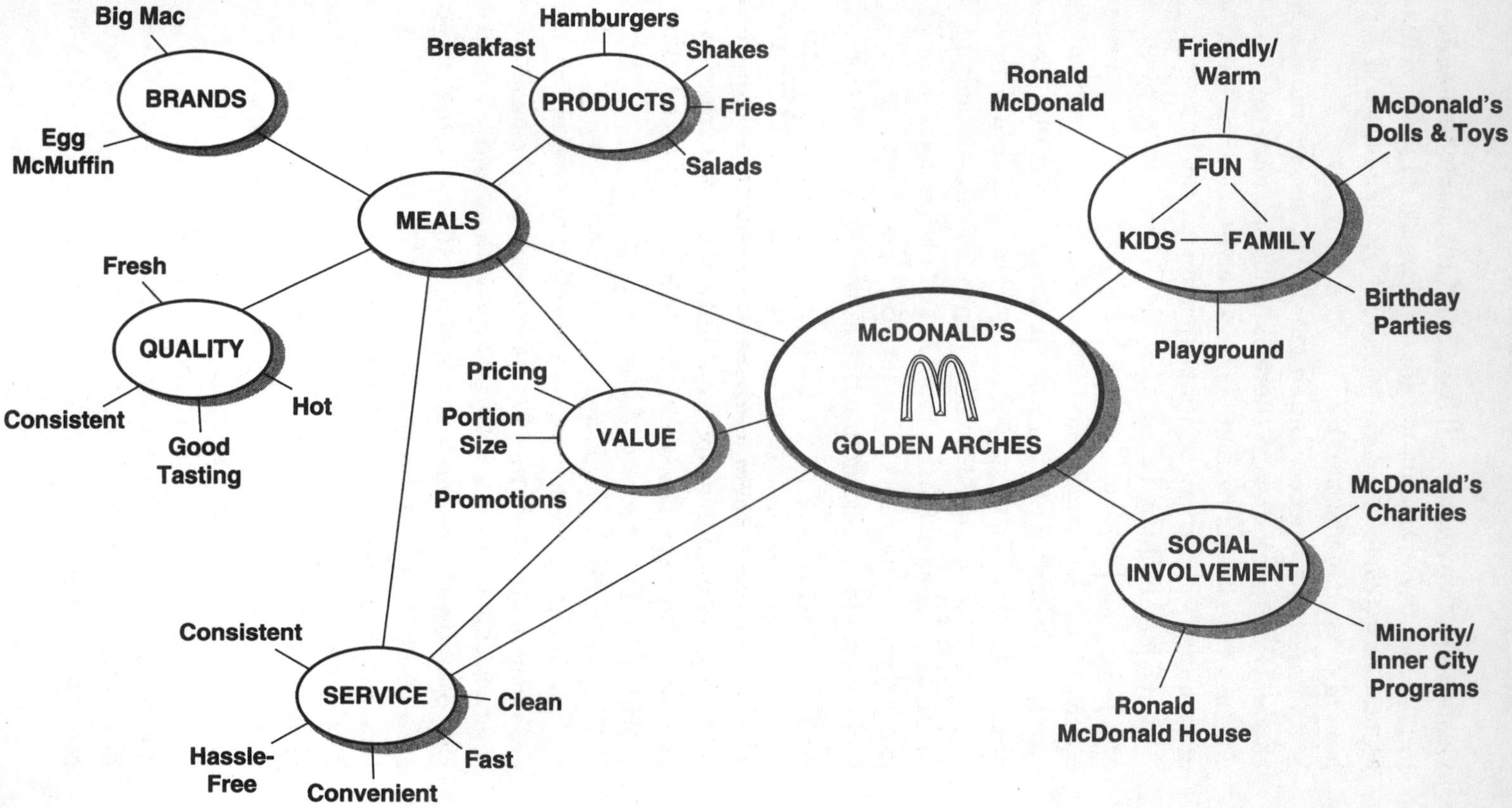

BRANDS
- Big Mac
- Egg McMuffin

QUALITY
- Fresh
- Consistent
- Good Tasting
- Hot

MEALS

PRODUCTS
- Breakfast
- Hamburgers
- Shakes
- Fries
- Salads

VALUE
- Pricing
- Portion Size
- Promotions

SERVICE
- Consistent
- Clean
- Fast
- Convenient
- Hassle-Free

McDONALD'S GOLDEN ARCHES

FUN
- Friendly/Warm
- Ronald McDonald

KIDS—FAMILY
- McDonald's Dolls & Toys
- Birthday Parties
- Playground

SOCIAL INVOLVEMENT
- McDonald's Charities
- Minority/Inner City Programs
- Ronald McDonald House

Gestalt psychology, this phenomenon is often summed up by the phrase "The whole is greater than the sum of its parts." This applies as well to brand identity.

FIGURE 3–10
Look for Patterns

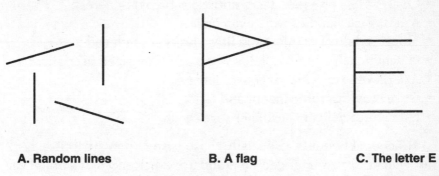

| A. Random lines | B. A flag | C. The letter E |

PROVIDING A VALUE PROPOSITION

The bottom line is that unless the role of a brand is simply to support other brands by providing credibility, the brand identity needs to provide a value proposition to the customer. What is a value proposition?[9]

> *A brand's value proposition is a statement of the functional, emotional, and self-expressive benefits delivered by the brand that provide value to the customer. An effective value proposition should lead to a brand–customer relationship and drive purchase decisions.*

The central concepts of functional, emotional, and self-expressive benefits are explained below.

FUNCTIONAL BENEFITS

The most visible and common basis for a value proposition is a functional benefit—that is, a benefit based on a product attribute that provides functional utility to the customer. Such a benefit will usually relate directly to the functions performed by the product or service for the customer. For laser printers, functional benefits might be their speed, resolution, quality, paper capacity, or lack of downtime. Other examples are as follows:

- Volvo is a safe, durable car because of its weight and design.
- Quaker Oats provides a hot, nutritious breakfast cereal.
- A BMW car handles well, even on ice.
- Huggies deliver comfort and fit, so leaks are reduced.
- Gatorade helps replace fluids when one is engaged in sports.
- A 7-Eleven store means convenience.
- Coke provides refreshment and taste.
- Nordstrom delivers customer service.

Functional benefits, especially those based upon attributes, have direct links to customer decisions and use experiences. If a brand can dominate a key functional benefit, it can dominate a category. Crest, for example, led the toothpaste category for decades with a cavity-reducing claim supported by the endorsement of the American Dental Association (originally obtained in the 1950s). Competitors were forced to position their brands along inferior dimensions such as fresh breath and white teeth.

The challenge is to select functional benefits that will "ring the bell" with customers and that will support a strong position relative to competitors. The latter task involves not only creating a product or service that delivers but also communicating that capability to customers. Communication, of course, is always a nontrivial task; sometimes, it may be extremely difficult.

Limitations of Functional Benefits

As noted in the discussion of the product-attribute fixation trap, product attributes and functional benefits have limitations—they often fail to differentiate, can be easy to copy, assume a rational decision-maker, can reduce strategic flexibility, and inhibit brand extensions. One way to overcome these limitations, already explored, is to expand the brand identity perspective beyond product attributes by considering the brand-as-organization, person, and symbol. Another is to expand the value proposition to include emotional and self-expressive benefits as well as functional benefits.

EMOTIONAL BENEFITS

When the purchase or use of a particular brand gives the customer a positive feeling, that brand is providing an emotional benefit. The strongest brand identities often include emotional benefits. Thus a customer can feel any of the following:

- Safe in a Volvo
- Excited in a BMW or while watching MTV
- Energetic and vibrant when drinking Coke
- In control of the aging process with Oil of Olay
- Important when at Nordstrom
- Warm when buying or reading a Hallmark card
- Strong and rugged when wearing Levi's

Evian is simply water, which has fairly uninteresting functional benefits. In its advertising (shown in Figure 3–11), however, the brand is overlaid with a substantial emotional benefit. Through the slogan "Another day, another chance to feel healthy" and the visual imagery, Evian associates itself not only with working out (a common use occasion for the brand) but with the satisfied feeling that comes from a workout.

Emotional benefits add richness and depth to the experience of owning and using the brand. Without the memories that Sun-Maid raisins evoke, that brand would border on commodity status. The familiar red package, though, links many users to happy days of helping Mom in the kitchen (or to an idealized childhood, for some who wish that they had such experiences). The result can be a different use experience—one with feelings—and a stronger brand.

To discover what emotional benefits are or could be associated with a brand, the focus of research needs to be on feelings. How do customers feel when they are buying or using the brand? What feelings are engendered by the achievement of a functional benefit? Most functional benefits will have a corresponding feeling or set of feelings.

Fusing Functional and Emotional Benefits

The strongest brand identities have both functional and emotional benefits. A study by Stuart Agres supports this assertion.[10] A laboratory

FIGURE 3–11
An ad with emotional benefits

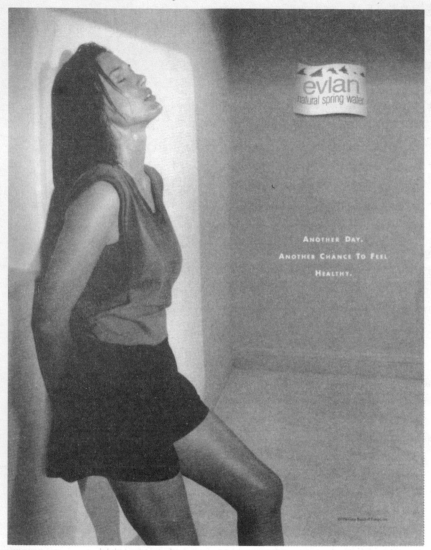

Reproduced with permission.

experiment involving shampoo showed that the addition of emotional benefits ("You will look and feel terrific") to functional benefits ("Your hair will be thick and full of body") enhanced the appeal. A follow-up study found that 47 TV commercials that included an emotional benefit had a substantially higher effectiveness score (using a standardized commercial laboratory testing procedure) than 121 commercials that had only a functional benefit.

Scott Talgo of the St. James Group talks of fusing functional and emotional benefits in order to create a composite. For example, Quaker Oats could combine the functional benefit of a nutritious, warm breakfast with the feelings that accompany serving (or being served) such a breakfast to create a fused "nurturing" brand image. Similarly, Rice-A-Roni's "the San Francisco treat" slogan combines the functional benefit of adding flavor to rice with the excitement and romantic feelings associated with San Francisco.

SELF-EXPRESSIVE BENEFITS

Russell Belk, a prominent consumer behavior researcher, once wrote, "That we are what we have is perhaps the most basic and powerful fact of consumer behavior."[11] What Belk meant was that brands and products can become symbols of a person's self-concept. A brand can thus provide a self-expressive benefit by providing a way for a person to communicate his or her self-image.

Of course, each person has multiple roles—for example, a woman may be a wife, mother, writer, tennis player, music buff, and hiker. For each role, the person will have an associated self-concept and a need to express that self-concept. The purchase and use of brands is one way to fulfill this need for self-expression. For instance, a person may define himself or herself as any of the following:

- Adventurous and daring by owning Rossignol powder skis
- Hip by buying fashions from the Gap
- Sophisticated by using Ralph Lauren perfume
- Successful and powerful by driving a Lincoln
- Frugal and unpretentious by shopping at Kmart
- Competent by using Microsoft Office
- A nurturing parent by serving Quaker Oats hot cereal

Nike has substantial self-expressive benefits associated with its brand. The advertisement in Figure 3–12 shows the "Just do it" concept. As a Nike user, you express yourself by performing to your capability.

FIGURE 3–12
A Nike Ad

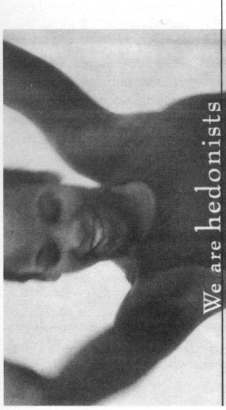

We are all basically hedonists.
And we all want, all we've ever wanted,
is to have

a good time.

We want our feet to have a good time.
We want our hands to have it.
Our lungs, our heads, our knees,
the insides of

our calves.

And we will jump up and down and scream until we get it.

Any woman who works out knows what pleasure is.
The clapping of the hands.
The rhythm of the feet.
The crowd you are swallowed in and released by and the way you
stand out.

And fit back in.

She works out because she has found what she wants.
And what wants her.
It is, she repeats, a good time. A good time.

And they have even set this good time

to music.

If it feels good then just do it.

We are hedonists and we want what feels good.

For more information call 1-800-945-6453.

When a brand provides a self-expressive benefit, the connection between the brand and the customer is likely to be heightened. For example, consider the difference between using Oil of Olay (which has been shown to heighten one's self-concept of being gentle and mature, but also exotic and mysterious) and Jergens or Vaseline Intensive Care Lotion, which don't provide such benefits.

Self-Expressive Versus Emotional Benefits

Sometimes there is a close relationship between emotional and self-expressive benefits. For example, there is only a subtle difference between feeling rugged when wearing Levi's jeans or expressing the strong, rugged side of yourself by wearing them. The differences between the two perspectives, however, can be important. Proving one's success by driving a Lincoln might be significant, whereas "feeling important" may be too mild an emotion to surface in a brand identity analysis or in its execution. Thus it is helpful to consider self-expressive benefits separately.

In general, in comparison to emotional benefits, self-expressive benefits focus on the following:

- Self rather than feelings
- Public settings and products (for instance, wine and cars) rather than private ones (such as books and TV shows)
- Aspiration and the future rather than memories of the past
- The permanent (something linked to the person's personality) rather than the transitory
- The act of using the product (wearing a cooking apron confirms oneself as a gourmet cook) rather than a consequence of using the product (feeling proud and satisfied because of the appearance of a well-appointed meal)

The self-expressive benefit of a brand—and its background in psychology and consumer behavior research—is discussed in detail in Chapter 5, where the self-expression model is developed. In that discussion, a distinction is drawn between actual self-concept (how people actually perceive themselves) and ideal self-concept (how people would like to be perceived).

THE ROLE OF PRICE

A brand's price is also related to the benefits that the brand provides
(see Figure 3–13). A price that is too high relative to the benefits will
undercut the product or service's value proposition, as brands are not
evaluated independent of price. A brand that is seen as overpriced by
customers will not be rewarded even if there are clear and meaningful benefits.

FIGURE 3–13
The Value Proposition

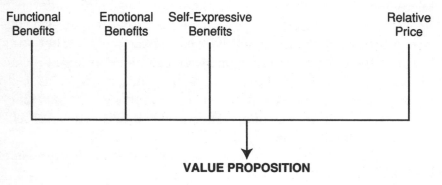

Price, however, is a complex construct. While a higher price can
reduce the value proposition, it can also signal higher quality. As part
of brand identity, price can define the competitive set—such as
whether the brand is upscale (BMW 700 or Nordstrom), middle
market (Toyota Camry or Macy's), or downscale (Honda Civic or
Kmart). Within a brand's competitive set, a high relative price signals a higher-quality or premium position, and a low relative price
signals a lower-quality or value position.

The issue really is whether the value proposition is driven by benefits or by price. The goal of identity creation and management is
usually to focus on benefits rather than price. If price is an important
part of the identity, however, the challenge is to make sure that the
benefits are anchored by elements other than price. One approach is
to note explicitly that the brand, although comparable or superior to
others in its set, has a lower price. (The Oldsmobile Aurora, for example, is as good as premium imports but is less expensive.) The
price is then evaluated in the context of the competitive set.

PROVIDING CREDIBILITY

A brand does not always need to drive the purchase decision; sometimes it plays an endorser role. For instance, Nike, Chevrolet, Kellogg's, and Sony play endorser roles for Nike Air Jordan, Chevrolet Lumina, Kellogg's Corn Flakes, and Sony Walkman. In each case, the endorser brand's primary role is to provide credibility for the subbrand rather than a value proposition. Chapter 4 will discuss the function of organizational attributes such as innovation and trust in providing credibility. In Chapter 8 the various brand roles, including endorser roles, will be presented.

THE BOTTOM LINE: A BRAND–CUSTOMER RELATIONSHIP

A brand–customer relationship can be based upon a value proposition. For example, a customer may be loyal to Maytag because it delivers, at a fair price, the functional benefit of reliability and the emotional benefit of feeling secure and confident. Or the relationship may need to emanate directly from the brand identity, especially when the value proposition does not effectively capture the relationship. The Saturn brand–customer relationship (based on treating customers with respect and as a friend), for example, is not captured well by the car's functional, emotional, or self-expressive benefits.

Many brand–customer relationships emerge when the brand is considered as an organization or as a person, rather than as a product. For example, organizational associations (such as concern for consumers or for the environment) might translate into a respect or liking that forms the basis for a relationship. A likable personality such as that of the Pillsbury Doughboy also could underlie a relationship. Relationships between a brand and customers can be based on a host of positive feelings (such as admiration, friendship, having fun, and being a part of the same community) that cannot be accurately conceptualized in terms of value propositions. Chapters 4 and 5 will elaborate on these perspectives.

Sometimes the brand–customer connections can be strong. For example, consider Stew Leonard's high-energy, family dairy/grocery store in Connecticut. One of its customers had a Stew Leonard shopping bag placed in her casket. The relationship between the woman and the store was such an important part of her life that she sought to continue it in death.

WORKING WITH MULTIPLE BRAND IDENTITIES

In some cases, a brand identity is so persuasive and universal that it will work in all markets. For example, British Airways expects its "World's Favorite Airline" tag line to work throughout the world. Coca-Cola also has long used a core identity across segments and countries. To the extent that an identity can be common across markets, economies of scale will result, and inconsistencies (which can be costly and even debilitating) can be avoided. In most cases, however, a brand identity will need to be adapted to different market or product contexts.

For example, Hewlett-Packard needs to adapt the identity of the HP name to fit diverse markets, including engineers who buy test equipment and workstations, business professionals who buy mini-computers and laser printers, and consumers who buy the Omnibook subnotebook computer. The Levi's identity needs to be adapted to Europe and Japan (where it is seen as "them" rather than "us," and upscale rather than utilitarian). Nike needs to refine its identity to distinguish between the sports and fitness sides of its business.

Courtyard by Marriott draws on the core identity of the Marriott name for associations of consistency, dependability, and friendliness. For business travelers, the Courtyard brand adds identity elements drawn from the slogan "Designed by business travelers for business travelers." For the leisure traveler, Courtyard offers a set of associations around a value theme. For both segments, the Courtyard name defines a set of hotel attributes that help manage expectations.

When multiple identities are needed, the goal should be to have a common set of associations (as suggested by Figure 3–14), some of which will be in the core identity. The identity for each market would then be embellished, but in a way that is consistent with the common identity elements. Thus Levi Strauss might develop a core urban-hip user imagery that plays in most countries. In the United States, though, the gold-miner heritage and rugged brand personality would be more prominent, whereas in Europe the brand personality would be more upscale and less blue-collar.

The non-overlapping associations should avoid being inconsistent. One approach that ensures consistency is to have the same identity, but emphasize different elements in each market: In one market a brand personality will be in the forefront, while in another the product attributes will be more prominent. When there are real differences, the goal should be to make them as consistent as possible without undercutting their impact and effectiveness.

FIGURE 3–14
Multiple Identities

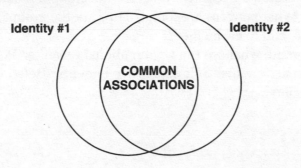

TOWARD UNDERSTANDING BRAND IDENTITY

The understanding and management of brand identity are keys to building strong brands and thus creating brand equity. This chapter has presented an overview of brand identity—in other words, what a brand stands for. A brand identity potentially consists of twelve elements organized around four perspectives: the brand-as-product, brand-as-organization, brand-as-person, and brand-as-symbol. The identity structure includes a core and extended identity and a system of cohesive, meaningful groupings of the identity elements.

The brand identity concept will be elaborated in the next two chapters. Chapter 4 will cover organizational attributes and their role in providing credibility as well as a value proposition; Chapter 5 will discuss brand personality. In Chapter 6, the balance of Figure 3–1 will be presented: the brand position, the execution or the communication program, the tracking of the results, and the strategic brand analysis that in practice starts the process.

QUESTIONS TO CONSIDER

1. Consider your key brands from the perspective of a product, an organization, and a person. From each perspective, which elements could be used as part of the brand identity? Consider each

of the twelve brand identity dimensions: product scope, product attributes, quality/value, uses, users, country of origin, organizational attributes, local versus global, brand personality, brand–customer relationships, visual imagery/metaphors, and brand heritage.

2. For each brand, what is the brand identity? Identify the core identity and extended identity. What are the groupings of identity elements? What patterns are found? How are the groups linked to the brand and to each other?

3. For each brand, what are the key functional benefits? What are the emotional benefits? Self-expressive benefits? Relationships with customers?

4

ORGANIZATIONAL ASSOCIATIONS

Corporate brands will be the only successful area of new brand building in the future . . . as technology increasingly functions as the great leveler, consumers increasingly depend much less on their evaluation of a single product.
—Stephen King of JW Thompson, UK

Companies have to wake up to the fact that they are more than a product on a shelf. They're behavior as well.
—Robert Haas of Levi Strauss

THE BODY SHOP STORY[1]

In 1976, The Body Shop, an international manufacturer and retailer of skin and hair care products that breaks all the rules, began life in Brighton, England, when Anita Roddick opened her first store. Most cosmetic brands have identities based on glamorous user imagery and powerful functional, emotional, and self-expressive benefits supported by dramatic packaging and heavy advertising. In sharp contrast, The Body Shop sold its products with a hype-free presentation, reflecting values that set it apart from its competitors. The firm's "profits with principle" philosophy continues to provide a dramatic source of differentiation.

The Body Shop's unique approach to product development is based in part on history. People throughout the world have been using naturally based products to care for their skin and hair for centuries; why not capture some of this knowledge, refine it, and make it available to others? The Body Shop followed this thinking in developing such products as its Honey and Oatmeal Scrub Mask, Cucumber Cleansing Milk, Seaweed and Birch Shampoo, and Cocoa Butter Body Lotion.

The use of ingredients from less industrialized countries not only provides a basis for unique product ideas but also generates much-needed jobs and resources to improve lives in these countries. For example, the Brazil Nut Conditioner and Rainforest Bath Beads are made with Brazilian nut oil processed by the Kayapo Indians of the Amazon rain forest. In Nepal, The Body Shop obtains paper made from water hyacinth. The resulting relationships—based on the Body Shop principle of "Trade, Not Aid"—help create livelihoods for economically stressed communities, mostly in what The Body Shop calls the "majority world" (known to others as the Third World).

The Body Shop's involvement in the majority world extends beyond trade. In 1989, for example, The Body Shop collected a million signatures on petitions to "Stop the Burning" in the Amazon rain forest, where fires were being set to clear vast areas for development. The Body Shop's mission is not merely to sell cosmetics, but to create a global community.

As The Body Shop and its products have evolved, its antiglitz, antiwaste, natural-ingredient philosophy has remained visible. Products are still developed without the use of animal testing. Simple, practical packages (featuring refillable plastic bottles with simple labels) are reminiscent of the unglamorous, no-tail-fins Volkswagen Beetle of the 1960s. No-hype salespeople, informative brochures, and The Body Shop's innovative Product Information Manual provide customers with information about the company's products and causes.

Perhaps the most differentiating characteristic of The Body Shop is its pursuit of social and environmental change. A passion for social causes pervades the culture of the firm, and The Body Shop "walks its talk" with a host of visible, meaningful efforts that include opposing animal testing, helping economically stressed communities, campaigning to help save the rain forest, and promoting recycling. The Body Shop is also an advocate for endangered species (the Animals in Danger line of children's soaps and bath products promote awareness of this issue) and a participant in exploring alternative energy resources (its goal is to supply its own energy needs with wind power). The Body Shop charter reminds employees that "goals and values are as important as our products and profits" and that "The Body Shop has soul—don't lose it."

The Body Shop identity influences employees as well as customers. Founder Anita Roddick believes that employees, like customers, are "hyped out" and need a sense of purpose that is more ennobling and involving than mere organizational profits. The charisma of The Body Shop's corporate mission provides that purpose. Employees, who are considered part of an extended family, are informed about products and environmental issues through instructional courses and newsletters, and they play an active role that ranges from educating others to participating in demonstrations.

This singular, dedicated posture provides a point of real differentiation that stimulates loyalty and commitment from customers. The Body Shop's customers are likely to be concerned with the world around them and to seek more involvement. Participating in The Body Shop is one way for customers to gain this involvement—and, in so doing, to express themselves. The acts of shopping at the store, interacting with the salespeople, using the refillable containers, and supporting the environmental positions all help provide a bond with the organization. The bond stems from a common belief that business should do more than make money, create decent jobs, and sell good products. Rather, it should help address major social problems by not only donating money but leveraging its resources to illuminate and call attention to the issues. In fact, Roddick's intent is to provide customers with a sense of "excitement and passion."

FIGURE 4–1
Body Shop Visual

Reprinted with permission of The Body Shop.

The Body Shop is a good example of a brand for which the identity is largely based on organizational associations, particularly those involving values and programs. Many Japanese firms also have identities that draw heavily on organizational associations.

THE STORY OF BRANDING IN JAPAN[2]

Japanese firms, in general, look at brand strategy very differently than firms in other nations. First, they are preoccupied, even obsessed, with their image. Second, they often put their name on a wide variety of products, making their corporate brand the ultimate range brand (the general name for a brand that ranges over product classes). Finally they are concerned with the internal impact of the brand identity on employees and prospective employees, as well as the external impact on customers and prospective customers.

IMAGE OBSESSION

Japanese firms care intensely about how people view them, and the identity dimensions on which they focus are remarkably similar across firms. Their highest priorities are innovativeness, being successful, and social responsibility (that is, being good corporate citizens and being sensitive to the environment). A reputation for quality is less of a concern, but only because it is not regarded as a differentiator; all firms in Japan are expected to deliver quality.

Innovativeness. For many Japanese firms, a reputation for innovation is crucial in terms of providing credibility for new products. The goal is to have an expectation in the marketplace—among the distribution chain as well as end consumers—that any new product the firm introduces will have a worthwhile advantage. Such perceptions also generate a sense of excitement and accomplishment for the firm, thus enhancing its prestige. The Japanese consumer is thought to admire firms that have the technological capability, imagination, and initiative to advance the state of the art.

For example, in 1986 Asahi Breweries was considered a tired, perennial also-ran, the maker of a third-place beer that was sliding into fourth. However, the introduction of Asahi Dry in 1987 caused the brand's share to bounce from roughly 9 percent (where it had languished for decades) to well over 20 percent—largely at the expense of Kirin, the industry leader. Asahi Dry completely changed the image of the company to that of a young, exciting, innovative industry leader. This new image affected not only the gain in market share but also the intensity of brand loyalty. Asahi Dry was able to fight off a host of imitators, in part because Japanese customers rewarded the successful innovator by buying the "authentic dry beer."

Many Japanese firms carefully avoid me-too products because of the impact on perceived innovativeness. For example, Kao Corporation (a soap company much like Procter & Gamble) strives to ensure that any new product includes a technological advancement that supports the brand's innovative identity. Kao even put its name on a line of technologically advanced floppy discs, which was a market success even though high-tech product was far from Kao's traditional domain of soap and skin care. The credibility of the Kao name (and the large, successful company it represented) supported the new product, and the nature of the product helped, the innovativeness image of Kao.

The old image of Japanese firms being quick to copy but not very good at innovation is certainly incorrect today. Japanese firms, in fact, focus on developing core competencies that lead to innovativeness. Their R&D organizations (comparable to Bell Labs or the Xerox think tank) will tend to be more visible than would those of U.S. firms. The goal is to develop credible innovativeness signals in addition to actually supporting innovation. Along these lines, Canon has developed centers that focus on not only R&D but also creativity.

Success and Leadership. Japanese firms believe that customers want to do business with successful, well-known firms, not only to be reassured about likely product quality but also to associate themselves with the prestige of a successful firm. People in Japan want to be associated with the best. There are numerous cases in Japan of brands doing well in test markets only when a corporate brand was used to endorse the product, because the prestige and credibility of a large corporation was a necessary ingredient.

Good Citizenship. Japanese firms are interested in proving they are good citizens by being responsive to the environment and supporting the arts and other civic programs and causes. They understand that it is not enough to be "green;" they must also make sure that others understand and know about the firm's values. Hitachi, for example, ran a four-color, eight-page insert in *Fortune* explaining what it was doing to help preserve the environment. This series served to position Hitachi with respect to environmental issues, and it also provided insight into the company's values and programs. Customers are likely to feel closer to a corporation that they respect and that shares their own values.

Stretching the Mind. Japanese firms are aggressive at personalizing their organizations by focusing on issues and values that are far afield from the product and services involved. For example, in 1992 Mazda ran a ten-page insert in *Time* in which a dozen essayists and photographers set forth their own individual views on the meaning of life.

What kind of a company would introduce such a basic philo-
sophical question and ask others (both essayists and readers) to
participate in a meaningful way? Perhaps Mazda hoped customers
would supply the answer: a firm with broader interests and concerns
than simply making and selling cars, one whose leaders have an intellectual bent. Mazda may have felt a market segment would respect,
admire, and bond with such an organization because of a similarity in
interests, beliefs, and self-image. Of course, quantifying such an
impact is difficult.

Relationship Marketing. Relationship marketing is a hot topic in American business. To the U.S. firm, a relationship is based on getting close
to customers, understanding their problems, and developing responsive programs. It is ironic that the Japanese, by focusing on organizational values instead of specifications and action programs,
may understand the nature of customer relationships better than
Americans.

An Internal Focus

In Japan, corporate brand-building efforts often are aimed primarily
toward current and prospective employees. An impact on customers
is seen as almost a bonus, and certainly not as the only benefit. Japanese firms consider it vital that employees feel pride in their firm
because of its values, purpose, past success, and future goals. They
believe that workers who feel this pride will then be more effective
and motivated and will buy into the group activities and culture that
are at the heart of the Japanese management style. Corporate advertising in Japan is thus largely justified on the basis of its internal
impact. In contrast, employees in the United States and Europe are
rarely considered to be an important audience for a corporate advertising effort.

Stimulating Strategic and Organizational Change. In Japan, firms often
engage in corporate identity (CI) programs, the goal of which is to
obtain a consensus among a broad cross-section of employees as to
what the corporate identity should be. The process not only results in
a corporate identity for which there is "buy-in" among employees but
it also provides a vehicle to stimulate change and renewal within the
organization. For example, in 1985 a broad set of groups within Asahi

Breweries discussed the identity and vision of the firm. The result was a new attitude that made Asahi Dry and other programs feasible. One tangible sign of the new Asahi was a decision to change the firm's rising-sun logo, which was more than a century old.

THE PERVASIVE CORPORATE BRAND

In Japan, firms put their names everywhere; Mitsubishi alone puts its name on literally tens of thousands of brands. The parent name thus becomes elastic, meaning very different things in different contexts. The common core, though, is that behind each subbrand is a large, successful firm that is capable of being a leader in product and sales wherever it competes.

Firms such as Sony, Honda, Canon, Mitsubishi, and Toshiba further this message by investing in name-exposure activities. These corporate names are found in lights in most of the leading cities in the world. In one particularly compelling instance, a huge Toshiba neon sign overlooks (and dominates) a crowded Thai village. Aggressive sponsorship of events such as the Olympics also helps make the names of large Japanese firms a common part of the environment.

Suntory makes whiskey, but it also has its name on beer and even soft drinks, and only through great willpower did it keep its name off its chain of fast-food restaurants (which serve American-style hamburgers, pizza, and fried chicken). There is also a Suntory art museum, an elegant and important Suntory auditorium in Tokyo, and a host of prestigious firm-sponsored events. Thus the Suntory name is indeed a valuable commodity in Japan, one that is driven by more than its products.

THE PERMANENCE OF THE CORPORATE BRAND FAMILY

In Japan the corporation and its structure of products has a real permanence, because businesses are rarely sold. Thus it is easier for a Japanese firm to invest in a corporate brand, secure in knowing that a major change in its business scope is unlikely. In contrast, U.S. corporations such as GE, General Mills, and Xerox make only a temporary commitment to the family of products and brands within their portfolios. Their willingness to buy and sell businesses, thereby changing their corporate identity, makes it more difficult to justify investing in U.S. corporate brands.

THE BRAND AS ORGANIZATION

Brands in nearly all product classes are struggling to find points of distinction in the face of deteriorating market contexts. Powerful retailers and customers are focusing on price in an era of belt-tightening. A price emphasis is further fostered by aggressive or desperate competitors and by defensive players unwilling to cede market position. Product innovations are quickly copied or attract only small niches. How can brands differentiate themselves and maintain an advantage?

One answer is to base the brand identity in part on the organization behind the brand. The basic premise is that it takes an organization with a particular set of values, culture, people, programs, and assets/skills to deliver a product or service. These organizational characteristics can provide a basis for differentiation, a value proposition, and a customer relationship, as the stories of Saturn (described in Chapter 2) and The Body Shop illustrate.

Values and Culture

Saturn's organizational values of treating the customer with respect and as a friend provide the basis for a relationship. Most customers sense these values and developed attitudes and perceptions accordingly. The Saturn commitment to building a world-class economy car, another organizational characteristic, is also visible enough to affect customers' perceptions of the car. Similarly, The Body Shop's concern about such causes as the rain forests, animal testing, package recycling, and Third World economic development also draw the admiration and respect of customers.

People

The people at Saturn and The Body Shop, as encountered by customers either in person or through ads, are seen to be committed to the values and culture of the organization. They provide a credibility that could not be obtained by simple announcements of product attributes and corporate programs.

Programs

The Body Shop engages in visible activism that provides substance to its values and culture and a way for customers to participate either actively or vicariously. Saturn's many customer-involving retail programs and its invitation to all owners to come to Spring Hill for a summer celebration reflect the values and culture of an organization concerned with much more than selling cars.

Assets and Skills

The Body Shop's access to Third World ingredient sources makes its interest and involvement in those countries' problems more credible. Saturn developed a manufacturing plant in Spring Hill from scratch in order to deliver a "different kind of car." Saturn also has a unique retail operation that visibly reflects its customer-friendly philosophy.

Organizational Versus Product Associations

Viewing the brand as organization generates *organizational associations* that can be attached to the brand as part of the brand identity. For example, Saturn is viewed as an organization that is committed to world-class quality. This perception is qualitatively different from the view that the Saturn car is a superior product; it instead reflects the organization's values, programs, and assets and skills. The implication is that an organizational commitment to quality will result in or support a claim of product quality, but it is nevertheless a different focus. Thus, just as a brand can have associations with respect to attributes, users, symbols, use contexts, country or region, and brand personality, it can also have organizational associations.

THE CORPORATE BRAND

A corporate brand such as Sony, GE, or Siemens does not necessarily need to have organizational associations as an important element of its identity. Rather, the brand-as-product perspective could dominate its identity. For example, Sony might mean quality consumer electronics, and GE Jet Engines might mean efficient engines.

For a corporate brand, however, organizational associations are usually important for two reasons. First, a corporate brand does represent an organization with a CEO and people employed in design, production, and consumer contact. Thus it is natural to focus on organizational values, employees, programs, and assets of the organization.

Second, the corporation is almost always involved with many product classes, each of which will usually have a set of product brands.

Siemens, for example, has its name on 100,000 products being marketed in 100 countries. Organizational associations such as innovation or quality provide a common denominator that can be applied over these products. The result is substantial economies of scale in building organizational associations. There is also the risk, however, that one visible product could tarnish the corporate name by delivering poor performance.

A corporate brand that is applied to many products also provides economies of scale and scope in creating visibility and awareness, since the cost involved is spread over multiple products and categories. Further, the name is exposed wherever these products are advertised or sold. Multiple products therefore translate directly into more exposure for the brand name.

ORGANIZATIONAL ASSOCIATIONS NEED NOT REFLECT A CORPORATION

Organizational associations are not at all limited to corporate brands. The issue really is whether the organizational associations are an important part of the brand identity.

Sometimes, in fact, brands that can productively focus on organizational associations should not use the corporate brand. Hidden Valley salad dressings would suffer greatly under the Clorox brand umbrella because the parent corporation is tied to bleach, which is incompatible with a food product. (Hidden Valley labels list HVR Company as the manufacturer.) Similarly, L'Eggs hosiery would not gain from an association with its parent company, Sara Lee. Hidden Valley and L'Eggs, however, could still involve organizational associations in their brand identity. As described in Chapter 2, Saturn has emphasized such associations in its brand positioning even while distancing itself from General Motors.

The visibility of organizational associations can vary greatly. For many product brands (such as Tide or M&Ms), the focus is on product attributes or user imagery, and the organization is invisible. The brand is really an abstract entity rather than a reflection of an organization. For others (such as Saturn and many service firms), organizational associations are often part of the core identity.

Organizational associations differ from but can be influenced by product associations, as will be discussed in Chapter 8. Even the nature of the products involved will matter. For example, a firm making big-screen TVs will be perceived as being more innovative and high-tech than one making audio equipment.

ORGANIZATIONAL ASSOCIATIONS

Most brand identities provide value propositions that are tied to a product benefit, a use occasion, or a user group. These associations are usually product-class specific and involve tangible attributes, often with sharp visual imagery. In contrast, associations driven by the values/culture, people, programs, and assets/skills of the organization are qualitatively different. Less tangible, more subjective, and less tied to a product class, these associations have the potential to play a significant but different role in generating and supporting value propositions and customer relationships.

Sometimes associations, such as being community-minded, are uniquely attached to an organization. Other characteristics, such as perceived quality, could be viewed as product attributes (the product has quality designed in) which provide functional benefits (the customer benefits from superior quality) or as organizational attributes (the organization behind the brand has quality and quality programs as priorities). Which perspective dominates will depend on the source of the association links.

A host of organizational associations are available to managers. In order to provide an understanding of the way these associations work, a representative few of the most prevalent and useful will be discussed below:

- Society/community orientation
- Perceived quality
- Innovation
- Concern for customers
- Presence and success
- Local vs. global

SOCIETY/COMMUNITY ORIENTATION

Some organizations are simply "good citizens" and prove it in many ways including environmental sensitivity, sponsorship of worthwhile charities, interest and involvement in their communities, and even how they treat employees. Organizational associations are almost indispensable in developing society/community-oriented associations. For example, Ben & Jerry's is a funky, Vermont-based, socially responsible ice cream firm with programs and policies that include the following:

- Giving 7.5% of its profits to social and environmental causes
- Creating a spin-off firm called Community Products, which markets products such as Rain Forest Crunch ice cream (using Brazilian nuts) that promote environmental awareness and provide dollars for social causes
- Paying top executives only seven times as much as the lowest-paid worker (this practice, not uncommon in Japan but highly unusual in the United States, was eventually relaxed in an effort to attract an outside CEO)
- Registering voters at a Ben & Jerry's outlet, and giving away ice cream cones as an inducement
- Establishing a Harlem franchise that employs twelve homeless workers and donates 75 percent of its profits to a local shelter

Ben & Jerry's, which started in 1978, now challenges Häagen-Dazs with sales in the hundreds of millions. It is difficult to estimate, of course, how much of its success is due to superior products and marketing, and how much is due to customers' affinity for the firm's values and programs, but it can be argued that the cost of pursuing worthy causes is fully compensated by the publicity generated by the programs and awards. (The announcement of Rain Forest Crunch ice cream drew forty media members to a press conference.) Certainly, the organizational associations have enhanced customer loyalty, although it is very difficult to say how much.

Levi Strauss earns respect for the way it treats employees and   for its support of community institutions like the University of California and the Oakland A's baseball team. Saturn retailers are simi- larly admired for their involvement with zoos, playgrounds, and other local charities. There are undoubtedly customers who forge   a richer relationship with such firms simply out of respect and admiration.

Going "green" is another way of being a good citizen. This trait can be associated with environmentally sensitive ingredients or recyclable packaging, but a green image rooted in corporate values can be more difficult to copy, more visible, and more credible. It can be difficult, however, to know what the green route is—there may not be a consensus as to the "greenness" of a package, for example. Moreover, many effective green activities (such as reducing toxic emissions from plants) are not visible. Thus one challenge is to create brand value from what can be a huge investment.

Payoffs

As noted above, the question is whether doing good pays off in the market. Certainly being a "good citizen" may generate feelings of respect, admiration, and liking that can help the brand by contributing to customer relationships. Consider the annual McHappy Days celebration/party in Lyon, France, which attracts some 100,000 people and raises money to send medical teams to refugee camps in Cambodia and Thailand. In the view of the McDonald's franchise owner and sponsor, the event generates a special feeling toward McDonald's in Lyon. A 1994 survey of nearly 2,000 U.S. adults provided some substantiating evidence that doing good pays off, even considering the tendency for people to exaggerate actions that reflect positively on their character.[3]

- When choosing between products of equal price and quality, 78 percent of the respondents said they would buy from a firm that contributed to medical research, education, and similar causes rather than one that did not.
- Two-thirds said they would switch brands to a manufacturer that supported a cause they deemed worthwhile.

In another U.S. survey, 83 percent of respondents said that they prefer buying environmentally safe products.[4] Yet another found that 23 percent of American shoppers claimed to make purchases based on a company's environmental profile and programs.[5]

"Cause" programs can add interest and visibility to a brand. Ronald McDonald House, a program (see Figure 4–2) that provides homelike accommodations for families of seriously ill children, has contributed to the McDonald's identity in this way. Consumers in focus groups tend to perk up when Ronald McDonald House becomes the topic for discussion. By provoking not only admiration and respect but also interest, the Ronald McDonald House illustrates how a social program can add vitality to a mature brand.

FIGURE 4–2
Ronald McDonald House

This house was built by a three-year-old girl with leukemia.

In 1969, little Kim Hill was diagnosed as having leukemia, forcing her to leave home to seek special medical attention. Endless commutes and sleepless nights in hospital waiting rooms led Kim's family to help develop the first Ronald McDonald House.®

Today, more than 100,000 families each year use a Ronald McDonald House as their home-away-from-home while their kids are treated in nearby hospitals. But it wouldn't be possible without the generous support of local businesses and community volunteers. If you'd like to contribute some time or money to our house here, please give us a call.

Because to a critically-ill child, having loved ones nearby is often the best medicine of all. Just ask 22-year-old Kim Hill.

Ronald McDonald House

Reprinted with permission from McDonald's.

Finally, it appears that firms with better records for social responsibility get rewarded in the stock market. Although the evidence (from dozens of studies) is mixed, the consensus seems to be that a positive reputation in this area does not hurt and in some contexts helps the stock return. More unambiguous is the fact that a negative incident will have less impact on a firm with a good reputation. A classic case is the way Johnson & Johnson's reputation undoubtedly helped the firm regain the confidence of customers and investors after the Tylenol poisoning incident.

Have a Program

To capitalize on the interest in social responsibility, programs and actions must be translated into perceptions that help the organization to stand out from the crowd. To do this, a firm must obey the fundamentals of branding:

- *Have a focus*. In its pro bono work around the world, DDB Needham focuses on water—in particular, on the availability of water and the problems of pollution. It has participated in world conferences and helped develop communication programs. Other firms have focused on education, the inner city, an arts program, parks, AIDS research, or bicycling trails and events. A focus enhances both impact and visibility.

- *Be consistent over time*. With any branding effort, consistency over a long time period results in cumulative benefit to the firm. Brands with consistent involvement in a specific charity are likely to gain enhanced impact and visibility. Reebok, for example, has been associated with human rights for many years; among other things, it has sponsored Amnesty International's "Human Rights Now" world concert tour. This long-term involvement is likely to have much more impact on customer perceptions of Reebok than would a scattered charity-of-the-month program.

- *Link the program to the brand*. One way to strengthen the program/brand link is to participate in programs that are related to the firm's business. Thus Herman Miller, a furniture maker, reduces waste in its woodworking and encourages well-managed, sustainable forests. The California Casualty Insurance Company, which services teacher organizations, sponsors education programs. Kodak provides cameras, film, and other equipment to help parents put together ID kits for their children (to be used in case of an abduction). This program provides a natural link to Kodak and cameras that donating money to a symphony would lack.

• *Be Branded*. A program that is branded is all the more effective. Liz Claiborne's campaign against violence toward women is called Women's Work. The Coors program to fight breast cancer, termed High Priority, has its own logo. A brand, of course, is a powerful device to crystallize the meaning and enhance the impact of a program.

PERCEIVED QUALITY

Perceived quality is a key consideration in nearly every consumer choice context. Quality can be communicated directly by showing, through demonstration or argument, that a brand's product attributes are superior to a competitor's. Visual quality cues can be employed to signal quality more indirectly. An alternative, as was shown in the discussion of Saturn in Chapter 2, is to discuss quality as a part of a firm's values, culture, people, and programs.

When organizational associations are used to make the quality claim, the focus is on the firm rather than on the products. Thus the "GM Mark of Excellence" is a corporate-wide effort spanning all General Motors brands and reflecting an organizational commitment to quality. It is also backed by programs such as Mr. Goodwrench and several visible total-quality programs that provide substance and credibility.

Many firms are committed to quality or to being "the best" at what they do. For example, Johnson & Johnson, consistently rated as one of the most admired corporations in the annual *Fortune* magazine survey, has quality and trust as its core identity. Nestlé uses the "Makes the very best" tag line for its corporate campaign, which is derived from its more familiar "makes the very best chocolate" consumer slogan.[6]

Retail Brands

Many retail chains, from supermarkets to clothing stores to automobile supply firms, market products under the name of their chain or under a brand that is closely associated with the chain. Because such store brands usually span a host of products, they are really positioned with respect to quality. Many of these brands are value brands, with acceptable quality but a relatively low price. Increasingly, however, store brands are being developed that are actually positioned as premium brands with top quality. Their value propositions thus are defined with respect to the best brands in the product class.

These retail brands often rely on packaging cues and customer trial to establish perceived quality and brand loyalty. Organizational associations, however, could also be a good vehicle to communicate quality both credibly and distinctively. Organizational associations are sensible because, after all, the retail chain is an organization. Further, any organizational associations used to enhance store brands will likely also help develop store loyalty.

Loblaw's, a large Canadian supermarket chain, used organizational associations to create the upscale President's Choice brands. The brand name indicated that the products were the personal choice of the very visible president of the Loblaw chain, who presumably would not put the President's Choice name on an unworthy product. The president himself communicated facts about the organization and its commitment to quality that helped create a quality position for the President's Choice line. He also personally developed links to the customers by being visible in stores and creating a cookbook for customers.

The Tesco supermarket chain in England is another example of the use of organizational associations to create a quality position. Tesco ran a set of ads starring the comedian Dudley Moore as a buyer who was charged with finding a source for superior chickens. His search found him chasing loose "range" chickens in a forest in Bordeaux, being arrested for poaching salmon in Scotland, and being chased by large, costumed chicken characters in Chile. In the process, Moore stumbled onto sources of Italian grapes, Scottish Salmon, and Chilean Cabernet. His humorous exploits suggested the organization's willingness to go to great lengths to achieve top quality for its premium line of Tesco brands.

INNOVATION

As noted earlier, innovation is perhaps the key corporate brand association for Japanese firms. It is also important to Western firms, especially for those competing in a product class in which technology and innovation are important to the customer. For example, Oral B in dental equipment, Gillette in razors, AT&T in communication equipment, Intel in microprocessors, and Lexus in automobiles all base their competitive strategy on being the best technologically. Rubbermaid, another fixture on the *Fortune* list of most admired corporations, provides value through innovation. Innovation is one of three cornerstones of the General Mills brand strategy, as well as a driving force at 3M. The developers of such products as Scotch tape, Post-it products, and Scotchguard protector, 3M derives more than 25 percent of its sales from products less than four years old. Figure 4–3 illustrates the 3M identity.

It is difficult to have a product or service that is demonstrably the best at any given time. There is always someone who can outspec you (to use Regis McKenna's term), and even if this has not happened yet, there are always some segments that are uninformed or unconvinced. Having strength on an intangible dimension like innovativeness provides an advantage that is more durable in such a market. For example, many buy Hewlett-Packard products because of HP's reputation as a technologically advanced firm, even if the product in question may not be the most advanced.

A reputation for innovativeness can also provide credibility in making new product claims, especially when such claims really make a difference to customers. The innovative firm will be given the benefit of the doubt because it has a track record of breakthroughs that support meaningful product claims.

Many firms—especially established, "tradition-rich" leaders like GE, Kodak, AT&T, or Coke—face the problem of being seen as a bit old-fashioned and boring. Being innovative can be a vehicle to appear more modern and up-to-date. A firm that makes products containing the most advanced features and capabilities will be seen as more contemporary.

CONCERN FOR CUSTOMERS

Many organizations, from Nordstrom to Lexus, enshrine a drive to always place the customer first as a core value. If a firm can credibly communicate such a philosophy, customers not only gain confidence in the products and services but also feel that someone cares for them. It is a lot easier to like someone who likes you.

Several corporate brands have made this concept of friendship one of the defining elements of their corporate brand identity. Gateway Computer has a tag line—"You have a friend in the business"—that distinguishes it from competitors who focus on price and features. The friend metaphor is very powerful because it implies that the

FIGURE 4–3
Innovation as a Corporate Thrust

You can hardly go through a single day without touching something a 3M abrasive hasn't touched first.

Your refrigerator, your pots and pans, your shoes, your car, your desk, a chair, a floppy disk, so many of the things you touch every day without thinking twice have been touched by over 90 years of development by 3M abrasive technology.

By continuously refining and redefining abrasives and their applications to virtually every facet of our lives, 3M has produced innovations ranging from powerful abrasives that grind metal, to abrasives that conform in order to smooth and finish three-dimensional surfaces, to precision abrasives so gentle they can polish eyeglass lenses.

In an environment that encourages people to reach and supports the cross-fertilization of ideas, 3M has changed forever the way we grind, shape, sand, clean, finish, polish and smooth. Because the one thing 3M has never changed is

From tough abrasives that grind large steel casings to others so delicate they can polish computer disks and fiber optics, 3M shapes and smooths countless items that touch our lives.

its commitment to imagine the unthinkable and invent the unknown. A commitment that has resulted in more than 60,000 products that make our world safer, easier, better. And often a good deal smoother. For information call: 1-800-364-3577, that is 1-800-3M-HELPS.

3M pioneered the combining of abrasives with non-woven fiber technology. The result: unique manufacturing applications and useful household products like the Scotch-Brite scour pad.

© 3M 1994

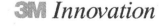

3M *Innovation*

Reprinted with permission of 3M.

brand will deliver what the customer wants: honesty, caring, dependability, and respect. In the next chapter, the brand-as-person metaphor will be explored, and the concept of a friend relationship between the brand and customers will be discussed further.

THE ROLE OF THE CEO

Some organizations are blessed with a charismatic leader—perhaps the corporate CEO—who can both represent and express the organizational associations effectively. Anita Roddick plays this role for The Body Shop. Such a person can often make corporate announcements more newsworthy and thus can gain inexpensive exposure. For example, the announcement of a new Microsoft product becomes major news when Bill Gates is invited to make a speech or appear on a national news program.

Personalizing the corporation by putting its founder/leader out front helps to create a relationship with the customer. Sam Walton, the highly visible leader of Wal*Mart, was perceived as a very appealing, even lovable person. The relationship of customers with Wal*Mart was in part a relationship with Sam Walton. In fact, in terms of representing Wal*Mart both internally and externally, the spirit of Sam Walton has remained very much a factor even after his death.

PRESENCE AND SUCCESS

The visibility and presence of the organization behind a brand can create an image of size, substance, and competence. Recall the discussion in Chapter 1 on the power of simple brand recognition—it even affected taste tests. Dealing with an organization that has the resources to back up its products and a long history of doing business is reassuring, especially in high-tech markets.

Visible success, as indicated by sales and/or sales growth, also provides customers with the reassurance of knowing that other customers have selected the brand. This comfort-in-numbers argument was behind the old (and now somewhat anachronistic) expression, "You can't get fired for buying IBM." Particularly in Japan, a background of success brings with it prestige, credibility, and the implication that the organization must be good at what it does.

An image of substance can also affect persuasion. In one study, Goldberg and Hartwick manipulated the corporate reputation of a firm that was introducing a beer in Canada.[7] The firm was described in terms of its years in business, sales, the number of people employed, and corporate citizenship activities, but not with respect to its product expertise. In addition, the firm was described to some subjects in the study as being older and larger, while to others it was described as younger and smaller. An advertisement from another market was then shown in which a comparative taste test was described—the test results presented were extreme (the new product was superior to one hundred alternatives) for some experimental groups, and less so for others. The respondents were then asked to evaluate the advertisement claims and the product. The study showed that extreme claims created skepticism for the younger, smaller firm but were accepted for the larger, older firm.

Event sponsorships are a unique vehicle for the organization to develop a presence and a sense of substance. As noted in Chapter 1, WordPerfect was an unknown, also-ran software company in Europe until it became the sponsor of one of the continent's top bicycle racing teams. WordPerfect acquired not only exposure (because television covered the leading teams extensively) but also much of the team's visibility and prestige. PowerBar had similar success with its sponsorship of bike races and so-called ironman competitions.

LOCAL VERSUS GLOBAL

A brand often needs to make a fundamental identity choice: Should it (1) be a global brand, with the accompanying prestige and credibility, or (2) try to connect with the local market? In many markets there are brands following each strategy option.

Going Local

One strategic option is to be perceived as a local brand from a local company. Lone Star beer, for instance, draws upon the fact that a particular market segment identifies with its Texas heritage. Buying and drinking Lone Star can thus be a way to express that pride and attachment, and Lone Star promotions designed with a local flavor can reinforce such users' Texas identity.

There is almost always a niche for the local competitor. BellSouth, Pacific Telesis, and U.S. West are regional telecommunication companies that compete with AT&T, MCI, and Cellular One. A differentiation path for the former firms is to emphasize their regional heritage to customers in hopes of creating a bond. A supermarket chain attempting to establish a high-end private brand against global brands is uniquely situated to go local. It can engage in local United Way festival promotions or give a percentage of saved receipts to schools for computers, thereby indicating where its ties and loyalties (unlike those of its competitors) lie.

Use of the local route, though, is not necessarily restricted to local firms. Some of the most successful U.S. brands in Europe are accepted as part of the local culture and are not viewed as being foreign. For example, although Holiday Inn is obviously a U.S. firm, many of its European hotels appear to be local inns and are often accepted as such, particularly in Germany. Heinz is considered by the English to be "their" brand, even though it is a U.S. brand with a German name. GM's Opel is also very localized, again especially in Germany.

The go-local approach need not be overt. There was a very American element in Saturn's message, but customers needed to pick this up on their own. Unlike with Chevrolet, there was no "Heartbeat of America" tag line to make the point visible and explicit. The most successful local brands do not have to tell anyone that they are local; rather, people need only observe the brands' attitude, actions, and sometimes their accent.

The go-local strategy provides a link to customers. At the extreme, it can suggest that the brand is part of the neighborhood and stands against the carpetbagger (from the big city or from a foreign country) who does not care about or understand the local culture. At least seven country-of-origin studies have found a home-country bias—for instance, that "Made in the U.S.A." in general contributes more to brand evaluation in the United States than elsewhere.[8] Han and Terpstra suggest that pride/patriotism and product serviceability are among the reasons for the bias.[9]

A local linkage is especially effective if an element of the global competitor's marketing program is insensitive or does not resonate with (or even offends) local sensibilities. A serious effort to go local can also result in a better understanding of the needs and attitudes of the locality, which in turn can lead to product refinements and more effective brand identity implementation efforts.

Going Global

The other identity option, of course, is to go global. The fact that brands like Budweiser and Kirin are national in scope—or that Nestlé, Kodak, Ford, AT&T, and Nissan are truly global—provides the prestige and reassurance of a brand that has a larger audience and mission. Even for products such as detergents, it is better to be backed by a major company such as Kao (the Japanese soap company), than to be an orphan brand (that is, one not tied to a range brand or corporate brand).

A global brand signals longevity, resources to invest in the brand, and a commitment to the brand's future. A global firm will be presumed to be advanced technologically, able not only to invest in R&D but also to draw on the advancements in the countries in which it competes. AT&T is presumed, for example, to be at the forefront of telecommunications technology because of its ability to compete both nationally and across the world.

A global brand also has considerable prestige because of its ability to compete successfully in different markets. Suntory, for example, carefully positioned Midori (a melon liqueur) as a global brand when marketing it in Japan, correctly predicting that a perceived Japanese source would be a handicap. The global brand is often the established market leader; further, it can put forth a personality of being worldly and cosmopolitan, characteristics that can be very important for some product categories.

We next turn to how organizational associations work to provide value by considering their internal and external impact.

HOW ORGANIZATIONAL ASSOCIATIONS WORK

The brand-as-organization perspective is summarized in Figure 4–4. This perspective draws upon the visibility of the organization, as well as its culture and values, people, programs, and assets/skills, to identify organizational associations that might become an important part of the brand identity. The end benefit for the brand is to provide:

- A value proposition or customer relationship based on the organizational associations

FIGURE 4-4
How Organizational Associations Provide Value

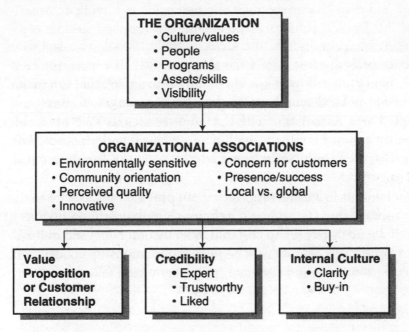

- Credibility to other brands
- A vehicle to clarify and crystallize the organizational culture and values inside the organization

PROVIDING A VALUE PROPOSITION OR CUSTOMER RELATIONSHIP

Organizational associations created by Saturn, The Body Shop, Kao Soap, and others can contribute directly to a value proposition because the associations are valued by customers. In particular, organizational associations can provide functional benefits. An organization with a reputation for having a product-quality culture provides value in the form of higher delivered quality and a guarantee against unpleasant usage experiences. A concern for customers, such as that attributed to WordPerfect, can reassure customers that the product will be supported.

Emotional benefits can be stimulated by organizational associations. Feelings of respect and admiration, for example, can be connected to an organization because of its programs and values. The experience of buying a Saturn can result in a relaxed, comfortable feeling, and many Saturn owners also feel pride in buying an American car. McDonald's charity involvement can stimulate feelings of affection and respect.

Organizational associations can also provide self-expressive benefits. Linking oneself (perhaps via a loan) with a bank that is a major sponsor of the local symphony could reinforce one's self-concept of loving the arts. Associating with the value-conscious Wal*Mart culture could support a self-concept of being frugal and practical. And patronizing The Body Shop is one way to express a commitment to social causes.

Most benefits in a value proposition can provide the basis for a customer relationship. In addition, relationship associations such as a sense of friendship (perhaps related to a customer-focused culture) exist at Saturn and elsewhere. The personal relationship concept will be revisited in the brand personality chapter which follows.

PROVIDING CREDIBILITY

A key way in which organizational associations work, particularly in the context of the corporate brand, is by providing credibility to brands being endorsed.[10] The corporate brand is often used to endorse a product brand as part of a dual brand strategy, as in the case of the Ford Taurus, Nike Air Jordans, Campbell's Healthy Request, Chevron FastPay, or General Mills Cheerios. Each brings different associations to the dual brand (see Figure 4–5). The natural role of the product brand is to generate brand-as-product associations, whereas the corporate brand's natural role is to provide organizational associations that add credibility to the product claims. The corporate brand is like the flag bearer in front of the army, bestowing credibility on the army forces but depending on the army itself to fight the battle. Chapter 8 will explore these different brand roles more carefully.

The Credible Organization: Expert, Trustworthy, Liked

Attitude research in psychology has shown that believability and persuasive power is enhanced when a spokesperson is perceived as being expert, trustworthy, and well-liked. These same characteristics should

FIGURE 4–5
Relative Roles of Corporate and Product Brands

	CORPORATE BRAND	PRODUCT BRAND
Brand Example:	Ford	Taurus
TYPE OF ASSOCIATIONS:	Organizational	Functional benefits
Association Example:	"Quality is Job 1"	Well designed
PRIMARY FUNCTION OF ASSOCIATIONS:	Provide credibility	Provide value Proposition

be relevant when evaluating whether a claim made by an organization is credible. To what extent is the organization seen as expert or trustworthy, and to what extent is it liked?

An *expert* organization is seen as especially competent at making and selling its products. Thus the visible R&D facility at Canon indicates technological expertise, which makes product claims for a new camera more credible. Indicators that Ford delivers quality cars provide similar credibility to its new offerings.

A *trustworthy* organization will be trusted and believed when it makes claims. An organization viewed as trustworthy would be perceived as honest in its communication and dealings with customers, dependable, and sensitive to consumer needs. Some firms, such as Hewlett-Packard and Levi Strauss, are trusted because their policies toward societal problems and/or their employees are interpreted as a general commitment to "doing the right thing." That sense of trustworthiness carries over to communication about product capabilities. Trust, frequently a part of the core identity of a corporate brand (for example, Johnson & Johnson), provides a strong basis for a relationship between an organization and its customers.

An organization could be *liked* because of admiration for the firm's contributions to the community, or the organization could be regarded as fun because of the activities in which it participates. Swatch, for example, by hanging a giant watch on a tall bank in

Frankfurt or by sponsoring an offbeat contest, creates an organization one (in the target market) has to like. MetLife shares some of the feelings people have toward Snoopy because of its use of the Peanuts characters. There is less of an inclination to disagree or argue with someone you like well, and the same tendency can be hypothesized to exist when a brand is the "someone" in question. The message of a liked brand will tend to be accepted, whereas the claims of a disliked brand will be viewed with skepticism.

Impact of Organizational Associations on Credibility: Some Evidence

Kevin Keller and I conducted an experiment to explore the impact of corporate image on customer acceptance of a corporate brand extension (that is, a new product outside the current range of a firm's products).[11] Four different corporate images (innovative, environmentally conscious, community minded, or neutral) were created for corporations given neutral names (e.g., Meridian); the settings were baked goods, personal care products, dairy products, and over-the-counter drugs.

A major finding was that an innovative corporate image was a powerful asset, in part because of its impact on the brand extension. Innovativeness was the only corporate image dimension to enhance the perceived fit of the corporate brand extension and the evaluation of the product attributes. The implication is that an innovative corporate image gives a firm license to stretch the brand name further. An innovative corporate image also had the largest impact on the perceived quality of the extension, a finding that occurred across several positioning strategies attached to the extension.

Moreover, an innovative corporate image had a substantial positive impact on corporate credibility, making the firm appear to be more expert (with respect to designing and making the product), more attractive (likable, prestigious), and more trustworthy. Thus respondents seemed to be attracted to the innovative profile beyond simply respecting the firm's ability to innovate.

The image of being either environmentally sensitive or community minded made only a modest difference, much less substantial and extensive than the innovativeness dimension. Both images did enhance the attractiveness and trustworthiness dimensions of corporate credibility. In addition, the environmentally sensitive corporation generated a small impact on the perceived expertise of the corporation and on the perceived quality of the corporate brand extension. This, however, was partially because this firm was seen as somewhat innovative due to its environmental leanings.

INTERNAL IMPACT

There is little doubt that it is important for employees to buy into organizational values and programs. Over the years, both current business practices and social science research into employee motivation have supported this basic premise. Consider the current acceptance of group or team efforts, empowerment, and the flat organization; all require clear organizational values and goals, and employees motivated to accomplish them.

A brand identity that includes organizational associations is more likely to represent the basic goals, values, and strategies of the organization. Thus it can play a key role in articulating these elements to employees, retailers, and others who must buy into the goals and values and implement the strategies. An identity with organizational associations is more likely to provide internal guidance on some basic questions, such as the following:

- What is the purpose of the organization? Why does the company exist? What does it stand for? Are there any broader concerns and issues involved besides making products and profits?
- What are the values and culture of the organization? What is important? What is the relative importance of being environmentally sensitive, having the highest quality, being innovative, having a concern for customers, being successful or connecting locally? What is the organization really good at doing?
- What is the vision for the future? What will be the values, culture, and goals then?

WHEN TO USE ORGANIZATIONAL ASSOCIATIONS

Proactively using organizational associations can add cost and complexity. The worst scenario is that they could add little value and succeed in diverting resources and focus from what otherwise would be a strong product brand. When should organizational associations be used? A strong role is appropriate when the brand involves an organization that has people, a culture, programs, and values that have substance and will do the following:

- create a value proposition that will be meaningful to customers and differentiate the brand
- promote customer relationships based on the feelings engendered by the organizational associations
- help a variety of products, thereby efficiently providing all of them with an identity umbrella
- provide employees of an organization with a sense of purpose and meaning that motivates them

If these conditions hold, the corporate brand should be a source of strength to the businesses it touches, and it should be treated as such.

ORGANIZATIONAL ASSOCIATIONS AS A SUSTAINABLE ADVANTAGE

An organization is usually more enduring, complex, and permanent than a particular product line. A perception of an organization is therefore more difficult for competitors to combat than specific brand attributes, which can be easily surpassed. Thus organizational associations can be a major source of a firm's sustainable advantage.

QUESTIONS TO CONSIDER

1. What is the soul of the organization? What are its values? What should they be in the future?
2. Are there organizational associations that will provide either a value proposition, a relationship, or credibility? Consider community/ societal commitment, perceived quality (as an organizational characteristic), innovation, customer concern, success/leadership, and a global versus local focus.
3. Exactly how will the organizational associations be developed, and how will they provide value to the firm?

5

BRAND PERSONALITY[1]

A brand that captures your mind gains behavior. A brand that captures your heart gains commitment.
                    —Scott Talgo, brand strategist

What other brand name do you see tattooed on people?
          —Bob Dron, Harley-Davidson dealer, Oakland, California

THE HARLEY-DAVIDSON STORY

One measure of brand loyalty is the percentage of customers who tattoo a brand's symbol on their body. By that measure, Harley-Davidson has the highest loyalty of any brand in the world. In fact, the most popular tattoo in the United States is the Harley-Davidson symbol.

Many Harley owners, even those who do not have tattoos, see Harley-Davidson as an important part of their lives and identities. Over 250,000 of them belong to one of roughly eight hundred chapters of the Harley Owners Group (H.O.G.). The H.O.G. members receive a bimonthly newsletter and attend weekly or monthly meetings, as well as motorcycle outings sponsored by dealerships. A "Ladies of Harley" subgroup caters to the 10 percent of Harley owners who are women. Approximately forty-two state rallies are held each year in addition to a series of major national club rallies that includes a Spring Bike Week in Daytona Beach and a summer gathering in Sturgis, South Dakota, that draws tens of thousands. In June 1993, more than 20,000 H.O.G. members (plus another 80,000 Harley-Davidson enthusiasts of all kinds) went to Milwaukee to celebrate the firm's ninetieth anniversary.

Harley-Davidson is much more than a motorcycle; it is an experience, an attitude, a lifestyle, and a vehicle to express who one is. One Harley visual image, that of a bike alone on the open road somewhere in the vastness of America, clearly expresses rugged individuality and personal freedom. Another is of a powerful machine accelerating along a winding road. Still another is of a relaxed group of down-to-earth bikers who share beliefs, values, and experiences. One rider describes riding as "a singular experience . . . being out in the air, in the open . . . the different scents . . . a special experience . . . leaning into turns . . . [I] love that feeling of nimbleness and freedom."[2] One theme here is that the Harley experience is ageless and timeless; you don't have to be a teenager to experience a Harley-Davidson.

Two Oregon researchers (who bought Harleys and studied the ownership experience as participant observers) have uncovered three core values of Harley owners.[3] The dominant value is personal freedom, which includes both freedom from confinement (as opposed to riding in a car or staying at home) and freedom from mainstream values and social structures. The Harley-Davidson eagle logo is one symbol of this freedom. Others are the biker clothing and saddlebags, which are reminiscent of the Wild West folk hero. This aspect of the Harley spirit is captured in the ad shown in Figure 5–1.

FIGURE 5–1
Ad Typifying Harley-Davidson Lifestyle

IF YOU DIDN'T HAVE TO ANSWER TO ANYONE, WHAT WOULD YOU DO?

Machines like this don't just happen. But in building the Heritage™ Softail Classic, we really had to answer only to ourselves.
Maybe it's time you thought about doing the same thing.
Call 1-800-443-2153 for the location of a Harley-Davidson® dealer near you.

Source: Harley-Davidson. Photo by Jon Mason.

A second value is patriotism and the Harley-Davidson American heritage. Harley is visibly American, a brand that fought off the Japanese competition. At rallies the American flag and pro-USA messages abound. At the extreme, some Harley bikers engage in forms of Japan-bashing (Japanese cycles are termed "rice grinders"), and some seem to feel that riding a Harley-Davidson motorcycle is a stronger expression of patriotism than is obeying the law.

The third value is being macho, inspired in part by the outlaw bikers in *The Wild Ones*, the famed Marlon Brando picture of the 1950s.[4] Expressions of manliness abound; a popular Harley T-shirt proclaims "Real Men Wear Black." Harley-Davidsons are the biggest, heaviest, loudest and thus the most macho motorcycles on the road. There is an abundance of black leather, heavy boots, chrome, weaponry, and other signals of maleness at Harley rallies. The imagery also involves heavy beards, long hair, cowboy boots, and, of course, the tattoo.

While Harley-Davidson has maintained a consistent brand personality based largely on the macho, American, and Western folk hero associations, it has been successful at broadening its user imagery by drawing on the freedom value. The modern user may simply be a respectable outdoors person who enjoys traveling wherever the road leads. In recent advertising, Harley users are shown on the open road and in front of remote cabins, with the riders living the kind of laid-back, relaxed life most only dream about. The Harley motto— "Live to ride, ride to live"—appeals to many nonmacho potential buyers in mundane jobs.

One of the unique aspects of Harley-Davidson is the involvement of the firm's personnel and dealers with customers and their experiences. The H.O.G. activities are all sponsored or supported by Harley executives, employees, and dealers, who become part of the action. For example, Harley managers—from the CEO to the chief engineer on down—participated in rides from U.S. cities to the 1993 Milwaukee rally. As a result of this involvement, H.O.G. members generate a personal bond with the Harley-Davidson organization. And Harley people get to know their firm's customers intimately. They see the Harley experience firsthand, including what features are clicking, how the bikes are being modified, and what suggestions H.O.G. members have. At rallies, a town hall meeting provides an opportunity for members to communicate their thoughts.

Owners of Japanese motorcycles generally have a very different perspective toward life and their bikes. They tend to talk about the features of the bike rather than the riding experience. In fact, Japanese bikes are engineering marvels. They are quiet, smooth, capable of higher speeds than Harleys, and full of such features as digital instruments, rear speakers, reverse gear, fans, and even air conditioners. Their owners tend to look down their noses at the anachronistic design and noisy, throaty roar of Harleys. To a Harley-Davidson owner, however, the sound, feel, and look of his or her bike is part of the experience. Even the infamous Harley vibrations are treasured by aficionados. The owner of a Japanese motorcycle focuses on functional benefits, whereas the Harley-Davidson owner is much more concerned with emotional and self-expressive benefits.

Harley-Davidson is an extremely healthy company; it sells nearly 100,000 bikes a year (which is as many as it can make). Amazingly, only a decade ago this same company was facing death at the hands of Japanese firms, who were delivering a better product with a lower cost structure. There was a real concern at one time that the United States would no longer have a serious motorcycle manufacturer. However, Harley-Davidson coupled a serious quality improvement program with its strong brand-enhancing activities to come back.

Harley-Davidson customers can also express themselves by wearing Harley clothing. The Harley MotorClothing division is part of an accessories business that exceeded $200 million in sales in 1993 marketing jackets, boots, gloves, and other accessories and licensing such items as bathing suits (with "Harley" studded across the front) and silk underwear.

The concept of a Harley-Davidson brand personality—a macho, America-loving, freedom-seeking person who is willing to break out from confining societal norms of dress and behavior—provides a metaphor that helps to explain the Harley phenomenon. The experience of riding a Harley, or even the association that comes from wearing Harley clothing, is a way for some to express a part of their own personality. It can also create feelings of freedom, independence, and power that provide emotional benefits. For others, having a relationship with an organization and a product with a strong personality is satisfying and rewarding, as is bonding with a group that shares the same values and lifestyle.

BRAND PERSONALITIES

A *brand personality* can be defined as the set of human characteristics associated with a given brand.[5] Thus it includes such characteristics as gender, age, and socioeconomic class, as well as such classic human personality traits as warmth, concern, and sentimentality.

For example, Virginia Slims tends to be feminine in comparison to the masculine Marlboro. Apple is considered young while IBM tends to be seen as older (in part because it has been around longer). After Eight mints tend to be upper-class, while Butterfinger tends to be blue-collar. Guess is considered sophisticated in contrast to the rugged Wrangler. Nike is considered athletic, while LA Gear tends to be perceived as more fashionable. American Express is pretentious relative to Discovery Card, which is more down-to-earth.

Brand personality, like human personality, is both distinctive and enduring. For example, one analysis found Coke to be considered real and authentic whereas Pepsi was young, spirited, and exciting and Dr. Pepper was nonconforming, unique, and fun.[6] Further, the personalities of all three brands had endured over time, sometimes in spite of efforts to augment or change them.

The brand personality concept has considerable face validity (brand strategists and researchers are comfortable with it). Respondents in qualitative and quantitative research studies are routinely asked to profile the personalities of brands. Their responses come easily and generally are interpretable and consistent across people. Differences between groups (such as users and nonusers) are often reasonable and provide useful insights. Frequently, for example, users will perceive a brand to have a strong personality, whereas nonusers may not: Oral B may be regarded as a serious, competent brand by the former, whereas the latter may regard it as being bland.

Further, customers often interact with brands as if they were people, especially when the brands are attached to such meaningful products as clothes or cars. Even if they do not give their possessions a personal nickname (as many do their cars), it is not uncommon to hear people talk of objects as if they were human: "Sometimes my computer feels better after I let it rest awhile," or "Sometimes I think my car breaks down just to irritate me."[7]

MEASURING BRAND PERSONALITY

The same vocabulary used to describe a person can be used to describe a brand personality. In particular, a brand can be described by demographics (age, gender, social class, and race), lifestyle (activities, interests, and opinions) or human personality traits (such as extroversion, agreeableness, and dependability).

A recent study developed and tested the Brand Personality Scale (BPS), a compact set of traits designed to both measure and structure brand personality.[8] The development of the BPS involved more than 1,000 U.S. respondents, 60 well-known brands with distinct personalities, and 114 personality traits. Five personality factors (termed the Big Five) —Sincerity, Excitement, Competence, Sophistication, and Ruggedness—emerged even when the sample was subdivided by age or gender and when subsets of the brands were used. The Big Five explain nearly all (93 percent) of the observed differences between the brands. Figure 5–2 describes the Big Five in terms of an extended set of traits in order to provide an understanding of their scope and richness.

As Figure 5–2 illustrates, the Big Five describe the personalities of many strong brands well. Campbell's, Hallmark, and Kodak are very high on Sincerity, and Levi's, Marlboro, and Nike are high on Ruggedness, for example. Like a person, however, a brand can have a complex personality that ranges across the Big Five. Levi's, for example, is relatively high (in the top 20 percent of the brands studied) on Sincerity, Excitement, and Competence as well as being the top-rated brand on Ruggedness. McDonald's rates high on both Sincerity and Competence. And Hallmark, perhaps because of the diversity of its greeting cards, is not only extremely high on Sincerity but one of the highest brands on Excitement and Competence as well.

Each of the Big Five factors have been divided into facets to provide texture and descriptive insight regarding the nature and structure of the Big Five. The fifteen facets are given descriptive names in Figure 5–2. Thus, Sincerity breaks down to Down-To-Earth, Honest, Wholesome, and Cheerful, while Excitement contains the facets Daring, Spirited, Imaginative, and Up-To-Date. Again, brands can span personality facets; thus Benetton scores well on Up-To-Date and Daring, whereas Absolut is high on Up-To-Date and Imaginative.

The fifteen facets suggest strategic options. A strong Sincerity brand, for example can emphasize Cheerful (sentimental, friendly, and warm) instead of Honest (sincere, real, and ethical) qualities. Or a brand high in Competence can stress Intelligent (technical, corporate, and serious) rather than Successful (leader, confident, and influential) characteristics. In each case, the personality objective and the implementation strategy would be very different.

FIGURE 5–2

A Brand Personality Scale (BPS): The Big Five

Sincerity (Campbell's, Hallmark, Kodak)

  Down-To-Earth: family-oriented, small-town, conventional, blue-collar, all-American

  Honest: sincere, real, ethical, thoughtful, caring

  Wholesome: original, genuine, ageless, classic, old-fashioned

  Cheerful: sentimental, friendly, warm, happy

Excitement (Porsche, Absolut, Benetton)

  Daring: trendy, exciting, off-beat, flashy, provocative

  Spirited: cool, young, lively, outgoing, adventurous,

  Imaginative: unique, humorous, surprising, artistic, fun

  Up-To-Date: independent, contemporary, innovative, aggressive

Competence (Amex, CNN, IBM)

  Reliable: hardworking, secure, efficient, trustworthy, careful

  Intelligent: technical, corporate, serious

  Successful: leader, confident, influential

Sophistication (Lexus, Mercedes, Revlon)

  Upper Class: glamorous, good-looking, pretentious, sophisticated

  Charming: feminine, smooth, sexy, gentle

Ruggedness (Levi's, Marlboro, Nike)

  Outdoorsy: masculine, Western, active, athletic

  Tough: rugged, strong, no-nonsense

The BPS study also measured the degree of positive or negative attitude toward each brand in comparison to other brands in the product category. Of interest was the fact that personality variables were significantly related to attitude, with the specific relationship varying by brand. Excitement and Competence were related to positive attitudes for Apple and American Express. Ruggedness was a positive driver for Levi's and a negative one for McDonald's. Respondents who regarded

Mercedes or Porsche as sophisticated were more likely to have a positive attitude toward the brand. Overall, however, the personality traits, most associated with positive attitudes were primarily from the Sincerity factor, (e.g., real, sincere, genuine, original) and the Competence factor (e.g., reliable, leader).

The potential of the Sincerity factor may explain in part why several brands have turned to genuineness or authenticity as a core identity. Chevrolet developed the ad theme "Genuine Chevrolet" when its research found a reservoir of goodwill based on the Chevy heritage of the 1950s and 1960s.[9] Jockey underwear uses a "Genuine Jockey" position to draw on its heritage and help fight private-label competitors. Other examples include the "one and only" Wonderbra from Sara Lee Foundations and Docker's Authentics. One motivation for going "genuine" is to draw on a strong brand heritage and capture the reassurance and emotional links that such a heritage provides. In general, Sincerity is often used by heritage brands such as Kodak and Coke.

Excitement is another personality trait that has worked in several contexts such as cars, athletic equipment, cosmetics, and even coffee. The fact that Folgers had a personality of being exciting and smart looking and Maxwell House had a nondescript, weak personality was credited with some significant sales shifts from Maxwell House to Folgers in the early 1990s.

HOW A BRAND PERSONALITY IS CREATED

Just as the perceived personality of a person is affected by nearly everything associated with that person—including his or her neighborhood, friends, activities, clothes, and manner of interacting—so too is a brand personality. Figure 5–3 suggests the breadth of factors, both related and unrelated to the product, affecting perceptions of a brand personality.

Product-related characteristics can be primary drivers of a brand personality. Even the product class can affect the personality. A bank or insurance company, for example, will tend to assume a stereotypical "banker" personality (competent, serious, masculine, older, and upper-class). An athletic shoe like Nike or Reebok might tend to be rugged, outdoorsy, and adventurous, as well as young and lively. A package or feature can also influence the brand personality, just as

FIGURE 5–3
Brand Personality Drivers

PRODUCT-RELATED CHARACTERISTICS	NON-PRODUCT-RELATED CHARACTERISTICS
Product category (Bank)	User imagery (Levi's 501)
Package (Gateway computers)	Sponsorships (Swatch)
Price (Tiffany)	Symbol (Marlboro Country)
Attributes (Coors Light)	Age (Kodak)
	Ad style (Obsession)
	Country of origin (Audi)
	Company image (The Body Shop)
	CEO (Bill Gates of Microsoft)
	Celebrity endorsers (Jell-O)

the white box with black splotches (reminiscent of Holstein cows) provides a down-to-earth personality for Gateway Computer.

Product attributes often affect the brand personality. If a brand is "light" (such as Coors Lite, Weight Watchers, or Dreyer's Light) the brand personality might be described as being slender and athletic. A high-priced brand such as Tiffany might be considered wealthy, stylish, and perhaps a bit snobbish. As will be discussed, the brand personality can also reinforce and represent an attribute. For instance, if Weight Watchers is given a slender, active personality (perhaps reinforced by using Lynn Redgrave in an active pose as a symbol), a customer will find it easier to remember and believe that Weight Watchers products have low-calorie, weight-control attributes.

Non-product-related characteristics that can also affect a brand personality include advertising style, country of origin, company image, CEO identification, and celebrity endorsers. AT&T's "Reach out and touch someone" slogan and Calvin Klein's Obsession advertising both helped define a strong personality for the brands. A German brand like Audi might capture some perceived characteristics of German people (such as being precise, serious, and hardworking), and the company image of The Body Shop might suggest a social activist working hard to stimulate change. The personality of a visible CEO such as Charles Schwab or Microsoft's Bill Gates can also transfer to the brand, as can that of a celebrity endorser such as Bill Cosby for Jell-O. Four other non-product-related brand personality drivers—user imagery, sponsorships, age, and symbols—will be discussed next.

User Imagery

User imagery can be based on either typical users (people you see using the brand) or idealized users (as portrayed in advertising and elsewhere). User imagery can be a powerful driver of brand personality, in part because the user is already a person and thus the difficulty of conceptualizing the brand personality is reduced. For example, Charlie has a feminine, strongly independent brand personality driven by its user imagery. The upscale personality of Mercedes and the sexy, sophisticated personality of Calvin Klein are similarly influenced by user imagery.

Sponsorships

Activities such as events sponsored by the brand will influence its personality. Swatch, for example, reinforces its offbeat (even outrageous), youthful personality with targeted sponsorships that have included the Freestyle Ski World Cup in Breckenridge, the First International Breakdancing Championship, Andrew Logan's "Alternative Miss World Show" in London, street painting in Paris, and the "Museum of Unnatural History" tour through Europe. Häagen-Dazs helped create a prestigious, upscale personality with its sponsorship of several opera performances under the theme "Dedicated to Pleasure, Dedicated to the Arts."

Age

How long a brand has been on the market can affect its personality. Thus, newer entrants such as Apple, MCI, and Saturn tend to have younger brand personalities than brands such as IBM, AT&T, and Chevrolet, and it is all too common for a major or dominant brand to be seen as stodgy and old-fashioned, a brand for older people. Active management of the brand to counter such pressure is discussed in Chapter 7.

Symbol

A symbol can be a powerful influence on brand personality because it can be controlled and can have extremely strong associations. Apple's bitten apple, the Marlboro cowboy, the Michelin man, and the Maytag repairman all help to create and reinforce a personality for their brands.

In the early 1980s, IBM had an image problem—it was a business computer from a stuffy corporation, not a brand with which an individual buying his or her first computer would necessarily be comfortable. IBM attacked this problem by using the Charlie Chaplin character to lighten up its personality and to reinforce the user-friendly attribute of its PC Junior personal computers. The Chaplin character was initially effective, but it unfortunately was discarded after it came to be associated with the PC Junior product, which was a failure. Thus IBM still struggles with an image problem to this day.

A similar problem faced MetLife in the 1980s. It wanted to appear friendly and caring but instead was perceived to have the personality of a life insurance company: faceless, bureaucratic, and cold. The firm's solution was to attach the Peanuts characters to the brand through consistent and heavy advertising over a long time period. Figure 5–4 provides an example of that advertising. The characters serve to soften and lighten the prototypical life insurance image and to differentiate MetLife from its competitors.

The Peanuts characters were borrowed by MetLife, as was Bart Simpson by Butterfinger (see the insert). Other cartoon-character symbols that have helped create brand personalities are owned by the brand, however, making the task of linking the symbol to the brand much easier. These include the Jolly Green Giant, the Keebler elves, and Charlie the Tuna.

Unlike real people, cartoon-character symbols rarely generate unfavorable surprises, and they do not age. The Pillsbury Doughboy, for example, is likable and will reflect the desired attributes, such as freshness, in exactly the same way for as long as the company desires. In addition, the character can be revised as needed; for example, the doughboy has gotten thinner, more active, and more enthusiastic over the years.

A key attribute of cartoon symbols like the Pillsbury Doughboy is that they can make assertions without stimulating counterarguments

FIGURE 5–4
MetLife ad

WE'RE THE OLD MASTERS OF
FINANCIAL SECURITY.

GET MET. IT PAYS.
❖ MetLife®

from the audience (such as "Is that cake healthy for my child?"). For starters, it would make no sense to argue with a fictional character, who will not talk back. Further, the character is simply too likable to be a target of discontent or anger.

THE BUTTERFINGER STORY

Butterfinger was a rather tired candy bar brand in 1989 when RJR Nabisco decided to sell it to Nestlé. Although the candy bar was perceived as being outdated and without personality, it did have a license to use the Bart Simpson character. Nestlé used the irreverent, mischievous personality of Bart to create a new personality for the brand.

The advertising presented the ongoing adventure of Bart versus a bully, a school principal, and Homer (Bart's father), all of whom were trying unsuccessfully to "lay a finger" on Bart's Butterfinger. Promotions involving the Bart Simpson character have supported the personality and the Bart connection. In addition, a link with snowboarding and music tours has strengthened the bar's relationship with the 12-to-24-year-old target market. In a flat category, sales of Butterfinger in supermarkets were up 14 percent in 1990, 36 percent in 1991, and 18.3 percent in 1992.

WHY USE BRAND PERSONALITY?

The brand personality construct can help brand strategists by enriching their understanding of people's perceptions of and attitudes toward the brand, contributing to a differentiating brand identity, guiding the communication effort, and creating brand equity.

ENRICHING UNDERSTANDING

The brand personality metaphor can help a manager gain an in-depth understanding of consumer perceptions of and attitudes toward the brand. By asking people to describe a brand personality, feelings and relationships can be identified that often provide more insight than is gained by asking about attribute perceptions. The arrogant and powerful personality ascribed by some to Microsoft, for example, provides insight into the nature of the relationship between Microsoft and its customers.

CONTRIBUTING TO A DIFFERENTIATING IDENTITY

Strategically, a brand personality, as part of a core or extended identity, can serve as the foundation for meaningful differentiation, especially in contexts where brands are similar with respect to product attributes. In fact, it can define not only the brand but the product-class context and experience. With its stagecoach symbol and associations with the Old West, Wells Fargo Bank is largely defined by its brand personality. In contrast, its competitor First Interstate is perceived in terms of bank attributes. Advertising agencies such as Young & Rubicam and Ogilvy & Mather routinely include a brand personality statement as part of their brand positioning strategy.

When Canon, a maker of high-end cameras, came out with a per-formance camera that could be used in action contexts, it needed to create excitement and energy for the new product. Moreover, it needed to differentiate the product not only from competitors but from the rest of Canon. The solution was a subbrand, the Rebel, with a distinct brand personality: independent (even a bit wild and off-the-wall), forceful, and colorful. Tennis player Andre Agassi, who captured the personality of the Rebel, was chosen as an endorser, as Figure 5–5 illustrates.

GUIDING THE COMMUNICATION EFFORT

Tactically, the brand personality concept and vocabulary communi-cates the brand identity with richness and texture to those who must implement the identity-building effort. Practical decisions need to be made about not only advertising but packaging, promotions, which events to associate with, and the style of personal interactions between the customer and the brand. If the brand is specified only in terms of attribute associations, little guidance is provided; to say that Prince tennis rackets possess high quality and an oversized head does not give much direction. To say that Prince as a person is a demand-ing professional, however, conveys much more. A brand personality statement provides depth and texture that make it easier to keep the communication effort on target.

CREATING BRAND EQUITY

The ways a brand personality can create brand equity are summa-rized by the three models shown in Figure 5–6. These models will be described in the following sections. The chapter will close by con-trasting brand personality with its close relative, user imagery.

FIGURE 5–5
Andre Agassi Endorsing Canon Camera

Reproduced with permission of Canon.

FIGURE 5–6
Brand Personality Creates Brand Equity

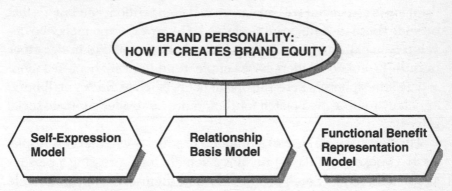

THE SELF-EXPRESSION MODEL

The premise of the self-expression model is that for certain groups of customers, some brands become vehicles to express a part of their self-identity. This self-identity can be their actual identity or an ideal self to which they might aspire. People express their own or idealized identity in a variety of ways, such as job choice, friends, attitudes, opinions, activities, and lifestyles. Brands that people like, admire, discuss, buy, and use also provide a vehicle for self-expression.

A brand can be used for expression even if it lacks a strong personality. A person can express frugality by buying a cheap brand, even one with a weak personality. Attaching even a fuzzy personality to a brand, however, usually provides insight into how that brand is being used for self-expression. If the brand has a strong personality, such as Harley-Davidson's, the personality can be hypothesized to play a key role in the self-expression process.

Since the work of William James in the nineteenth century, social scientists have examined ways in which people use goods and possessions not only to satisfy functional needs but to provide meaning and organization to their lives. Grant McCracken, a consumer anthropologist, notes that a brand's personality is part of its cultural meaning.[10] He argues that consumers look for products and brands whose cultural meanings correspond to the person they are or want to become—in other words, that they use these brand meanings to construct and sustain their social self.

McCracken also notes that cultural meanings change over time. In a study of beer consumption, he found that for college men, beer drinking is associated with maleness and competition, and brands that provide those meanings are preferred. However, some men who develop new patterns of masculinity after college come to prefer other brands. Professional men, for example, tend to drink beer in a more sedate atmosphere where European beers (such as Beck's or Tuborg) are likely to be a good match for their more controlled, upscale social selves.

The purchase and use of a branded product—whether it is Apple, Betty Crocker, or Nike—provides a vehicle for expressing a personality and lifestyle. Some people may find themselves uncomfortable when an activity is pursued or a brand is used that is not true to their actual or ideal self. In contrast, an activity or brand that "fits" can create comfort and satisfaction and can make people feel more fulfilled.

As a person, the Apple Macintosh is perceived by many as friendly, unpretentious, irreverent, and willing to go against the grain. This personality has developed partially because the Mac is an easy-to-use, intuitive computer that even greets its users, but also because of the brand's user imagery, the activities of user groups, and the Mac symbol (a rainbow-colored apple with a bite out of it) and advertising. A particularly strong personality statement was made by the famous Chiat-Day 1984 television ad which introduced the Mac; it showed a woman destroying a huge television screen on which a Big Brother–like figure spoke to a huge, zombielike crowd of people (representing conventional wisdom and the IBM world). The use of an Apple, for some, expresses a personal identity of being non-corporate and creative.

Betty Crocker as a person is a traditional, small-town, all-American mother who cares about cooking and about her family. The familiar symbol of the Betty Crocker face provides a strong visual image. For many, Betty Crocker reminds them of childhood memories of Mom baking in the kitchen, or sometimes of an idealized childhood they would like to have had. The use of Betty Crocker thus expresses the home/mother/nurturing side of some of its users.

Nike as a person is spirited, stylish, determined to excel and into health and fitness. The brand is very aspirational (in the sense that wearing Nike represents what the users aspire to be like rather than their current self-image), with a personality influenced by such endorsers as Michael Jordan, Andre Agassi, and Bo Jackson and by advertising such as the "Just do it" campaign. For some people, wearing the Nike brand can be a personal statement of who they would like to be.

STOLICHNAYA VERSUS ABSOLUT

Two brands have competed for decades in the upscale vodka market: Stolichnaya and Absolut. Despite many similarities between them (such as high quality, purity, and upscale image), they have created very different brand personalities.

Stolichnaya vodka as a person is experienced, self-assured, and successful in a traditional career such as law or banking. He is male, drives a Lexus, and has no compulsion to follow the latest trends. He recognizes quality.

The Absolut person, in contrast, is younger, more contemporary, and flashier. Also a male, he is more likely to go to trendy bars and work in a creative occupation such as advertising or the arts.

In each case, the brand personality has become the glue that holds together the identity and communication effort.

HOW THE BRAND HELPS TO EXPRESS A PERSONALITY

A brand can help people express their personality in several ways that vary in terms of the intensity and the process. These ways are discussed below.

Feelings Engendered by the Brand Personality

There can be a set of feelings and emotions attached to a brand personality, just as there are to a person. Some brands (such as MCI) can be aggressive and pushy, while others (such as Kodak and Campbell's Soup) can be warm and empathetic. Such use of a brand can cause feelings and emotions to emerge. Feelings might exist when using a Harley-Davidson or Apple, for example, that would not emerge when using a Yamaha or Dell. These feelings can be a part of self-expression. A warm person will be most fulfilled when a warm feeling occurs; similarly, an aggressive person will seek out contexts where aggression is accepted.

One study has suggested that a brand personality can transform the use experience.[11] Respondents were asked to imagine themselves either taking a break on a mountain after a daytime hike or relaxing at a small evening barbecue with close friends. During the scene, the beer served was either Coors or Löwenbräu. Coors (with an outdoorsy, active, healthy personality) created feelings of warmth, friendliness, and wholesomeness in the mountain setting, but not in the barbecue setting. In contrast, for Löwenbräu (with an urban, social personality) the reverse was true.

The Brand as a Badge

A brand could serve as a person's personal statement even if that person were on a desert island with no others present. However, there often is also a potential for brands—particularly those that are visible or "badge" brands—to have a substantial social impact. The presence of a brand (or even the attitudes held toward it) can serve to define a person with respect to others, and when social identity is involved, what is expressed can be very important to the individual.

Thus product categories such as autos, cosmetics, and clothes lend themselves to personality expression because their use occurs in a social context with relatively high involvement. Individuals evaluating and interpreting another person's identity will observe the car driven and the clothes worn.

The Brand Becomes Part of the Self

The ultimate personality expression occurs when a brand becomes an extension or an integral part of the self. Imagine the full-time biker and his or her Harley; the bike and the person become impossible to disentangle. For an Apple user who is constantly at his or her keyboard, the computer is part of the person. For a couple who drink Dewar's at the end of each day, the Scotch is not so much an expression of who they are but a part of their lifestyle, personality, and being. Another person may need to slide on a pair of Levi's 501 jeans on a lazy Saturday afternoon in order to feel fully as if the weekend has arrived. The potential to create this oneness with some people can represent a significant opportunity for a brand.

In consumer behavior literature, Russell Belk suggests that objects can go beyond representing oneself to actually become a part of the self.[12] Belk mentions collection items, gifts, and family heirlooms as particularly strong examples of products that become a part of this "extended self." He further argues that brands that become a part of one's extended self (1) are central to one's identity, (2) have a deep emotional attachment to the self, and (3) are somehow "controlled" by the individual.[13]

MULTIPLE PERSONALITIES

In the 1950s and early 1960s, a self-expression model emerged that was stimulated in part by motivation research (in-depth interviewing using clinical psychoanalytic methods and theories). It hypothesized that a person's personality would match that of the product classes or brands he or she used. A series of studies explored this hypothesis empirically by relating a person's current and/or ideal self image with the brand personality of brands purchased. The general conclusion was that although a relationship existed, it was relatively weak or inconsistent.

There are several methodological explanations for these somewhat discouraging findings. The most compelling explanation, however, is that the assumption that a person has a single personality or self-image may be erroneous. Indeed, psychologists and sociologists have conceived of multiple-personality systems in which certain parts of a person's personality would emerge in different contexts (such as social gatherings, vacation, and work) and in different social roles (such as friend, colleague, boss, or parent).[14] For example, a male accountant may be perceived by colleagues as humorous, creative, and hard-working; by golf partners as relaxed and a good loser; by his children as absent-minded but a stable, supportive teacher; and by friends as a real "party animal." The personality that dominates will depend on the role that is being played and the situation in which that role is being expressed.

Each of these multiple personalities needs to be expressed, some more than others. Thus there may be a little bit of Harley-Davidson in a lot of males, and perhaps a lot of Harley in a few. A man may be accurately described as a meticulous lawyer who dresses neatly and leads an organized lifestyle, and his ideal self may not be much different. A desire to express that bit of Harley that exists within him, though, may result in the purchase of Harley clothing or even of a bike.

Similarly, it is not realistic to assume that most Apple users are pure "Apple types." Rather, it seems more reasonable to consider an Apple personality as reflecting a part of an individual's attitudes and lifestyle. For some people, buying and using an Apple can provide an outlet for a part of their personality. Competing brands such as IBM and Hewlett-Packard can provide an outlet for different personalities, and a person's choice of computer may depend in part on which brand provides the strongest and most appropriate expressive value.

To test the premise that people use brands to express their self, and that this self changes across situations, a laboratory experiment was conducted in which respondents indicated their preferences for brands with certain personalities in specific situations. The study found that brand preferences changed when the situations changed. For example, preferences were different in the context of a homey dinner with your family versus an important business dinner meeting with your boss. The effect was more pronounced among those who were high on a self-monitoring scale—those particularly aware of their situations and others in it—altered their behavior accordingly.[15]

Like a person, a brand can exemplify different personalities in different contexts and roles. For example, an Apple computer may be thought of as friendly, fun, and relaxed at home, but at work this personality may translate into being unprofessional or even lackadaisical. People's feelings toward a brand can thus differ depending on the context. It is noteworthy that Apple, with a strong brand personality, has been historically very successful in the home and at school but has struggled in the business environment.

In order to understand the brand's personality profile, it can be helpful to look at the brand's use context. Does the brand change personalities in different use contexts? Will attempting to generalize the brand's personality across contexts hide the potential for a strong personality impact?

BRAND PERSONALITY AND SELF-EXPRESSION NEEDS MUST FIT

In order to be effective, a brand personality needs to be desirable and important enough to matter to the person using the brand. The person should feel better because of an association with the brand—

more upscale when driving a Lexus, younger when drinking Pepsi, sophisticated when wearing Chanel perfume, or laid-back when drinking Miller Lite. A personality that is off target will not work. For example, a brand with a reliable, distinguished personality would not appeal much to someone who needs to express his or her youth.

Brand personality effects might be larger for visible, involving products like cars and clothes. When the fit between the brand personality, the context, and the self-expression need is right, however, any brand personality may facilitate identity expression. An oven cleaner might be given a tough, aggressive, can-do type of personality, and its use could play an expressive role as a result. Oscar Mayer, which shows its hot dogs being eaten by a child in a nostalgic setting, notes that everyone has a little bit of kid in them. The childlike aspect of anyone's personality can perhaps be expressed by eating Oscar Mayer hot dogs, especially if the setting is appropriate.

THE RELATIONSHIP BASIS MODEL

Some people may never aspire to have the personality of a competent leader but would like to have a relationship with one, especially if they need a banker or a lawyer. A trustworthy, dependable, conservative personality might be boring but might nonetheless reflect characteristics valued in a financial advisor, a lawn service, or even a car—consider the Volvo brand personality. The concept of a relationship between a brand and a person (analogous to that between two people) provides a different perspective on how brand personality might work.

To see how the relationship basis model works, consider the personality types of people with whom you have relationships and the nature of those relationships. Some of the types might be as follows:

- *Down-to-earth, family oriented, genuine, old-fashioned* (Sincerity). This might describe brands like Hallmark, Kodak, and even Coke. The relationship might be similar to one that exists with a well-liked and respected member of the family.
- *Spirited, young, up-to-date, outgoing* (Excitement). In the soft-drink category, Pepsi fits this mold more than Coke. Especially on a weekend evening, it might be enjoyable to have a friend who has these personality characteristics.

- *Accomplished, influential, competent* (Competence). Perhaps Hewlett-Packard and the *Wall Street Journal* might fit this profile. Think of a relationship with a person whom you respect for their accomplishments, such as a teacher, minister or business leader; perhaps that is what a relationship between a business computer and its customer should be like.
- *Pretentious, wealthy, condescending* (Sophistication). For some, this would be BMW, Mercedes, or Lexus (with gold trim) as opposed to the Mazda Miata or the VW Golf. The relationship could be similar to one with a powerful boss or a rich relative.
- *Athletic and outdoorsy* (Ruggedness). Nike (versus LA Gear), Marlboro (versus Virginia Slims), and Wells Fargo (versus Bank of America) are examples. When planning an outing, a friend with outdoorsy interests would be welcome.

Two elements thus affect an individual's relationship with a brand. First, there is the relationship between the brand-as-person and the customer, which is analogous to the relationship between two people. Second, there is the brand personality—that is, the type of person the brand represents. The brand personality provides depth, feelings and liking to the relationship. Of course, a brand–customer relationship can also be based on a functional benefit, just as two people can have a strictly business relationship.

THE BRAND AS A FRIEND

One important relationship for many brands is a friendship link characterized by trust, dependability, understanding, and caring. A friend is there for you, treats you with respect, is comfortable, is someone you like, and is an enjoyable person with whom to spend time. This type of relationship was a driver for much of the Saturn program as was discussed in Chapter 2. General Foods, in fact, defines brand equity as a "liking" or a "friendship" relationship between the customer and the brand. WordPerfect, a software company that has always been a leader in customer service, would rate high on the friendship dimension.

A friend relationship can involve very different brand personalities. Some friends are fun and irreverent. Others are serious and command respect. Others are reliable and unpretentious. Still others are just comfortable to be around. A focus on the friend relationship rather than the brand personality can allow more scope and flexibility in the implementation of the brand identity.

Fred Posner of Ayer Worldwide has observed that people live in a world characterized by stress, alienation, and clutter.[16] Noting that people cope by developing escape mechanisms and meaningful friendships, Posner suggests that brands can provide these roles by being either an "aspirational" or a "trusted" associate. Escape can take the form of aspirational relationships which provide a social lift or trusting relationships which provide some expertise or knowledge of a subject in which a given person is interested. Posner believes that either relationship can be the basis for real differentiation and competitive advantage. He further suggests that the chosen relationship should be the centerpiece of brand strategy and execution.

Dodge Neon, like Saturn, wants to be considered a friend, but its friend relationship is a bit different.[17] Aiming at the under-thirty crowd, Neon brand strategists have adopted a lighthearted tone reminiscent of the VW Beetle personality. The introductory ads (illustrated in Figure 5–7) showed a white Dodge Neon facing directly into the camera with the word "Hi" over the car, as if the car was talking to the reader. In contrast, the Saturn customer relationship is quite a bit more serious and adult in nature.

WHAT IF THE BRAND SPOKE TO YOU?

When considering brand personality, the natural tendency is to consider the brand to be a passive element in the relationship. The focus is upon consumer perceptions, attitudes, and behavior *toward* the brand; attitudes and perceptions of the brand itself are hidden behind the closed doors of the organization. Yet your relationship with another person is deeply affected by not only who that person is but also what that person thinks of you. Similarly, a brand–customer relationship will have an active partner at each end, the brand as well as the customer.

Max Blackston of Research International has argued that to understand brand–customer relationships, it is necessary to consider what a brand thinks of you.[18] One approach to obtaining this information is to ask what the brand would say to you if it were a person. The result can be illuminating. Blackston illustrates this approach

FIGURE 5-7
A Dodge Neon Ad

Reproduced with permission of Chrysler Corporation.

with a doctor–patient example. Consider a doctor who is perceived by all to be professional, caring, capable, and funny—characteristics that most would like in a doctor. But what if the doctor also felt you were a boring hypochondriac? The resulting negative relationship would be impossible to predict based only upon perceptions of the doctor's personality or external appearance.

Blackston's approach was used in a research study of a credit card brand. Customers were divided into two groups based on how they thought the personified brand would relate to them. For one customer segment (labeled the "respect" segment), the personified brand was seen as a dignified, sophisticated, educated world traveler who would have a definite presence in a restaurant. These customers believed that the card would make supportive comments to them like the following:

- "My job is to help you get accepted."
- "You have good taste."

A second "intimidated" segment, however, described a very different relationship with the brand. This group's view of the brand personality was similar to that observed in the respect segment, but had a very different spin. The credit card was perceived as being sophisticated and classy but also snobbish and condescending. This segment believed that the personified card would make negative comments such as the following:

• "Are you ready for me, or will you spend more than you can afford?"
• "If you don't like the conditions, get another card."
• "I'm so well known and established that I can do what I want."
• "If I were going to dinner, I would not include you in the party."

These two user segments had remarkably similar perceptions of the brand personality especially with respect to its demographic and socioeconomic characteristics. The two different perceived attitudes of the credit card toward the customer, however, reflected two very different relationships with the brand which in turn resulted in very different levels of brand ownership and usage.

Contexts in which it is often worthwhile to consider what a brand might say to a customer include those listed below.

Upscale brands with a snobbish spin. Nearly any prestige or badge brand risks appearing snobbish to some in the target market. This risk is often much greater for those on the fringe of or just beyond the target market. In part, this perceived attitude restricted the market for Grey Poupon, advertised as the mustard of limousine riders. The brand has since tried to soften this message in order to expand its market and the usage rate.

Performance brands talking down to customers. Talking down to customers is a common danger for performance brands. Consider the VW Fahrvergnügen campaign. The use of the German word provided some nice associations (especially if one knew German) but risked implying that the brand looked down on those who did not "get" the clever symbol and campaign. A discarded campaign for Martel—"I assume you drink Martel"—ran the risk of talking down to all customers who were drinking a competitor's brand.

Power brands flexing their muscles. A brand that has power over the marketplace, like Microsoft and Intel in the 1990s or IBM in the past, has a real advantage as a result of being the industry standard. The risk is that by promoting this advantage, the brand may be perceived as being arrogant and willing to smother small, defenseless competitors. One respondent in a focus group reportedly said that if IBM was a vehicle, it would be a steamroller and would park in a handicapped space.

Intimidated brands showing their inferiority. A brand might risk appearing inferior if it tries too hard to be accepted into a more prestigious competitive grouping. Thus Sears could attempt to associate itself with trendier retailers and simply come off as being pathetic. The humorous thrust of the Sears campaign from Young & Rubicam, in which a woman goes there for a Die Hard battery but ends up buying great clothes, helps avoid this pitfall.

Any active brand relationship, though, needs to be managed. Sometimes adding a sense of humor or a symbol can help. In one study for a cigarette brand, the brand personality profile was a sophisticated individualist, stylish and corporate but also aging. Further, there was a segment, most of whom did not use the brand, who saw it as snobbish. This segment rejected the brand in part because it felt rejected by the brand. To combat this problem, the brand kept its upscale imagery but added, with gentle humor, a sense of irony about its status and prestige to soften the hard edge of the image.

RELATIONSHIP SEGMENTATION

Research International routinely segments consumers by brand relationship. In a first-phase research effort, fifty to a hundred subjects are interviewed, usually by phone.[19] A series of open-ended questions are asked, including word associations, brand personalization, characteristics of liked and disliked brands, and a dialogue section (based on what the brand would say if it were a person).

The first analysis stage involves scanning the data and forming hypotheses about the types of relationships that exist. In the second stage, respondents are allocated to relationship categories on the basis of the hypothesized relationship groupings. In the process, the relationship typology is refined. The relationships are then formalized into specifications, and coders classify the respondents into those relationships. The groups are then profiled. Often the relationship groupings correspond to like, dislike, and neutral segments. The "dislike" group for credit cards, for example, perceived the brand as being snobbish; the "like" group, in contrast, felt that they were accepted by the brand.

THE BRAND AS AN ACTIVE RELATIONSHIP PARTNER

Susan Fournier of Harvard, who has worked extensively with the brand-as-relationship concept, notes that brand actions have distinct implications for both the imputed brand personalities and for the brand–customer relationship.[20] This concept is inspired by act frequency theory, which posits that key indicators of a person's personality can be revealed by a systematic observation of trait-relevant behavior.[21] It is in behavior that the true personality emerges—in short, you are what you do.

Just as a person's behavior affects others' perceptions of his or her personality, so too does a brand's actions affect its perceived personality. Consider the brand behaviors and the personality traits shown in Figure 5–8.

Brand behavior and imputed motivations, in addition to affecting brand personality, can also directly affect the brand–customer relationship. A relationship of dependency (where you could not get along without the product) would be damaged by an out-of-stock condition, which would temporarily deny access. A friendship relationship based upon a warm and accessible brand personality might be changed if the brand were radically repositioned as being technologically advanced. The reinforcement of a ritual or routine, in contrast, could strengthen a relationship characterized by familiarity and comfort.

Thus brand personality is not just a customer perception to be manipulated. Rather, the attitude and behavior of the brand is important. The brand identity and strategy, although seemingly behind the scenes, should be considered as a part of the relationship. Such a perspective enhances the likelihood that brand programs will be developed that will support the brand identity.

FIGURE 5–8
Brand Behavior and Brand Personality

BRAND BEHAVIOR	PERSONALITY TRAITS
Frequent changes in position, product forms, symbols, advertising, etc.	Flighty, schizophrenic
Frequent deals and coupons	Cheap, uncultured
Advertises extensively	Outgoing, popular
Strong customer service, easy-to-use package, etc.	Approachable
Continuity of characters, packaging	Familiar, comfortable
High price, exclusive distribution, advertises in upscale magazines	Snobbish, sophisticated
Friendly advertising, endorsers	Friendly
Association with cultural events, PBS	Culturally aware

BRAND RELATIONSHIP QUALITY

Certainly a goal of brand strategists is to create segments with high brand loyalty. In the context of the relationship metaphor, the goal is a high brand relationship quality (BRQ). But what are the dimensions of BRQ? How can it be measured?

Insight into brand relationship quality comes from psychologists who have studied in some depth the nature of relationships and the characteristics of ideal relationships. Drawing on this body of work plus research on the success of leadership brands, Susan Fournier has developed seven dimensions of brand relationship quality.[22] These dimensions are associated with strong relationships between people and suggest how brand–customer relationships should be conceived, measured, and managed. The seven dimensions are as follows:

1. *Behavioral interdependence.* The degree to which the actions of the relationship partners are intertwined is indicated by the frequency of, importance of, and involvement in the interaction.

- This brand plays an important role in my life.
- I feel like something's missing when I haven't used the brand in a while.

2. *Personal commitment*. The partners are committed to each other. There is a desire to improve or maintain the quality of the relationship over time, and guilt is felt when it is compromised.
   - I feel very loyal to this brand.
   - I will stay with this brand through good times and bad.

3. *Love and passion*. Intense emotional bonds between partners, and the inability to tolerate separation, reflect the love and passion that exists. In relationships where customers develop passionate links to brands, substitutes create discomfort.
   - No other brand can quite take the place of this brand.
   - I would be very upset if I couldn't find this brand.

4. *Nostalgic connection*. The relationship is based in part on the memory of good times.
   - This brand reminds me of things I've done or places I've been.
   - This brand will always remind me of a particular phase of my life.

5. *Self-concept connection*. The partners share common interests, activities, and opinions.
   - The brand's and my self-image are similar.
   - The brand reminds me of who I am.

6. *Intimacy*. A deep understanding exists between partners. The customer will achieve intimacy by knowing details about the brand and its use. One-on-one marketing programs enhance intimacy by fostering mutual understanding.
   - I know a lot about this brand.
   - I know a lot about the company that makes this brand.

7. *Partner quality*. This dimension reflects the evaluation by one partner of the performance and attitude of the other, including the evaluation by the consumer of the brand's attitude toward him or her.
   - I know this brand really appreciates me.
   - This brand treats me like a valued customer.

The first three dimensions can be viewed as being variants of brand loyalty. The remaining four, however, introduce qualitatively different measures of relationships. The two statements associated with each dimension provide items for a possible measurement scale.

THE FUNCTIONAL BENEFIT
REPRESENTATION MODEL

The self-expression model and the relationship basis model provide contexts in which brand personality can be the basis for a brand strategy and a link to the customer. A brand personality can also play a more indirect role by being a vehicle for representing and cueing functional benefits and brand attributes. When it works best, it can capture the value proposition driving a brand strategy, as the examples below suggest:

- The Harley-Davidson personality of a rugged, macho, freedom-seeking person suggests that the product is a powerful, liberating vehicle. The product attributes would be much less convincing without the personality behind them.
- Hallmark as a person is sincere, warm, genuine, and ageless. This strong personality helps create the impression that a Hallmark card will reach recipients at an emotional level.
- The Benetton brand personality, which is trendy, provocative, and imaginative, affects people's perceptions of Benetton and its stores.

THE SYMBOL

When a visual symbol or image exists that can create and cue the brand personality, the ability of the personality to reinforce brand attributes will be greater. Consider the following examples:

- The Pillsbury doughboy is a happy chef who loves to bake fresh bakery goods. The doughboy's tummy and smile reflects the "poppin' fresh" quality of the Pillsbury products.
- The Michelin man's enthusiastic personality suggests a tire with strength and energy (see Figure 5–9).
- The Wells Fargo stagecoach reflects an independent, rugged organization that delivers reliability. This perception may persist even if competitors actually deliver superior reliability and personalized service. Because of the stagecoach, Wells Fargo wins the battle for perceptions.
- The Energizer rabbit is an upbeat, indefatigable personality who never runs out of energy, just as the battery it symbolizes runs longer than others.

A brand personality that represents a functional benefit or attribute may be relatively ineffective if it lacks a visual image established in the customer's mind. For example, Pepto-Bismol personified might be a kind mother who takes care of you in a soothing, gentle way. If this metaphor was captured by a familiar visual image, it would be more likely to stimulate customer perceptions that Pepto-Bismol is soothing and gentle.

FIGURE 5–9
The Michelin Man

COUNTRY OR REGION ASSOCIATION

A country or region of origin can add credibility to an identity. It can also generate a strong personality that provides not only a quality cue but also an important point of differentiation that can lead to effective marketing and communication programs.

- Killian's Red, for example, has created a strong Irish personality for the brand that inspires promotions and provides links to the Irish tradition of making and enjoying fine brews.
- Jack Daniel's whiskey has drawn upon its Tennessee background to create a personality that reflects the pace and flavor of backwoods Tennessee culture, as Figure 5–10 illustrates. The result is an "authentic" position and an opportunity to develop links to customers. For example, Jack Daniel's has a Squire club, the members of which own a square inch of land in the Tennessee back country and receive regular reports on their property.

THE POWER OF NATIONAL AND
CULTURAL STEREOTYPES

Psychologists have demonstrated that national and cultural stereotypes influence perceptions and evaluations. Applying this logic, Leclerc, Schmitt, and Dube showed that using French rather than English pronunciations of a name affected attitudes toward and perceptions of products such as fragrance, nail polish, glassware, and stuffed toys.[23] They suggest that the French stereotype of aesthetic sensitivity, sensory pleasure, and sophistication was a driving force behind this result.

The bottom line is that it is usually easier to create a personality that implies a functional benefit than to communicate directly that such a benefit exists. Further, it is harder to attack a personality than a functional benefit.

BRAND PERSONALITY VERSUS USER IMAGERY

User imagery is defined as the set of human characteristics associated with the typical user of the brand.[24] In both academic and practitioner research, there is a tendency to equate brand personality and user imagery; researchers often will measure brand personality by asking questions about the user of the brand. The implicit assumption is that the two elements are identical and that respondents will find it easier to conceptualize user imagery than brand personality.

For some brands, the differences between user imagery and brand personality are indeed minor. In most of these cases the brand is targeting a specific user profile, and that well-developed user profile is the primary driver of brand personality. Dewar's scotch, for example, used a famous series of profiles to define simultaneously the user imagery and brand personality. With brands and subbrands driven by athletic endorsers, Nike may also have very similar user imagery and brand personality.

For many brands, however, a significant difference between brand and user personality can be important to the brand strategy. For example, the Levi's brand personality is driven largely by the firm's heritage of providing clothes for miners and by the brand attributes (tough, durable, simple) and use contexts (Western/cowboy). In contrast, the Levi's 501 user imagery—driven largely by adver-

FIGURE 5–10
Jack Daniel's Back Country Image

What do you enjoy doing on Saturdays? Whatever it is, we hope it includes a sip of Tennessee Whiskey.

SATURDAYS in Jack Daniel's country are for old friends, familiar places and good conversation.

Some head off to Mulberry Creek in search of smallmouth bass. Some get together to barbecue. And a few always seem to gather at Clark's Store. There they'll speak profoundly on any number of subjects, including the oldtime way we make whiskey here in the Tennessee hills. Talking with friends about Jack Daniel's is one fine way to pass an autumn Saturday. Sipping it with friends, we believe, is another.

SMOOTH SIPPIN'
TENNESSEE WHISKEY

Tennessee Whiskey • 40-43% alcohol by volume (80-86 proof) • Distilled and Bottled by
Jack Daniel Distillery, Lem Motlow, Proprietor, Route 1, Lynchburg (Pop 361), Tennessee 37352
Placed in the National Register of Historic Places by the United States Government.

Reproduced with permission of Jack Daniel Distillery.

tising—tends to be urban, hip, contemporary, and both male and female.

USING USER IMAGERY TO BECOME CONTEMPORARY

The Levi's example illustrates a rather common case in which a younger, contemporary market is out of step with the brand personality. Addressing this problem by changing the heritage-related brand personality would be difficult and destructive. At best it would dilute or destroy the existing personality which still has value; at worst, it would undercut the relationship between the brand and an important segment.

User imagery provides a vehicle for retaining the brand personality and at the same time responding to the target market. The brand personality still provides a diminished role, perhaps by cueing and reinforcing the product attributes. When the user imagery is inconsistent with the brand personality, a tension can result that is potentially intriguing and interesting. One might argue that the most interesting brands have incongruent elements to them—consider Oil of Olay, which is practical yet exotic, and After Eight Mints, which are sophisticated yet accessible.

Several questions are raised by the strategy of developing user imagery that is distinct from the brand personality. Will the user imagery come to dominate the relationship, eventually diluting the heritage brand personality and its related attribute associations (durable work clothes, in the case of Levi's)? Is it possible to reinforce the brand personality while still building the user imagery? These issues will be revisited in Chapter 7, where the issue of managing brands over time is addressed.

USER IMAGERY AND REFERENCE GROUPS

Brands can create a value proposition and a basis for a relationship by focusing on a particular social or reference group through user imagery. The possibility of belonging to a user group or obtaining the approval and acceptance of a group may provide an added emotional tie for the consumer. Certainly, the success of Miller Lite's original "Tastes great/less filling" campaign resulted in part from inclusion of customers in an attractive but accessible group defined by retired star athletes.

When a brand's personality differs from its user imagery, the reference group can be based on either or both. Members of the hip-hop culture embraced such shoe and clothing brands as Timberland, Car Hart, Ben Davis, and Dickees. They were attracted by the brands' personality, usually related to authenticity, farming, good value, simple people and simple times. At the same time, a new user imagery was created—namely, the prototypical hip-hop individual. Thus a driver for many customers was to be accepted by the group represented by this user imagery.

ON CREATING USER IMAGERY

User imagery can be driven by actual users, those who are seen "around town" using the brand. Of course, actual user profiles may not be desirable or controllable. When the Izod alligator symbol spread beyond the yuppie target segment, or when the hip-hop culture started wearing the blue-collar Ben Davis lines, the user profile departed from the target market. Sears has long struggled with the burden of trying to sell fashionable clothing and accessories in the face of a middle-America, downscale user imagery. Oil of Olay would like to emphasize its exotic, upscale, and youthful brand personality and to de-emphasize the fact that its actual users are older and more downscale.

One way to de-emphasize undesirable actual-user imagery is to promote idealized or stylized users in advertising or other marketing efforts linked to the brand. Thus when Miller Lite felt limited by a user personality of ex-jocks in their thirties or forties, new campaigns explicitly attempted to change the user personality by making it younger. Celebrity endorsers can also provide the basis for user imagery. Nike, for example, used Charles Barkley and Scottie Pippen to create user imagery for the Nike Force and Flight basketball shoe brands.

BRAND PERSONALITY
AS A SUSTAINABLE ADVANTAGE

In summary, a brand personality can help a brand in several ways. First, it can provide a vehicle for customers to express their own identity. Self-expression is usually more vivid when the brand has a strong personality, because it is a personality that is being expressed. Second, a brand personality metaphor helps suggest the kind of relationship that customers have with the brand, a relationship that is modeled after person-to-person relationships. Third, brand personalities serve to represent and cue functional benefits and product attributes effectively.

The important aspect of a brand personality is that it is often a sustainable point of differentiation. Consider the personalities of Harley-Davidson, Saturn, Hallmark, Tiffany, Obsession (by Calvin Klein), Jack Daniel's, United Airlines, or Mercedes-Benz. In each case, the brand personality is unique within the product class. As such, it provides a powerful vehicle to develop an identity, a communications effort, and in fact a whole marketing program. Further, it is sustainable because it is very difficult (and usually ineffective) to copy a personality.

Brands that have a personality should consider enhancing it and making it a point of leverage within the brand identity. Those without personalities are usually vulnerable, exposed to attacks like stationary fortresses.

QUESTIONS TO CONSIDER

1. What is your brand personality as currently perceived by customers and other relevant groups? Which of the Big Five are most descriptive of your brand? Which of the fifteen facets? What is the nature of the personal relationship between the brand and the customers? How do the brand's personality and customer relationship differ from those of competitors?

2. What is your target brand personality in terms of the Big Five (and the fifteen facets)? How central is it to the brand identity? Is it part of the core identity? Or is it part of the extended identity, providing texture and richness to a brand identity statement that is driven by other dimensions?

3. How does the brand personality work to help the brand? What models are operating—self-expression, relationship basis, or functional benefit representation?

4. How has the brand personality been created? How will it be managed in the future?

5. Is your brand personality and user imagery the same? If it is different, is that a problem? Will it be possible to reinforce both over time if they are different?

6

IDENTITY IMPLEMENTATION

Where absolute superiority is not attainable, you must produce a relative one at the decisive point by making skillful use of what you have.

—Karl von Clausewitz (*On War*, 1832)

The primary focus of your brand message must be on how special you are, not how cheap you are. . . . The goal must be to sell the distinctive quality of the brand.

—Larry Light, brand strategist

I n the prior three chapters, conceptualizations of brand identity, the value proposition, and brand–customer relationships have been set forth. The goal has been to develop a textured, inclusive picture of what the brand stands for (how strategists would like it to be perceived).

The focus now turns to implementing the identity and value proposition by developing a three-step brand identity implementation system as suggested by Figure 6–1. The first step in implementation is a *brand position* statement that specifies what part of the identity is to be actively communicated. The second step is the *execution* of the communication program, which includes selection of the media to be used and creation of actual advertisements or programs. Finally, the communication program is monitored during a *tracking* stage. Each of these will be discussed in turn.

The chapter then turns to the *strategic brand analysis*, which supports the development of the brand identity system and its implementation, and closes with a summary discussion of the potential power of an identity and position.

THE BRAND POSITION

With an identity in place and a value proposition specified, implementation begins. Communication objectives need to be established, and execution planned and implemented. The place to start is with a brand position statement—the cornerstone of the communications program. A brand position is defined as follows:

> *Brand position is the part of the brand identity and value proposition that is to be actively communicated to the target audience and that demonstrates an advantage over competing brands.*

The four salient characteristics of a brand position as reflected by the phrases "part," "target audience," "actively communicated," and "demonstrates advantage."

A PART OF THE IDENTITY/VALUE PROPOSITION

When a brand position exists, the brand identity and value proposition can be developed fully, with texture and depth. They do not

176

FIGURE 6–1
Brand Identity Planning Model

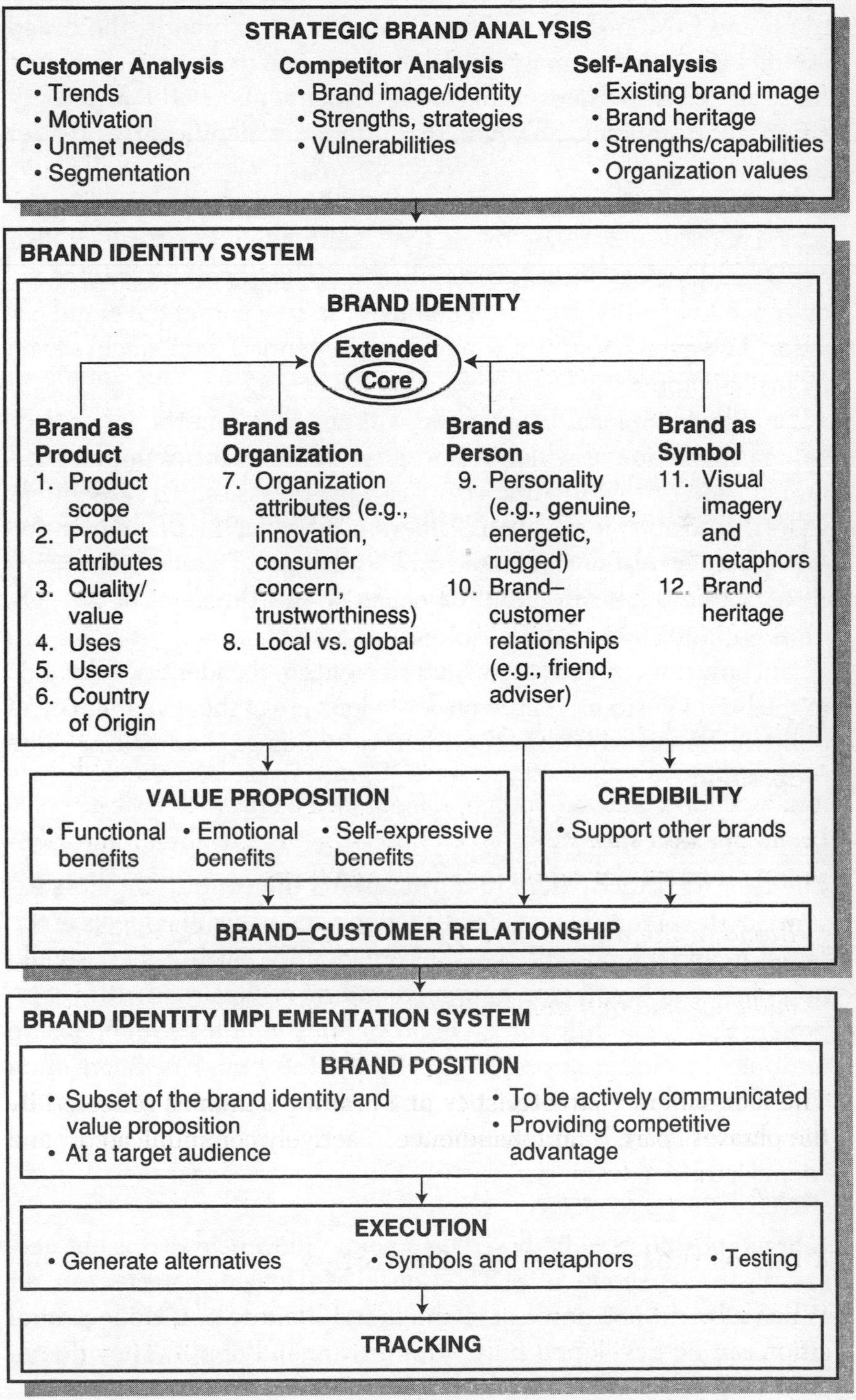

STRATEGIC BRAND ANALYSIS

Customer Analysis
- Trends
- Motivation
- Unmet needs
- Segmentation

Competitor Analysis
- Brand image/identity
- Strengths, strategies
- Vulnerabilities

Self-Analysis
- Existing brand image
- Brand heritage
- Strengths/capabilities
- Organization values

BRAND IDENTITY SYSTEM

BRAND IDENTITY

Extended
Core

Brand as Product
1. Product scope
2. Product attributes
3. Quality/ value
4. Uses
5. Users
6. Country of Origin

Brand as Organization
7. Organization attributes (e.g., innovation, consumer concern, trustworthiness)
8. Local vs. global

Brand as Person
9. Personality (e.g., genuine, energetic, rugged)
10. Brand–customer relationships (e.g., friend, adviser)

Brand as Symbol
11. Visual imagery and metaphors
12. Brand heritage

VALUE PROPOSITION
- Functional benefits
- Emotional benefits
- Self-expressive benefits

CREDIBILITY
- Support other brands

BRAND–CUSTOMER RELATIONSHIP

BRAND IDENTITY IMPLEMENTATION SYSTEM

BRAND POSITION
- Subset of the brand identity and value proposition
- At a target audience
- To be actively communicated
- Providing competitive advantage

EXECUTION
- Generate alternatives
- Symbols and metaphors
- Testing

TRACKING

have to be concise statements of what is to be communicated, because the brand position takes on that role. For some brands, the brand identity and value proposition do combine into a compact statement that can serve (perhaps with minor adjustments) as the brand position. In most cases, however, the former are significantly broader than the latter.

To illustrate, elements that are extremely important to the identity may not play a role in the active communication strategy. For McDonald's, cleanliness is certainly one of the important parts of the culture and identity. It would be unlikely to be a part of the brand position, however, because it would not differentiate McDonald's from its major competitors.

Brand position can be changed without changing the identity or value proposition of which it is a subset. Saturn, for example, positioned itself during the first year as a world-class car. In subsequent years the position focused on a different subset of the brand identity: the customer relationship based on friendship and respect. The identity or value proposition did not change—just the focus of the position, and thus the communications program.

But how does one choose which elements of the identity to include in the brand position? Three places to look are at the core identity, at points of leverage within the identity structure, and at the value proposition.

Look to the Core Identity

The core identity by definition represents the central, timeless essence of the brand. Thus the most unique and valuable aspects of the brand are often represented in the core identity. Further, there should be a cluster of brand elements surrounding each core identity component that (in addition to giving it richness and texture) opens up multiple execution alternatives. Finally, the brand position often should include the core identity just so communication elements do not stray from the brand's essence.

Identify Points of Leverage

A brand position can be based on a point of leverage that is not necessarily in the core identity. The Ronald McDonald character can, for example, provide a point of leverage for McDonald's. He is central to the focus on fun and kids, and he is also the basis for Ronald McDonald House, which provides an interesting message that engenders respect and visibility. Thus a possible brand position for McDonald's might well emphasize Ronald McDonald as follows:

- The restaurant that Ronald McDonald, with his presence and programs, makes a fun place for kids and families. (Target—kids and their parents)

Sometimes a subbrand, feature, or service can provide a point of leverage. For example, the visible air cushion in the early Nike Air line served to represent the advanced-technology aspect of the Nike identity. Subbrands-features, and services that play this role are termed *silver bullets* and are described in detail in Chapter 8 when the brand system concept is introduced.

The Value Proposition: Benefits That Drive Relationships

A customer benefit that is part of the value proposition and a basis of a brand–customer relationship can be another prime candidate for a brand position. Nike, for example, provides a functional benefit of improved performance and a self-expressive benefit based on using a shoe endorsed by a celebrity athlete. An endorser such as Michael Jordan can provide the basis for a brand position as follows:

- The shoe that Michael Jordan uses to provide the extra edge of performance. (Target—weekend athletes)

THE TARGET AUDIENCE

The brand position should also target a specific audience, which may be a subset of the brand's target segment. For example, a mountain bike company might define a target audience of serious, highly sophisticated, West Coast bikers, whereas the target segment might be a much larger group.

There can also be a primary and secondary target audience. Male drivers of sports sedans might be the primary target audience for Toyota Camry, but women may be an important secondary target audience. The position strategy should thus consider the secondary audience and, in particular, not antagonize it in any way.

ACTIVE COMMUNICATION

To say that the brand position is to be actively communicated implies that there will be specific communication objectives focused on changing or strengthening the brand image or brand–customer relationship. These objectives, if feasible, should be accompanied by measurement. For example, if the goal is to create or improve the "friend" relationship, an agree–disagree scale could be developed using items such as "Gateway is your friend" and "Gateway will be there for you." Such scales could be used both in testing communication programs and in tracking their impact.

Brand Position and the Brand Image

Brand image reflects current perceptions of a brand. Like brand identity, brand position is more aspirational, reflecting perceptions that the strategists want to have associated with the brand. In creating a brand position, a useful step is to compare the brand identity with the brand image on different image dimensions.

DIMENSION	BRAND IDENTITY (GOAL)	BRAND IMAGE (CURRENT REALITY)
Product:	Premium beer	Premium beer
User:	Young (in spirit *or* body)	Middle-aged
Personality:	Fun, humorous	Fun, humorous
Functional benefit:	Superior flavor	Superior flavor
Emotional benefit:	Social group acceptance	(none)

Comparison of the identity with the image will usually result in one of three very different communication tasks being reflected in a brand position statement. Any brand image can be:

- augmented (if a dimension needs to be added or strengthened)— e.g., add social group acceptance
- reinforced and exploited (if the image associations are consistent with the identity and are strong)—e.g., reinforce fun and humorous personality
- diffused, softened or deleted (if the image is inconsistent with the brand identity)— e.g., soften middle-aged-user imagery

Augmenting an Image

A brand image might be too restrictive—that is, it may be geared to one age group or application, while the identity points the way to adding other segments or applications. A firm might want to market to the home as well as the office, or to those requiring style as well as durability. The brand position might therefore attempt (1) to add associations to the brand image and (2) to soften restrictive perceptions.

Clinique, for example, has a strong image of being fresh, clean, and pure, with a white-coat clinical approach to skin care and cosmetics. The typical user is perceived to be a young woman with oily skin. The challenge for Clinique is to maintain its current image strengths but to soften the youthful image (to make the brand accessible to mature women) and to reach out beyond the specialized focus on oily, problem skin to a broader audience. For instance, Clinique would like to inject elements of elegance into the line, not to compete with the "elegant" position of competitors but to expand beyond their strong clinical position.

Reinforcing an Image

The brand image should not dictate the position (or identity), but neither should it be ignored. Often, an effective brand position will reinforce and exploit an image strength. In fact, a decision to create a new position that does not build on a brand's strengths is usually difficult and risky.

Subaru's greatest asset has been its association with all-wheel drive (supported by the image of Subaru transporting skiers to the slopes) and the performance and safety that all-wheel drive affords. At one point, an attempt was made to reposition the brand to appeal to a more general market, where it would compete more directly with the Honda Accord and Toyota Camry. The (perhaps predictable) result was that there was no longer a point of difference between Subaru and its competitors, and the effort failed. Subaru, somewhat damaged, then returned to a brand position based on its accepted image of superiority in making all-wheel-drive cars.

Diffusing an Image

Sometimes specifying what a brand is *not* is as important to the integrity of the communication program as specifying what it is. In the comparison shown above, the beer's brand image was of a typically middle-aged user, while the brand identity included younger drinkers. Specifying that the brand is not exclusively for middle-aged users suggests visual imagery to avoid as well as imagery to include.

DEMONSTRATE AN ADVANTAGE

Finally, brand position should demonstrate an advantage over competitors. The bottom line is that the position should specify a point of superiority that is a part of the value proposition. The point of advantage should resonate with customers and be differentiating—that is, represent something different from what competitors provide.

Resonate with the Customer

A key position objective is to develop a point of advantage that resonates with the customer because of a compelling value proposition or because of a meaningful brand–customer relationship. If the point-of-advantage appeal is off target, unpersuasive, or inconsequential, the result will be a weak, vulnerable brand.

Strategists should seek a position that will resonate with the customer not only today but for a long time into the future. A brand strategy will require substantial investments, and the return on these will be limited if the position is short-lived. In contrast, as Chapter 7 (on managing brands over time) will make clear, there are enormous payoffs to having a consistent strategy over time. Thus one goal is to create a brand identity and position that has the potential to endure.

Differentiate Oneself from Competitors

The brand position also needs to provide a point of difference with respect to competitive offerings. There are several ways to differentiate. The brand can position itself against a competitor's functional benefit by claiming to be superior or comparable at a lower price, or it can claim to provide a different functional benefit. Alternatively, a position can be based on something other than a functional benefit—an emotional or self-expressive benefit, an organizational attribute, a brand personality, or a customer relationship. Adding a brand personality often provides a key to competitive distinctiveness.

Matching Versus Beating Competitors

There is a natural tendency to believe that a brand needs to be superior on all dimensions. In fact, though, a more appropriate and feasible goal may be to avoid having an inferior image that is a liability. Assume, for example, that Compaq's portable computer brand is competing in a segment for which the primary dimensions of competition are features and company support. It may be unwise to attempt to be perceived as superior on the company support dimension, where competitors such as Dell have strong positions; rather, achieving parity or near-parity might be better strategy. The goal might be to have customers believe that Compaq is close enough to Dell on customer support that other considerations can dictate the purchase decision and satisfaction with the product.

FOUR QUESTIONS

The brand position statement should thus address four sets of questions, as suggested by Figure 6–2:

1. Which elements of the brand identity and value proposition should be a part of the position, a part of the active communication program? Which will resonate with customers, and differentiate the brand from competitors?
2. Who is the primary target audience? Who are secondary target audiences?
3. What are the communication objectives? Does the current image need to be augmented or strengthened, reinforced and exploited, or diffused or deleted (that is, what does the brand *not* stand for)?
4. What will be the points of advantage? What will be the points where parity or near-parity is the best the brand image should strive for?

POSITIONING IN ACTION

The following are six examples of position statements drawn from the work of BMP DDB Needham, a British advertising agency:[1]

- Miller Lite is a genuine standard-strength lager from America that is smoother and easier to drink. (Target—eighteen- to twenty-four-

FIGURE 6–2
Brand Position

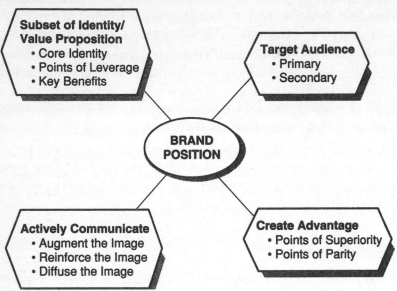

year-old, male standard-lager drinkers, particularly those more interested in personal appearance)

- Alliance & Leicester, a savings and loan, is big, warm, and friendly; something the ordinary person can identify with and feel secure about. (Target—existing and potential depositors/investors)
- Alliance & Leicester allows you to arrange a mortgage before buying a house; it reduces the anxiety, provides reassurance, and becomes a father figure. (Target—first-time home buyers, age twenty to forty, who are unconfident or even frightened about the whole process)
- Hellmann's mayonnaise is a versatile, everyday, idiot-proof (easy to use in recipes and sandwiches), condiment/ingredient with a range of uses well beyond salad dressing. (Target—current Hellmann's users, and nonusers of mayonnaise)
- Clarks Desert Boots are the original (a design originating decades ago), and yet they reflect contemporary style (like an Armani suit worn with a T-shirt). (Target—young men at the forefront of fashion)
- Krona is the first margarine with a taste and texture indistinguishable from butter. (Target—homemakers currently using butter who are sensitive to price increases)

Note that there are two positions for the brand Alliance & Leicester, each clearly aimed at very different target audiences. The brand personalities, however, do overlap (a reassuring "father figure" overlaps with "big, warm, and friendly"). There would be even more overlap between the complete brand identities.

Black Velvet

Black Velvet whiskey, the identity of which was introduced in Chapter 3, has the following positioning statement:

- Black Velvet is an exceptionally soft and smooth imported whiskey, *not* to be known as a Canadian. (Canadian is a type of whiskey.) It has a unique touch of class which provides affordable luxury at a cut above popular-priced whiskeys. (Target—spirits drinkers)

The point of advantage is the soft, smooth taste, which distinguishes Black Velvet from the sharp bite of Scotch whiskeys. The images of softness and smoothness are driven by the product and by the Black Velvet lady, who is shown in advertisements and posters (see Chapter 7). The imported position suggests that Black Velvet is a premium brand known worldwide, and the "unique touch of class" plus the soft, smooth taste suggest that it provides personal reward and relaxation. Note what Black Velvet is not—a Canadian. The need is to attract interest among drinkers of Bourbon and Scotch whiskey rather than being restricted to drinkers of Canadian whiskey.

BE FEASIBLE

The brand position must be attainable; there is nothing more wasteful than trying to achieve a position that is out of reach. Strong niche brands often fall into this trap when they attempt to break out of their niche. Subaru, as noted earlier, had a strong niche based upon its all-wheel-drive technology and Japanese quality associations, but faltered when it tried to become a mainstream brand with undifferentiated models. A brand position that extends beyond the current brand image must be supported by an organization that has the will and ability to create a product or services that reflect the new identity. Then the challenge is to convincingly communicate the new brand position. The Subaru story illustrates the difficulty of both tasks.

ACHIEVING BRILLIANCE IN EXECUTION

The most strategically logical position will not be worth implementing if a brilliant execution cannot be found. Too often communication is developed—sometimes by committee—that although on target is heavy-handed and does not break out of the competitive clutter. The keys to avoiding this mistake are patience and an insistence on achieving brilliance. It is too easy to compromise and believe that a commitment to spend money on a brand is enough. It isn't.

I have often been asked, "Should we increase our communication budget by X million dollars to create a brand?" The answer can be yes or no, depending on the quality of the execution. One study showed that the quality of the advertising is five times more important than the expenditures. Another showed that Marlboro got dramatically more impact for its communication budget than did other brands, undoubtedly due to its established symbols and personality.[2]

A brilliantly executed communication program breaks through the clutter by shocking, entertaining, or involving the audience. At the same time, it must implement the positioning strategy and connect that implementation to the brand name. Achieving brilliance is difficult; indeed, even recognizing when you have achieved it is not easy. Some guidelines are offered below.

GENERATE ALTERNATIVES

The more alternative executions you generate, the better are your chances of creating something brilliant. Alternatives can be in the form of either multiple creative approaches for the same media vehicle or disparate media avenues.

Getting a number of creative advertising teams independently involved—even using different agencies if necessary—can generate multiple creative options. Coca-Cola has rather aggressively used multiple agencies to create some great individual ads. The trick is to have a strategy that guides and coordinates, to be ready to deal with egos and a reluctance to share credit, and to believe in the concept enough to actually spend the extra money multiple teams require.

Considering nontraditional media often leads to effective communication and sometimes to breakthrough results. Brilliance may be

available only to those who to look in unconventional areas such as
the following:

- *Event sponsorships* provide relatively unobtrusive but high-impact
  name exposure coupled with positive associations. Spending on
  event sponsorships in the United States (two-thirds of which involved sports events) approached five billion dollars in 1994. Recall
  the impact of the WordPerfect sponsorship of a bike racing team in
  Europe, which was mentioned in Chapter 1.
- *Clubs and usage programs* provide new ways to generate personalized customer relationships. The Swatch collector's club, Nestlé's
  Buitoni Club, Harley-Davidson's Harley Owners' Group (H.O.G.),
  and the Apple Macintosh user groups all play a key role in creating
  and maintaining a loyal customer base.
- *Direct response marketing* allows customers to bypass retailers and
  link directly to firms via catalogues, infomercials, the Internet or
  other means.
- *Public relations efforts* offer low-cost exposures with enhanced
  credibility. Nintendo developed a new generation of video games
  that was newsworthy enough to get more than 300 million exposures on news and special-interest programs. Silicon Graphics
  spent no money on advertising until fall 1994 by relying on a public
  relations staff that got the firm on the cover of *Business Week*,
  among other achievements.
- *Publicity stunts* generate visibility. Swatch helped introduce a
  watch by hanging a 175-yard-long giant watch from a skyscraper in
  Frankfurt and Tokyo.
- *Promotions* have the potential to damage brand equity by focusing
  attention on price, but they can also support the brand. Recall the
  Saturn promotion in which winners got to visit Spring Hill to see
  their car being made.
- *Product shows and event stores* provide ways to make a unique and
  involving personality statement. Examples include Cadbury World
  (which offers exposure to the history of chocolate, plus samples, to
  more than a half million visitors per year), Apple Computer's Mac-
  World Expo, the GE Houses of the Future, the Coca-Cola Road
  Trip trailer, and the Nike Town stores.
- *Packaging* carries a major part of the identity for many brands.
  Loblaw's President's Choice Decadent Chocolate Chip Cookie, for

example, has an identity communicated largely by its rich, appealing package design. Packaging and display were also key to the L'eggs identity.

SYMBOLS AND METAPHORS

The best strategies will tend to have strong, memorable symbols. Some may already be in use or are in the heritage of the brand. Others can be created. Consider the functional benefit associations of Heinz's "slowest-pouring ketchup" and the Energizer bunny, the emotional benefit associations of the Pillsbury Doughboy and Allstate's "Good Hands," and the self-expressive benefit associations of "Marlboro country" and the Tiffany box. One of the leading teas in the United Kingdom has for more than three decades told its taste story with highly entertaining commercials featuring chimps at a tea party.

A strong metaphor can also leverage communication expenditures. Apple used the "desktop publishing" metaphor (unfortunately, without owning it) to communicate the user-friendliness and graphics capability of the Macintosh. Gumout, the gasoline additive from Pennzoil, uses a medicine metaphor: using Gumout to clean a car's fuel system is like taking a decongestant for a cold or flu. When a metaphor clicks, becoming virtually impossible to get out of one's mind, it can not only improve recall but also frame the way customers look at the product class and its brands.

TESTING

Most communication efforts can be tested, if imperfectly. Tests can be conducted in laboratory conditions and in the field. Testing usually pays even when it appears to be expensive in dollars and time.

In a laboratory test, a potential advertisement, package, event sponsorship concept, or other communication alternative can be exposed to target audience members to get their reaction. With the power of modern graphics capabilities, a host of options can be tested in a very realistic video environment. One testing goal is not only to determine the positive impact on the identity/position but also to discover any unforeseen negative reactions. For example, the Black Velvet lady could be perceived as unapproachable if she were overdressed with heavy diamonds, or the Merrill Lynch bull could be perceived as risky and uncontrolled instead of strong and aggressive if the setting was wrong.

A field test is much more definitive but also more expensive, and only a limited number of options can be tested. An ice cream firm tested a major increase in communication expenditures by looking at the sales of matched supermarket pairs (one supermarket in each pair was in a test city that was exposed to the new communication, and the other was in an adjacent city). Consistent results gave the company confidence to extend its brand-building strategy.

TRACKING

The final step shown in Figure 6–1 is tracking. It is highly desirable to invest in monitoring the brand position (and perhaps other elements of the brand identity over time).

Tracking can be based on quantitative surveys, where structured questions and scales allow an assessment of how customer perceptions have been affected by the brand positioning effort. Tracking can also be based on qualitative research, which systematically elicits customer perceptions through regular focus groups or in-depth interviews. A key to qualitative research is to be exposed to a cross-section of the target audience and to know what to ask. The value of a rich, textured identity is that it leads to dialogues with customers that get beyond functional benefits to a deeper understanding of relationships.

Chapter 10 will address the broader subject of tracking brand equity and measuring it not only over time but over product classes and brands. It will also explore the identity portion of brand equity and what questions can be tapped to measure it.

A STRATEGIC BRAND ANALYSIS

The development of a brand identity, a value proposition, and a brand position—statements of what the brand should stand for and its promise to customers—is a strategic decision in every sense. Thus a strategic perspective is needed. Brands need to be selecting markets and building assets for the future, rather than just engaging in tactical programs that address only the problems of the moment.

The brand strategy needs to be viewed from three perspectives: a customer analysis, a competitor analysis, and a self-analysis (see Figure 6–3).[3] The objective of a brand strategy, after all, is to create a business that resonates with customers, that avoids competitor strengths and exploits their weaknesses, and that exploits its own strengths and neutralizes its weaknesses. To create such a business, it is necessary to understand the viewpoints represented in these three analyses.

FIGURE 6–3
Strategic Brand Analysis

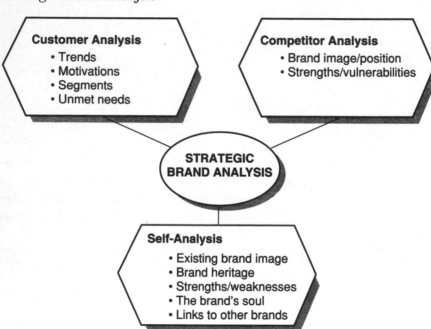

More specifically, the primary objective of the strategic brand analysis is to precipitate and improve strategic decisions about the brand such as the brand identity specification, the product classes with which it should be associated, its role within the organization's brand system (described in detail in Chapter 8), and the investment level that should support it. Another objective is to identify key strategic uncertainties that will affect brand strategy. For example, a strategic uncertainty might be whether a new product type (like flavored ice tea, ice beer, or minidisk recorders) will be accepted by the marketplace and grow or whether it will fade or be relegated to a niche market. Strategic uncertainties can help prioritize information gathering and analysis activities.

CUSTOMER ANALYSIS

A customer analysis can productively involve an analysis of customer trends, motivations, segmentation structure, and unmet needs.

Trends

A good way to start a customer analysis is by examining the dynamics of the market. What are the customer trends? This simple question is powerful because it often provides insight into changing motivations and emerging segments with strategic importance.

Working with the St. James Group, a brand strategy consulting company, Nestlé has looked at the beverage category and observed four trends: a greater concern for health, a growing preference for ready-to-drink beverages, movement from hot to cold beverages, and an increased demand for exotic flavors and variety that reflects both boredom and a greater exposure to foreign cultures.[4] These trends suggest position options for Nestlé's Juicy Juice and Perrier.

The analysis of sales volume trends and profitability prospects of submarkets can also provide insights. Which submarkets are growing and which are declining? Why? In coffee, for example, the per capita daily consumption has fallen from 3.1 cups in 1962 to under 1.7 in 1993. Although major supermarket brands such as Maxwell House (Kraft), Hills Brothers (Nestlé) and Folgers (Procter & Gamble) have suffered because of this decline, substantial growth and healthy margins have occurred in specialty coffee beans (for use in electric coffee grinders), gourmet brands, and coffeehouses.[5]

Customer Motivations

The goal of customer analysis is to determine which functional, emotional, and self-expressive benefits will motivate customers to buy and use the brand. The analysis methods described in Chapter 6 of

Managing Brand Equity can help strategists detect and understand these benefits.

Qualitative research is generally directed at detecting emotional and self-expressive benefits that might be relevant to the product class. The need is to get below the surface and probe those areas that are not as obvious to the customer but are influential in the brand choice and use experience.

The assessment of functional benefits involves three sets of questions:

• What functional benefits are relevant to customers?
• What is the relative importance of each functional benefit?
• How can customers be grouped with respect to functional benefits? Can benefit segments be identified?

Typically the strategist will develop a list of dozens of benefits—sometimes fifty or more. One task then is to reduce this list to a few major categories (or dimensions) of motivations that summarize how customers organize information and form attitudes about brands in the product class under analysis. In most product classes there are two, three, or four such dimensions. These can be useful in sorting out options for brand strategy.

In the retail oil industry, for example, there are two dimensions: product benefits (gasoline additives, quality) and the service station experience (helpfulness, efficiency, facilities). In many service, high-technology, and durable-goods contexts, there is often a product dimension, an organization or service dimension, and a price/quality dimension.

In the spirits industry, there are three dimensions: personal reward and relaxation (benefits received while alone), self-expressive benefits (received when the brand is consumed in a social setting), and the price/quality position. The ostentatious brands focus on self-expressive benefits and have high price points; the connoisseur brands focus on personal reward and relaxation and also have high prices; and the low-price brands focus on the cost-conscious segment. The balance of the market is positioned on some combination of these three dimensions.

Another goal should be to seek a motivation that can be leveraged into a unique advantage for a particular brand. Thus an oil firm that is the first to install an ATM or credit-card payment system might gain an advantage. Being environmentally sensitive may also provide a way for an oil company to differentiate itself, since most competitors are focusing on other customer motivations. IBM discovered a customer desire to have a subnotebook computer with a full keyboard; using a fold-out design termed the Butterfly, IBM supplied that feature.

Segmentation

How does the market segment? Certain segments may respond differently to communication programs and thus may justify different positioning strategies and perhaps different identities. Thus in the hotel industry, Hilton will likely want to have different positions for the business, leisure, and convention segments.

There are a limitless number of segmentation schemes to consider. The most useful, on average, include segmentation by benefits sought, price sensitivity, brand loyalty, and application. The task is to consider which segments are the most attractive target for the brand and most relevant to the brand identity development.

Unmet Needs

Of particular usefulness is a consideration of customer needs that are not being met by the existing product offerings. Unmet needs are strategically important because they can represent opportunities for firms that want to make major moves in the market.

Black & Decker gained in-depth insights into unmet needs by forming a panel of fifty do-it-yourselfers who owned more than six power tools.[6] Executives of Black & Decker visited panelists in their homes and saw firsthand how the tools were used and the problems and frustrations that were experienced. One of the problems observed was that cordless drills ran out of power before the job was done. The solution was a drill with a detachable battery pack that recharged in an hour. A sawdust problem prompted a saw and sander with a bag that acted as a mini-vacuum. To address safety issues, an automatic braking system was built into the saws. These advances provided part of the core identity of the Quantum line of midpriced tools endorsed by Black & Decker.

COMPETITOR ANALYSIS

Competitor analysis looks at the brand image/position and strengths and vulnerabilities of the major competitors. The need is to assess not only the current reality, but the future trajectory.

Competitor Brand Image/Position

A fundamental input into identity determination is how customers perceive competitive brands, especially with respect to benefits provided, brand–customer relationships, and brand personality. Knowing how competitors are perceived is key to developing a point of distinction. There are two sources of brand image data—customers and competitor communications.

Customers are the best source of the current brand image for competitive brands. Brand image information can be accessed by qualitative research (where customers talk about perceptions) or by quantitative surveys. In either case, the image may be a function of the market segment. Brand users, for example, will usually have different perceptions of a brand than nonusers or users of other brands.

It is also useful to understand how the competitor brands want to be perceived. Although annual reports and other accounts of strategic plans can provide some insights, the best source of information about a competitor's identity is usually its advertising and advertising plans. A profile of competitive ads is especially revealing.

Grouping Competitors' Positions

A careful analysis of all competitors' positions can often provide useful insights. Usually there are a few limited positioning strategies used in the industry; a good exercise therefore is to arrange advertisements into a "brandscape" of clusters representing firms with similar positioning strategies. Any positioning strategy needs to relate to this existing structure, even if plows new ground.

When choosing its own positioning strategy, a firm can evaluate the "formidability" (or competitor strength) of each cluster and then decide if it wants to use (or "join") the strategy represented by one of the clusters or to try something new. A positioning approach should generally be avoided if:

- The number of competitors is large.
- The individual competitors are strong in terms of market share and distribution clout. (Avoid clusters with dominant firms.)
- Competitors are well-positioned. (Avoid clusters with firms that have a lock on a position, or at least be prepared to neutralize it in some way—perhaps by adding a twist or refinement.)

For example, the exercise in the life insurance industry outlined in Chapter 3 revealed that competitor strategies were clustered around three metaphors. One was a strength metaphor, with the Rock (Prudential), the Castle (Fortis) and the Pyramid (Transamerica) as examples. The second was the plan-ahead metaphor, used by Fireman's Fund and others. The third metaphor was the "We care and will be there for you" theme used by Allstate (Good Hands), State Farm (Good Neighbors). The third grouping contained the fewest firms, but they were very strong and established competitors.

Changes in Competitor Images

In strategic brand planning, it is important to consider not only the current images of competing brands but also past changes and possible future changes in these images. An examination of the reasons for such changes can provide useful information about the competitive environment. For example, BMW was a car whose position revolved around the "ultimate driving machine"—the ultimate upscale car. In 1990, this concept ran into trouble, in part because the excesses of the 1980s had tarnished the so-called yuppie lifestyle. As a result, BMW introduced less expensive models and "de-yuppified" its position by stressing value and safety as well as the traditional BMW driving experience.

Competitor Strengths and Vulnerabilities

Another perspective on competitors comes from examining strengths and weaknesses. Going against a competitor strength with respect to a value proposition is risky; the brand and its identity, position, and execution will all need to be exceptional. There is little margin for error. It is easier to attack at points where the opponent's castle is not so well fortified.

Of particular interest, therefore, are competitors' vulnerabilities. For example, Arco is perceived as a low-price gasoline option which does not accept credit cards and appeals to the price-sensitive segment. The elements of the Arco organization—including its people, systems, programs, and culture—all support a low-cost operation, as does its source of Alaskan crude oil. A resulting vulnerability, though, is the appearance and operation of Arco service stations. A competitor who can persuade consumers to look at the gas purchase differently—

by considering the station experience, for example—might thus have an advantage in attracting Arco customers.

SELF-ANALYSIS OF THE BRAND

An important input to the development of a brand identity is a careful self-analysis of one's brand and organization. Areas of inquiry include the following:

- The current brand image
- The brand heritage
- The brand's strengths and weaknesses—what can be delivered under the brand's name.
- The soul of the brand and the organization
- Links to other brands

In each case, the brand can be viewed from the perspective of the brand as a product, an organization, a person, and a symbol.

Existing Brand Image

Self-analysis of the current brand image involves asking questions like the following: How is the firm's brand perceived? What associations are linked to the brand? How is it differentiated from the competing brands? How has its image changed over time? Does the image differ across segments? What benefits do customers feel they are getting? Does the brand have a personality? What is it? What are the intangible attributes/benefits? Does the brand as an organization have a presence? If so, what? What visual imagery does the brand evoke? Again, Chapter 6 of *Managing Brand Equity* covers approaches to answering these questions.

In assessing the brand image, it is useful to make sure that research and analysis extend beyond product attributes to other associations such as use context, user imagery, organizational associations, brand personality, brand–customer relationships, and emotional and self-expressive benefits. A common failing is to focus too heavily on product attributes and functional benefits.

Brand Heritage

In addition to knowing market perceptions, it is useful to understand the heritage of the brand. Who were the early pioneers of the brand? How did it originate? What was its image when it first started?

Often, knowledge of what the brand first meant can provide an insight as to what the identity should include.

A brand heritage analysis can also generate strategic insight about how to get a brand back on course. A host of brands have gotten into trouble by straying from their heritage, and returning to it can help restore the brand strength. Palmolive, for example, found that its heritage—rooted in images of palm trees, olive oil, and the mystery of the desert—still had a presence in the market and held the key to rejuvenating the drifting brand.

Strengths/Weaknesses

In order to be sustainable, a brand identity should be supported by organizational strengths. Sometimes these strengths need to be developed. The process starts by determining the strengths and weaknesses of the current product or service and the organization that lies behind it: What are we good at, and in what are we deficient? There needs to be a separation between what brand identity is de-

---

HIDDEN VALLEY RANCH DRESSING

Hidden Valley Ranch Dressing traces its heritage to a dude-ranch cook whose salad dressing was such a hit with his customers that he was pressured into packaging the spices so that people could add them to fresh buttermilk and enjoy the dressing at home. This packaged ranch dressing, under the Hidden Valley Ranch name, became a regional brand and was subsequently bought by Clorox for close to $1 million. Clorox successfully took it national and later added a bottled version that now has some eighteen variations.

The Hidden Valley Ranch brand identity is based upon its heritage—the original ranch dressing, made with fresh, natural ingredients in a special place. As is illustrated by Figure 6–4, television advertisements and the logo portray the lush, green "hidden valley" and the ranch. The ingredients and the associations with a unique location provide both functional benefits and the symbolic satisfaction of serving something out of the ordinary. Hidden Valley Ranch dressings are seen by consumers as coming from a special place, the hidden valley. In contrast, Kraft dressings are usually seen as being made in a factory. The Hidden Valley brand equity allows Clorox to charge a price premium while enjoying a market share second only to Kraft.

FIGURE 6-4
Hidden Valley Ad

Company: Clorox
Agency: Young & Rubicam/SF

Title: "Special Ingredient" :30
Comm'l No.: CXHV 0123
Date: May 25, 1990

and you'll discover that you
can't rush

SALLY KELLERMAN (VO): Spend
a little time in Hidden Valley

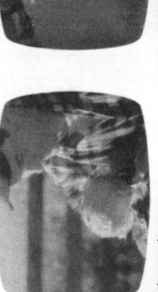

and there's just no substitute

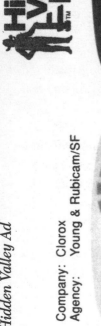

(MUSIC UP AND UNDER)

you can't cheat on freshness

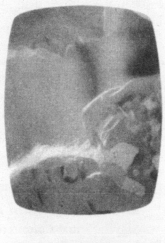

that valley fresh taste.

it's the Original.

the dressing that brings your salad

Hidden Valley Ranch . . .

for Hidden Valley Ranch . . .

Reproduced with permission from Clorox and Young & Rubicam San Francisco.

sired and what is attainable by the organization given its resources, capabilities, and priorities. It is a waste to attempt to develop an identity that cannot be supported in the marketplace.

Soul of the Brand

What is the soul of the brand and the organization? What is the brand vision? The dream? Most strong brands have a "soul" (the basic values of the brand) which provides character and meaning to the business. Some very basic introspection can be difficult but illuminating.

Links to Other Brands

A brand position decision cannot be made in isolation. Just as a basketball player's performance is defined with respect to his or her specified role on the team—a power forward (who must defend and rebound the ball well) is evaluated differently from a point guard (who must pass the ball well and run the offense)—a brand should

---

BRAND IDENTITY: PERSPECTIVES OF EMPLOYEES

There is a symbiotic relationship between organizational values and brand identity. The identity should reflect the values. But if the identity represents a clear vision that employees accept, it will also energize and guide the organization. Thus a strong identity can help shape organizational values.

Every organization should have an identity that employees—and other stakeholders, such as retailers and suppliers—know and care about. The following two sets of questions represent a test that can be used as part of the brand strategy analysis:[7]

- Do employees know what the brand stands for? What do they think is the brand identity? Is there a clear, shared vision, or is there uncertainty as to what the brand stands for?
- Do employees care? Do they feel an emotional commitment to the brand identity? Do they really care?

The answers are usually very revealing. The firms with strong, clear identities nearly always get quick responses; their employees know what the brand is about, and they care as well. When the employees don't even know the identity, there is a need to do better.

have well-defined roles and work within the context of other brands. An identity thus needs to be evaluated with respect to those role assignments.

In Chapter 8, some relationships between brands are explored. The goal is to create sets of brands that achieve synergy and clarity. Understanding brand roles is part of the analysis.

STRATEGIC BRAND ANALYSIS PHASES

The strategic brand analysis can be divided logically into several phases. In the first phase, the brand is analyzed using existing internal information: past customer research, market and brand sales data and patterns, the historical positioning of the brand, and known competitor identity strategies. As a part of this phase, those in the organization who have knowledge about the brand and its market should perform a thorough brand strategy analysis with the information at hand. The result should be the identification of identity options, and perhaps some positioning and execution routes as well.

In the second phase, information can be gathered using a variety of sources and methods including original customer research. The goal is to fill information gaps and explore branding options.

In the third phase, the target brand identity, value proposition, brand–customer relationship, and brand position are specified. In this phase, another set of customer studies may be useful for testing and refinement. These studies may explore implementation tactics as well as strategy options.

THE POWER OF BRAND IDENTITY AND POSITION

A well conceived and implemented brand identity and position can be a powerful asset to a firm, providing a source of sustainable advantage and a vehicle to help manage the brand. The following sections detail the specific contributions a brand identity and position can make (see also Figure 6–5).

GUIDES AND ENHANCES BRAND STRATEGY

A brand identity and position can do more than help customers organize information about the brand; it can also help managers systematize brand strategies. The manager who is intimately familiar with a

FIGURE 6–5
How Brand Identity And Position Creates Value

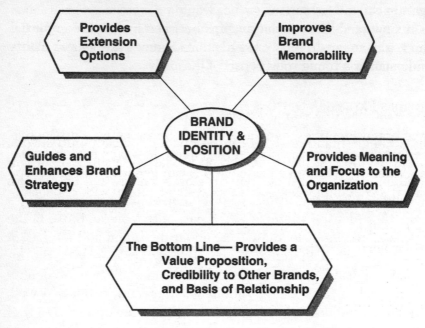

brand's identity and postition can quickly and efficiently choose those actions that are appropriate. Such a manager will also ensure that the company's advertising agencies and other marketing communication firms are similarly acquainted with the brand's identity.

As discussed in Chapter 1, creating and managing brands can be difficult in part because different organizations are involved. Promotions, packaging, advertising, direct marketing, event sponsorship, in-store displays, channel management, and customer relations are often handled by different people. Without a clear, strong identity and position, it becomes very difficult to maintain a consistent message across all these different functions.

A brand identity and position can also help managers generate new and suitable marketing strategies for a brand. For instance, the Mazda Miata was created to capture the identity of a 1960s sports car. This identity provides a clear and colorful basis for brainstorming about potential marketing strategies and themes for the Miata. Associations with handling and performance, for example, would be preferable to associations with advanced technology and safety. Print advertisements in car and fashion magazines would be more appropriate than ads in news and business magazines. And as a spokesperson for the brand, a race-car driver would be more strategically sound than a family man or a young sports hero.

PROVIDES EXTENSION OPTIONS

Some brand identities, such as A1 Steak Sauce being a distinctive meat condiment, are restrictive. In general, however, enriching the brand identity with linked associations can generate extension options. If, for example, Keebler's was associated only with chocolate-chip cookies, or even with cookies in general, its leverage potential would be limited. However, the Keebler's elf identity (which combines a sense of home-style baking with a touch of magic and fun) gives the brand more latitude to extend into other baked goods—and perhaps even into other types of food where homemade magic and fun might be perceived as a benefit.

IMPROVES BRAND MEMORABILITY

A strong, coherent brand identity and position will be easier to remember. The interesting is more memorable than the boring in brands as in people. Brands which have no personality will not tend to be recalled.

Also, an object that is made up of multiple elements that have coherence will be easy to recall. The mind is modeled by psychologists as a network with a set of connected nodes. An object can be recalled by accessing any of the nodes with which it is linked. Thus McDonald's may be brought to mind by any of its associations, such as Big Mac and Ronald McDonald. Because there are so many and because they are tightly linked, it is more likely that McDonald's will come to mind than another brand that has fewer linked nodes.

Finally, we know that consumers remember a product better when it has a strong symbol. The role of the symbol will be more powerful when it is personally meaningful and is associated with a visual image. In essence, the symbol becomes an easily accessible node in the mental network.

PROVIDES MEANING AND FOCUS TO THE ORGANIZATION

The impact of a strong identity and position within the organization is often ignored. When a brand identity and position is clear, it helps all employees—from customer service representatives to new product developers—to gauge their actions in terms of a central strategy. Thus, at Ford, saying that "Quality is Job 1" reflects a core organizational value that is communicated internally as well as externally.

In essence, the identity and position is a self-fulfilling prophecy. If you have a service quality identity, employees will realize that service is a priority inside the organization and expected by those outside. As a result, they will understand what to emphasize in their jobs and, as important, they are likely to feel commitment.

Certainly the Saturn brand identity helped the company deliver what it stood for. Saturn employees knew what their brand stood for and were motivated to make it happen. In contrast, when the identity is uninspired, confused, or communicated badly, employees are less likely to have direction or purpose.

A strong brand identity and position can also create a sense of pride and purpose that motivates employees—and even suppliers and distribution-channel participants—far beyond short-term financial performance goals. The Amoco concept of product purity in its gasoline, as symbolized by its clear gas and the visual imagery in its advertisements, helps make its refinery managers aggressively protective of the process and the output.

THE BOTTOM LINE: PROVIDES A COMPETITIVE ADVANTAGE

The brand identity planning model developed in Chapter 3 and shown in Figure 6–1 suggests that an identity can provide a value proposition, credibility to other brands and a basis for customer relationships. In performing one or more of these functions, a brand identity and position can provide a competitive advantage.

Further, the richness of a brand identity—its complex network of meanings—can set a brand apart from competitors and make it difficult to copy. Suppose, for example, that a new ice cream manufacturer hoped to steal some established customers from Ben & Jerry's by directly copying the brand. The challenge would be to copy not only the product but a set of associations, including the Ben & Jerry's philanthropy concept, New England craftsmanship, playful irreverence, and good quality. The task thus would be virtually impossible.

CHANGING A BRAND IDENTITY, POSITION, AND EXECUTION

Clearly, a central consideration in developing an identity, a position, and an execution is knowing when to change what has gone before. In fact, a brand is only developed from scratch once; most often, the identity, position, and execution are developed in the context of an existing brand "package." The next chapter explores the subject of change.

QUESTIONS TO CONSIDER

1. What emerges from an analysis of one's customers? One's competitors? From a self-analysis? What customer trends, motivations, and unmet needs are significant? Identify a small number of dimensions that summarize the customer motivations. Also identify a small number of dimensions that summarize the competitor images/identities. If the customer and competitor dimensions are different, explain. Are there other dimensions not now represented that could be the basis for a potentially effective identity/position?

2. What is the core identity? What are the points of leverage in the brand identity? How does the brand identity differ from the brand image? What differences create problems or liabilities? Can or should they be changed? What elements of the identity will resonate with customers? Differentiate the brand from competitors?

3. What are alternative brand positioning statements? Evaluate them according the following questions. Does a brand position:
   • Resonate with the customer? Will it endure?
   • Differentiate the brand from competitors? Does it represent something better or different that is valued?
   • Reflect and leverage the brand identity?
   • Represent a strategy that is feasible?
   • Represent a clear vision? Can people throughout the organization clearly articulate the brand identity?
   • Stimulate brilliant (or at least effective) implementation programs?

7

BRAND STRATEGIES
OVER TIME

If I could pray to move, prayers would move me:
But I am constant as the northern star,
Of whose true-fix'd and resting quality
There is no fellow in the firmament.
                    —William Shakespeare

For more than fifty years, Jell-O has presented the same honest face to its consumer. It's the ability of the Jell-O brand to evoke a scene of family, kids, and fun that makes it a far bigger product on the shelf.
                    —Michael Miles, Philip Morris Companies

THE GENERAL ELECTRIC STORY

In 1876, Thomas Edison founded a commercial research laboratory that would be the forerunner of General Electric. He realized early on that this laboratory would generate numerous inventions that would influence society and provide the foundation for a major corporation. The innovation stream was remarkable and relentless: One explicit goal was to create a minor invention every twelve days, and a major one every six months. The man who invented the light bulb, the motion picture, and the gramophone considered this lab to be his greatest invention.

One of Edison's early visions was to create a total system that would deliver the power and convenience of electricity to farms, households, and factories. He realized that the light bulb would not work unless electrical generation and distribution systems were developed. Among his innovations were turbine-driven power plants and the material and infrastructure technology involved in power distribution. That system and its parts were labeled by the brand name—General Electric.

In 1896, the familiar GE name and logo were created. Even in its earliest days, the company was positioned as having a personal relationship with customers. In early advertisements, the name GE was prophetically termed the "initials of a friend," and the promise and tag line of providing "better living electrically" was already in place.

A 1916 silent movie commercial showed customers using electric sewing machines, ranges, coffee makers, and toasters in their homes. Fast forwarding to 1955, a TV commercial featured Ronald and Nancy Reagan "living better electrically" by using modern appliances. GE appliances were making life easier and more enjoyable, and were providing self-expressive benefits for those who perceived appliances to be a symbol of economic success. The same brand position had survived more than forty years. An early print ad is shown in Figure 7–1.

In the 1960s General Electric diversified, It adapted its turbine expertise (from its electric generator business) to the design and manufacture of jet engines. In addition, its financial services business, founded during the Depression to finance home appliances, became very large. Light bulb technology led to products such as CT scanners, which became the basis for a medical electronic-imaging

FIGURE 7–1
An early GE print ad

business, and the knowledge of materials that developed from efforts to improve the insulation of power cables helped create an insulation and plastics business. As a result of this broad diversification, the concept of an electricity-focused company no longer fully represented GE.

A simple change in the slogan helped to chart a new vision: "Better living through technology" (rather than electricity) became the tag line. The new slogan enabled General Electric to evolve naturally toward a contemporary theme that was compatible with its heritage. Studies, however, showed that the name General Electric was associated with electricity and was considered relatively old-fashioned and narrow. A decision was thus made to sharply de-emphasize the General Electric name in favor of GE. The new GE name in block letters was perceived as high-tech, modern, and broader in scope.

The GE name alone, however, did not provide a strong link with the company's notable past. A solution was a variant of the classic "light bulb" logo, with GE written in script inside the bulb. The new symbol, representing both evolution and a link with the reliable and trustworthy General Electric heritage, was far better than starting over with a new name.

In the 1970s, two new themes—"Progress for people" and "Progress is our most important product"—emphasized the concept of progress rather than technology. The term *progress* provided a more aggressive and contemporary posture, as well as a greater focus on GE's contribution to better living. The basic idea, however, was still that people would benefit from GE technology. The strategic thrust of the firm thus was still seen through the eyes of the customers.

The increasingly varied businesses of GE created a key branding issue: To what extent should the GE name be the driver behind the business, the brand that would define the identity and drive customer purchase decisions? One option was to allow individual business units to develop their own identities and let the GE name fade to endorser status (much like the role Hewlett-Packard and Ford play for the HP LaserJet and the Ford Taurus). The firm concluded, though, that the development of separate business brands would be diverting, difficult, and expensive. Another very different option—to make the GE corporate name the lead, driver brand—was selected. The GE identity would contribute to a wide variety of businesses, each with a descriptive name that was attached to GE in a simple, consistent way:

GE Aerospace
GE Information Systems
GE Medical Systems
GE Capital Services
GE Transportation Systems
GE Electrical Distribution Control

GE Lighting
GE Appliances
GE Motors
GE Plastics
GE Industrial & Power
   Systems

During the late 1970s, though, an image study revealed a problem. Pictures of different types of people were placed in front of respondents, who were asked to select those who best represented the brand name GE. The pictures most associated with GE tended to be male, hard-hat types—not the image that a firm selling products to homemakers and the medical imaging industry wanted to see. Thus, in 1979, GE began a new ad campaign with the slogan, "GE—We bring good things to life." This campaign, which is still going on, featured emotional commercials focusing on the users of GE products. While true to the tradition of providing better living, the commercials were more contemporary and included women. A subsequent image study verified that this new tack did change the image: The GE brand was perceived to be much more contemporary, although still predominantly male.

Four principles that have guided GE through the years have contributed to its success. First, only one corporate brand has been used on virtually all products. The corporate brand thus has been the driver of the customer's link to the brand. Second, a single idea—better living from electricity/technology—has provided a core identity and a basis for a relationship with the customer for a long time period. Third, the focus has always been on customer benefits rather than on the products. It is the customers who are living better and enjoying good things in their lives. Fourth, the GE identity has been allowed to evolve while still being true to its heritage. Positioning and execution, particularly of the company's symbol and slogan, played a key role in the evolutionary process.

THE SMIRNOFF STORY

Vodka, which means "dear little water" in Russian, traces its roots back to the twelfth century. The Pierre A. Smirnoff Company became the leading vodka company in the nineteenth century by producing a consistent product using charcoal filtering and marketing it in color-ful bottles. The company's appointment in 1886 as the sole purveyor of vodka to the czar helped to ensure both prestige and market suc-cess for the brand. After the 1914 revolution, Vladimir Smirnoff, one of the founder's sons, failed in an effort to establish the brand in Poland and France. Ultimately he sold the business to Heublein, who subsequently built the brand throughout the world.

Smirnoff, and vodka in general, struggled in the United States until a South Carolina salesman began marketing the "no taste, no smell" alternative to whiskey in the 1930s. Smirnoff then began its ascent in the United States, aided by the popularity of cocktail-style drinks such as the Bloody Mary (tomato juice), screwdriver (orange juice), bullshot (bouillon), Black Russian (Kahlua and cream), Moscow Mule (ginger beer), gimlet (lime juice), and the vodka martini (vermouth), which was made famous—"shaken, not stirred"—by James Bond in the long-running movie series.

Although Smirnoff has achieved and held U.S. sales leadership, its share of the vodka category declined from more than 22 percent in 1974 to 17 percent in 1993. Even worse, during this time frame total vodka consumption was declining, although not as much as for the overall spirits category. Also, since the mid-1960s Absolut has carved out a 7.5 percent share of the vodka market; achieved market leader-ship on such vital image dimensions as taste, quality, and popu-larity; achieved a 50 percent unaided recall among category users; and been sold at a substantial premium. Stolichnaya (known as "Stoli"), another premium-priced brand, has gained a 3.3 percent market share.

Advertising has been an important factor in the vodka market. In particular, it has played a key role in establishing Smirnoff as the lead-ing brand in the United States. Smirnoff's advertising, however, has not been consistent over time. There were fourteen different adver-tising campaigns between 1953 and 1994 (and ten since 1978), each with different themes and visual imagery. At least five different brand personalities were put forth during this period. Some of these changes represented changed executions of positioning strategies, but most represented changed positions or identities.

Smirnoff provides an extreme case of changing positions or identi-ties. As such, it raises a host of issues that will be explored in this chapter: What is the rationale for change? Under what conditions should change occur? How can a timeless, effective positioning strategy be created? How can it be recognized? Figure 7–2 shows examples of four of the Smirnoff advertising campaigns, including the most recent one, and the full campaign chronology since 1953.

There were rationales for each of the Smirnoff campaign changes. The "self-expression" campaign, for example, was a reaction to the cultural changes of the Vietnam and Woodstock era. The "dining" campaign exploited an opportunity to expand usage. The "quality/value" theme was in direct response to a recession, and the "reigning vodka" theme attempted to defend the upscale position threatened by Absolut. The "home is where you find it" campaign was on target with the cocooners, an important emerging segment. The "pure thrill" approach was created to undercut Absolut, a key competitor with a strong visual image.

The question, though, is whether the motivation for each new campaign compensated for giving up advantages of consistency. The cumulative effect of a steady campaign would have added effectiveness and efficiency. Because of the endless changes, however, it was usually unclear what Smirnoff stood for. The Smirnoff identity was muddled in terms of its personality, its visual image, its value proposition, and the basis of its relationship with the customer.

But even if one assumes that a consistent campaign would have been more effective, the question remains: Which one? Should the firm have stayed with "Smirnoff style" or "Home is where you find it," or should it have had a consistent product-centered campaign such as the "reigning vodka" approach? Which could have achieved greatness? The answer is not obvious. Research would help, of course, but probably would not result in a definitive answer.

It does seem probable that the newest Smirnoff campaign will be successful and will endure. Further, it was designed to work throughout the world. Although country managers can develop their own scenes, the basic position and execution concept will be the same. This is a considerable achievement for Smirnoff.

Smirnoff is hardly the only brand to have undergone dramatic and frequent changes over time. Nissan, for example, not only changed its name from Datsun in 1982 but implemented numerous model changes before and since. An even better illustration is Burger King, which between 1975 and 1994 had some seventeen different advertising campaigns and five agencies. The early campaigns moved from

FIGURE 7–2
Smirnoff over the Years

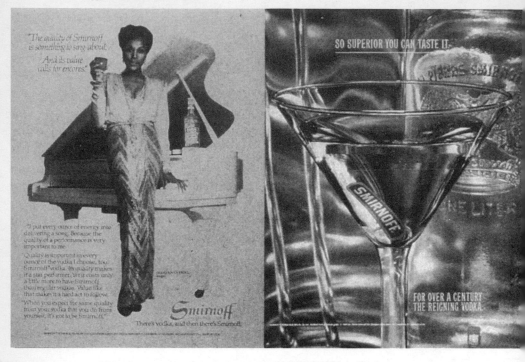

1981–83   1988–90

1946–53   Breathless. The first Smirnoff slogan, "It leaves you breathless," positioned Smirnoff with respect to dryness, a signal of quality in vodka martinis. The slogan also had an ulterior meaning: a vodka drinker avoids the risk of having alcohol on his or her breath. The ads of the 1940s showed the slogan above a martini, while those in the 1950s showed desert scenes with sand, camels, and very thirsty people. The slogan was to endure for eight campaigns through 1983, a run of more than 30 years.

1954–65   Sophisticated, witty people. Smirnoff's first personality campaign featured unusual and striking photos of sophisticated, urbane, and often famous people (such as comedians Groucho Marx and Phil Silvers). The copy was fresh, witty, and intelligent. One ad, for example, showed six celebrities—with Woody Allen in the front—on a wooden hobby horse having a (Moscow) "mule party."

1964–65   Variety of drinks. In order to create interest and to expand usage, this campaign introduced new drinks. One ad showed a person with a host of ingredients plus a bottle of Smirnoff, asking whether the reader had invented a Smirnoff drink lately.

1965–75   Self-expression. The late 1960s—the era of Vietnam and Woodstock—found young people wanting to break out of the mold. Smirnoff responded by extending the "variety" campaign to a lifestyle campaign that emphasized self-expression, with scenes of young couples relaxing.

1976–78   Dining. The use context changed to meals. Ads showed Smirnoff being used at a Paris café, a picnic, and a fancy restaurant (where the wine sat untouched while the Smirnoff flowed).

1978–79   Photogenic food. Smirnoff was shown in arresting, poster-quality photographs of food. One ad showed a stack of cheese with a Smirnoff-filled glass on top.

1979   Smirnoff style. A memorable, although short-lived personality campaign anchored by the slogan "Smirnoff Style" featured scenes of couples engaged in off-beat outdoor activities—honeymooning on an old sailboat, barbecuing in the snow, and having cocktails while sitting in inner tubes on a river.

1991–93   1994

1980 *Smirnoff style goes upscale.* Ads continued to show spontaneous and unusual behavior, but now the couples were much more upscale and sophisticated.

1981–83 *Value/quality.* With this campaign, Smirnoff responded to a recession in 1981 that made consumers more value oriented. A typical ad showed a celebrity (such as Broadway producer David Merrick) commenting on the product's quality and value, with the tag line "There's vodka, and then there's Smirnoff."

1984–87 *Friends are worth Smirnoff.* The message of this campaign was that customers should purchase premium brands that they are proud to serve to guests and friends. Warm indoor settings were shown, with friends enjoying themselves. The "It leaves you breathless" slogan finally disappeared.

1988–90 *Reigning vodka.* Reacting to the success of Absolut and others, who had successfully made inroads with a high-end position, this set of ads stressed the heritage and authenticity of Smirnoff vodka. The line "For over a century, the reigning vodka" was shown behind a picture of a full cocktail glass.

1989–91 *The contemporary campaign.* Attempting to create interest in the brand among younger drinkers, sharp visuals showed a glass with witty copy and a red Smirnoff label.

1991–93 *Home is where you find it.* "Cocooning," or enjoying the warmth and security of the home, was said to be a trend of the 1990s. This campaign responded with cozy scenes of families, friends, and lovers similar to those Hallmark or Kodak might use.

1994 *Pure thrill.* Developed by the London office of Lowe, these ads show scenes with a Smirnoff bottle in the foreground. The portion of the scene viewed through the bottle shows with vivid clarity a fantasy world that can be disturbing or humorous, but is always arresting. A penguin becomes a tuxedo-clad partygoer. A sedate room becomes the aftermath of a raucous party. A demure woman now has a tattoo. The "reality" as seen through the bottle reflects the purity of Smirnoff. The departure from the mundane world also suggests moving beyond fun to capture a sense of thrill, reflecting the experience users associate with successful social occasions in which new relationships and self expression are involved.

the "Have it your way" theme (which emphasized the ability of customers to special-order their hamburgers) to a focus on the flame-broiled cooking method. In 1986, the widely ridiculed "Search for Herb" campaign was launched to create interest and awareness; instead, it started a share decline. Six subsequent efforts, including the MTV-influenced "BK Tee Vee" (with a teen heartthrob screaming "I love this place!"), did nothing to arrest the fall.

WHY CHANGE IDENTITIES, POSITIONS, OR EXECUTIONS?

A key issue in managing brands over time is the decision to change an identity, position, or execution (to be termed *identity/execution* for the sake of brevity). Changing any one of the three can be expensive and potentially damaging. An identity change is more fundamental, but a change in position and execution can be disruptive as well.

There are, of course, contexts in which the identity, position, or execution should be changed—in fact, where the continuation of a defective or ineffective strategy may be a disaster. The sections below summarize five principal rationales for change.

RATIONALE 1: THE IDENTITY/EXECUTION WAS POORLY CONCEIVED

An ill-conceived or off-target brand identity/execution can usually be diagnosed early by measures of customer interest, brand perceptions, brand attitudes, and sales. Disappointing sales and share trends can be a particularly strong signal.

Sometimes it is obvious that an identity, position, or execution is defective. The AT&T "i" (for individualized calling) program, for example, was expected to provide added value and a basis for a relationship with its customers, but at best it only generated confusion; it was pulled after less than a year. Several of the Smirnoff campaigns (such as the "reigning vodka" series) also were considered to be ineffective and were thus short-lived.

RATIONALE 2: THE IDENTITY/EXECUTION IS OBSOLETE

Even if the brand identity/execution works, markets are not static, and brands do not exist in a time capsule. Contexts can change. Customer tastes and company cultures evolve, technology presents new challenges, and competitors enter and leave the market. Indeed, there can be fundamental paradigm shifts in the environment of the brand; as a result, an identity/execution that has been successful can become ineffective.

The Kentucky Fried Chicken brand, for instance, experienced great success with an identity based on Colonel Sanders—a native of the old South who cooked fried chicken with his secret formula of herbs and spices. In the mid-1980s, however, increasingly health-conscious customers associated Kentucky Fried Chicken with high fat and cholesterol content and began to patronize restaurants offering healthier alternatives. In 1991 Kentucky Fried Chicken decided to change with the times by adding rotisserie chicken to its menu and moving toward value positioning. It also shortened its name to KFC to avoid the association with fried food.

RATIONALE 3: THE IDENTITY/EXECUTION APPEALS TO A LIMITED MARKET

When the brand identity/execution is working well but addresses a market that is limited and perhaps shrinking, there may be a need to change the identity in order to reach a broader market. A brand can be repositioned to reach another segment, as Johnson & Johnson showed when it redefined its baby shampoo as a product for those who need a mild shampoo they can use every day. The market also can be expanded by establishing a new application, a classic example being the use of Arm & Hammer baking soda to deodorize refrigerators.

RATIONALE 4: THE IDENTITY/EXECUTION IS NOT CONTEMPORARY

Even a brand identity that is still relevant and meaningful may appear old-fashioned and stodgy. In General Electric's case, electricity became a dated concept that no longer represented technology and innovation. The GE solution was to eliminate electricity from its name and slogan and to express the value proposition differently. In the process, the concept of electricity systems and their role in people's lives (certainly a GE core identity element) was phased out. Several of the Smirnoff campaigns—including the "Smirnoff style" set—were efforts to make the brand more contemporary. The final section of this chapter will discuss approaches to making an identity more contemporary.

RATIONALE 5: THE IDENTITY/EXECUTION IS TIRED

Another problem with having a single brand identity/execution over time is that it may become boring to consumers, even if variants on the execution are used. As a result, it can fail to attract attention and ultimately lose its effectiveness. Further, when an identity remains the same for years, lively ideas for presenting that identity can become scarce. Competitors with more exciting identities and ways to communicate them have an advantage. Certainly, providing the Smirnoff creatives with few constraints resulted in some arresting advertising.

An identity/execution change can be newsworthy. A company that successfully repositions its brand is more likely to make headlines, thus stretching the brand's marketing dollars. Some marketing efforts that have caught the attention of the general media include Wendy's "Where's the beef?" campaign, Pepsi's controversial television advertisement featuring the singer Madonna, and Isuzu's use of a lying car dealer as a spokesman.

WHY CONSISTENCY (IF DONE WELL) IS BETTER

THE CONSISTENCY OPTION

Changes over time are certainly not inevitable. A host of successful brands have had remarkable histories of a consistent identity/execution. Consider Ivory soap, one nominee as the brand with the longest-running brand strategy. Its core identity since 1881 has been purity, with the twin slogans "99 ^{44}/100% pure" and "It floats."

Perhaps the most visibly consistent strategy is that of Marlboro. The Marlboro man, introduced in the 1950s and refined in the 1960s, is still going strong as a symbol throughout the world. With its strong brand personality (independent, outdoor-lifestyle, free spirited, rugged, and masculine) and its visual image of the cowboy and Marlboro country, Marlboro has become part of marketing folklore. Blessed with a strong identity and disciplined implementation, Marlboro has rarely had a misstep that has taken it away from its strategy.

One of the most consistent brand strategies for durable consumer goods has been that of Maytag; its position as "the dependability people" has been anchored by the "loneliest guy in town" campaign for almost three decades (see Figure 7–3 for an example). First aired in 1967, the campaign featured Jesse White, a prominent character actor, who explained why Maytag was so reliable. He punctuated his story with the tongue-in-cheek admission that, because he was the Maytag repairman, nobody ever called him (which is why he was so lonely). Since its introduction, the campaign's central message has changed very little, and the actor has changed only once: Gordon Jump, who played the bumbling station manager in the "WKRP in Cincinnati" television series, took over the role in the late 1980's. Maytag's is the longest-running campaign on television featuring a real-life character.

The Maytag identity leads to a strong functional benefit of quality and dependability, as well as emotional benefits (relief from worry and a reminder, for some, of their childhood homes). The functional benefit, in particular, is both relevant and important to customers, and it has staying power—it has not become obsolete because of technological change or consumer trends. In 1993, Maytag was rated as the preferred brand of washers, dryers, and dishwashers in the United States and Canada. It continues to command a significant price premium over competitors in an industry that has intense competition and severe margin pressures.

A brand with a similarly consistent strategy over time is Black Velvet Canadian whiskey. The early 1970s saw the introduction of the Black Velvet lady: a glamorous, beautiful blonde in a black dress pictured against a black background, with the tagline "Feelin' Velvet." Similar ads with different models have run ever since and have become the essence of the Black Velvet personality and identity. The slogan changed to "The Velvet Touch" in the mid-1980's, but the central image remains unchanged (see Figure 7–4). The Black Velvet lady provides a strong visual image that supports the "soft and smooth" core identity and also contributes emotional benefits (a feeling of being relaxed, rewarded, and sensual) and self-expressive benefits (serving a brand with a touch of class).

THE BENEFITS OF CONSISTENCY

Although change is sometimes appropriate and even necessary, there is no doubt that the goal should be to create an effective identity whose position and execution will endure and not become obsolete and/or tired. The result can be a consistency of meaning and message

FIGURE 7–3
The Loneliest Man in Town

MAYTAG COMPANY

 LEO BURNETT COMPANY, INC.

AS FILMED AND RECORDED   (1/93)   "Tools"   :15   MYWA4781

1. (MUSIC: UNDER THROUGHOUT)

2. (AVO): Maytag repairmen...

3. own the finest tools.

4. And sometimes....

5. (SFX: CRACK!)
(AVO): ...they even get to use them.

6. Maytag. The Dependability People.

FIGURE 7–4
The Black Velvet Lady

through time that can provide the ownership of a position, ownership of an identity symbol, and cost efficiencies, all of which combine to provide a formidable competitive advantage.

Ownership of a Position

A consistent identity/execution can lead to the virtual ownership of a position. Competitors are preempted and must therefore pick another route, often one that is inherently less effective. An effort by a competitor to usurp Maytag's position on the dependability dimension, for example, would not be believed. Worse, the competitor's communication efforts might actually be mistaken for those of Maytag by some, thus giving Maytag free advertising. Similarly, Black Velvet owns the sensual/smoothness dimension for whiskey, and Marlboro owns the masculine position for cigarettes. It would be difficult for competitors to be credible if they attached themselves to similar positions.

Ownership of Identity Symbol

Brand identity/execution consistency over time provides an opportunity to own an effective identity symbol, which might be a visual image, slogan, jingle, metaphor, or spokesperson. Such a symbol makes the brand's identity easier to understand, to remember, and to link with the brand. The competitive power of the position is thus enhanced.

The Maytag repairman and the Black Velvet lady are two examples of symbols that quickly and simply communicate the brand position. Others include United Airlines' theme music (which conveys a sense of stature and quality), McDonald's Ronald McDonald (who communicates an image of family fun), the Sprint pin-dropping image (which implies exacting technology), and Marlboro country. The Marlboro image is so well known that the company can sometimes place billboards that display only a "Marlboro Country" scene without the brand name or package. A competitor attempting to use a similar scene would likely only reinforce the Marlboro identity. Thus, when an identity symbol is strong, competitors must go another route.

In addition, when a simple, position-appropriate symbol becomes closely associated with a brand, the dangers of consumer boredom are somewhat reduced. While young brands need to entertain or do something outrageous in order to attract attention and become associated with a position, successful mature brands often need only to refresh existing associations. Ronald McDonald, for example, can be shown playing video games or wearing an updated outfit.

Cost Efficiencies

A consistent brand strategy supported by a strong identity symbol can produce an enormous cost advantage in implementing communication programs. All brands—especially new ones—are faced with the problem of creating and maintaining awareness, as well as creating and reinforcing an image or personality. The task of communicating, getting attention, and changing perceptions becomes less expensive, though, when it is reduced to cueing a visual image or slogan that is well known and closely associated with a brand.

Consider the cost burden if General Electric, a Maytag competitor, wanted to convince customers that it had surpassed Maytag in terms of dependability. Given the equity that Maytag has amassed on this dimension, GE would have to buy an exposure intensity much larger than Maytag employs, plus have an attention-getting message, to even hope for any impact. Even then, the goal still might not be feasible. In fact, it is likely that Maytag's strong reputation and loyal customer base has carryover effects to other appliance characteristics such as performance.

Now consider Maytag's recent task of adding the dependability dimension to its new refrigerator line. Maytag simply had the lonely repairman make a cameo appearance during the last few seconds of an ad introducing the refrigerator. That compact visual image cost so little and said so much. Just a glance at the repairman brought back all of viewers' past dependability associations.

A competitor of Marlboro, Ivory, or Black Velvet will have the same problem encroaching on their position. Consider the power and efficiency of the visual image of Marlboro country, a bar of soap floating in a clear stream, or the Black Velvet lady. It is likely that a competitor with no established position or visual imagery would have to spend five times as much (if not ten times or more) to make a significant dent.

Further, efforts to create a new identity are likely to be wasted in that they might not register or might only be effective at creating an identity that becomes obsolete. There is no cumulative effect. In contrast, an effort to support and reinforce a long-running campaign will more likely be productive.

A No-Brainer!

It really seems like a no-brainer! Being consistent over time with respect to a brand's identity, position, visual imagery, and theme or slogan is clearly a key to strong brands. The logic is compelling and the strategy is simple. But why, then, doesn't everyone do it? Why are there so few Marlboros, Maytags, Black Velvets, and Ivorys? Why are there so many firms that seem to panic when problems emerge?

CONSISTENCY OVER TIME: WHY IS IT HARD?

As already noted, at least five very legitimate rationales can make a change in identity, position, or execution appropriate or even necessary. However, there are substantial forces above and beyond these rationales that bias managers toward change and away from maintaining a consistent identity. Awareness of these forces (summarized in Figure 7–5) can help a firm avoid making ill-advised and premature changes in a brand identity/execution. One set of forces relates to psychological factors that influence managers' decisions regarding brands; the second involves strategic misconceptions or false assumptions about the existing brand identity/execution.

THE MINDSET OF THE MANAGERS

Problem Solver/Action Orientation

Those in charge of brands—from assistant brand managers to executive vice presidents—are generally bright, creative people within a culture that emphasizes finding and solving problems and detecting and responding to trends in the market. And there are always problems and new trends to address. Market share, even for the best of brands in the best of times, will face dips and competitive pressures. New trends in distribution, customer motivations, and innumerable other areas are continually emerging.

An aggressive, capable manager often believes he or she should be able to improve the situation, and that usually means changing one of

FIGURE 7–5

Resisting Pressures to Change Identities, Positions, and Executions

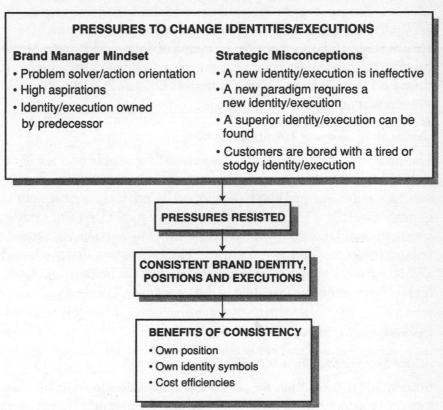

PRESSURES TO CHANGE IDENTITIES/EXECUTIONS

Brand Manager Mindset
- Problem solver/action orientation
- High aspirations
- Identity/execution owned
  by predecessor

Strategic Misconceptions
- A new identity/execution is ineffective
- A new paradigm requires a
  new identity/execution
- A superior identity/execution can be
  found
- Customers are bored with a tired or
  stodgy identity/execution

↓

PRESSURES RESISTED

↓

**CONSISTENT BRAND IDENTITY,
POSITIONS AND EXECUTIONS**

↓

BENEFITS OF CONSISTENCY
- Own position
- Own identity symbols
- Cost efficiencies

the drivers of brand equity. The prime candidate for change is the brand identity, position, or execution. The temptation is to dig in, diagnose the problem or trend, and take action—even when the "action" course may actually end up hurting the brand.

Consider the Black Velvet brand manager who is asked at the annual planning meeting how he or she plans to improve the brand's flat sales (even though the overall category is declining). A response of "Well, I thought I would do the same thing as the prior five brand managers have done" may represent an optimal strategy that builds and protects brand equity, but it is not impressive or, perhaps more important, much fun. "I have a dramatic plan for change that is likely to turn the brand around within twelve months" sounds both more professional and more exciting.

High Aspirations

The problem-solver/action orientation is usually accompanied by aspirations to improve the performance of the brand. Managers are generally not expected to do only as well as last year; the goal is always to do better, especially in terms of sales and profits. If the brand is to improve on prior performance, an obvious implication is that something must be done differently. Changing the identity/execution is one option.

Owned by Predecessor Identity/Execution

The pressure to change can best be resisted by people who are committed to the brand vision and its execution. However, the identity and its execution were likely developed by others (sometimes long gone), especially if the brand has had a reasonably long run. A new, transient brand manager will have no pride of ownership and little involvement in the identity/execution. The conclusion that the brand and its message are not responsive to the current market, and that a major improvement is possible, is thus personally painless.

STRATEGIC MISCONCEPTIONS

A New Identity/Execution Is Ineffective

Sometimes it takes time for an identity/execution to wear in. Customers need to get used to the concept, and the execution needs to be refined. A brand identity is not unlike a TV show that starts slow, develops a growing following, and only after two or three years becomes a hit. It can take that long for the audience to build, and for the characters to find their niche and become familiar to the audience. During that time, characters or other elements may be added, deleted, or modified as the show settles into its style.

Brand identities and their execution can also require some settling in. Marlboro, for example, started with a rugged man with a tattoo who only over time evolved into a cowboy. It took several years for Marlboro country to emerge. A decision on the effectiveness of the embryonic Marlboro identity might have been premature.

Then there is the "blinders trap," in which a great identity/execution is achieved but is not recognized as such. Greatness is harder to judge than one might think. Competent people may differ in their opinions because they judge the identity/execution with different assumptions about the market. Research results may be ambiguous because several criteria may be relevant to brand performance, and a given study may not measure all of them.

A New Paradigm Requires a New Identity/Execution

Managers, by instinct and training, are always examining the market for trends. A major challenge is to determine which of these trends represent a fundamental shift in the market. Will the change in consumer tastes endure and grow, or is it only a fad? Wine coolers (such as California Coolers) and clear, sweetened carbonated beverages (such as Clearly Canadian) are examples of fad products that failed to live up to their promise. Both they and the "forces" that drove their short-lived success have faded.

Even when a paradigm shift is accurately detected, it is not always clear that the brand strategy should change. The old strategy, even if found to be inappropriate for a major segment, may still represent a better strategy than alternatives. For example, when it came under attack by Healthy Choice, Weight Watchers could have chosen to stick to its professional weight control identity. This "consistency option" would have resulted in downsizing to a niche brand, which although painful, might have resulted in a healthier (albeit smaller) business.

Further, there is an upside to maintaining an existing identity in the face of a new paradigm. Customers lost may return after the glow of the new paradigm recedes and there is a resurgence of the old one. In addition, it avoids the risk that the revised identity will fail because it is too little, too late or because it was executed badly.

A Superior Identity/Execution Can Be Found

Managers evaluating whether to change identities sometimes overlook the fact that much more is known about the existing strategy and execution than about any proposed alternative. Thus the warts of the existing strategy are clear while problems with the untried proposal cannot yet be predicted, often making the proverbial grass seem greener almost anywhere else than where the firm is now. Nevertheless, alternatives are not necessarily better, and may at best result in similar share and profitability figures.

A similar pitfall is the aspiration trap, in which a brand team engages in an endless search for perfection and a dramatic improvement in performance when the probability of achieving either is actually very low. It can be a compulsive and futile waste of resources. The problem is that "genius" identities and executions are difficult to achieve, in part because people capable of generating them are rare, and the environment that allows such people to thrive is rarer still.

Customers Are Bored with a Tired or Stodgy Identity/Execution

Often it is those managing the brand, not the customers, who are bored with an identity or execution. The fact is that insiders can get bored and even irritated with an execution—and when they do, they assume that customers are as well. Many managers are likely to see more repetition of their brand's advertising than any target group. In fact, by the time a consumer first sees a new campaign, those who work with the brand have probably seen it (or alternative versions of it) hundreds of times.

Advertising giant Ross Reeves once claimed that if he had the second-best advertising in a market, he would always win, because the competition would get bored and change theirs. When asked why his agency was billing its Anacin client so much, given that it just kept running the same commercial, he replied that it was expensive to convince the client managers not to change the advertising.

If boredom is being claimed as a reason for changing strategy, the brand management team should do the research necessary to see if consumers really are the ones who are bored. And remember that consumer boredom is not necessarily bad: Brands from Bayer to Charmin have built a flourishing business by "boring" consumers with the same consistent message.

It is important to distinguish between the wearing out of a position or identity and the wearing out of a particular execution. An execution can be changed without changing the position or identity; I will explore how brands such as Jell-O have done this later in the chapter.

THE PANIC ATTACK

When change seems necessary, the most difficult thing to do is to remain calm and analytical. With all of the pressures described above, the gravitation toward change is difficult to resist, especially when the market is seeming to demand it and sales are slipping. However, precipitous action—which can sometimes resemble panic—is often the opposite of what is needed when considering a change to a long-standing brand identity.

The case of Miller Lite raises some important questions about change. Miller invented the light-beer category by positioning its brand not as a diet drink, but as one that was both great tasting and less filling—the perfect beer for heavy beer drinkers. Miller Lite built a strong image around male camaraderie (an identity that included not only masculinity but humor and sports-related fun), primarily using retired athletes as its spokesmen. The intent was to make the audience feel accepted as part of this group. The ad characters shared private jokes with and never looked down at their viewers. The Miller Lite brand–customer relationship was defined in part by this atmosphere.

This brand identity, supported by advertising and events, was remarkably successful from the 1970s to the late 1980s, but then its share started to fall (from roughly 12.5 percent to below 10 percent). The ability of Coors Light and Bud Light to attract young beer drinkers—the heart of the heavy-drinker segment—was at least a partial cause of Miller Lite's change in fortunes; the previously brilliant use of middle-aged ex-athletes had become a disadvantage in appealing to this younger segment.

As a result, Miller Lite changed agencies, dumped the classic Miller Lite campaign (and the identity that went with it), and replaced it with a lively, upbeat set of ads centered on the "It's It and That's That" tag line. The theme was intended to emphasize that Miller Lite was the first and therefore best light beer. Unfortunately, the new target audience—most of whom were not drinking when Miller Lite was first introduced—was not attracted to the campaign.

This failure clearly raises questions. What caused the decline of Miller Lite? If it was the success of competitors in appealing to the younger crowd, does that mean that Miller should have followed them? Did Miller Lite panic in turning its back on its long-standing identity? Did it turn its back on its brand equity? Would existing customers feel uncomfortable (even annoyed or angry) about their "friend" going toward a different target market? Would they feel abandoned for a younger person? Should Miller have simply continued with the old campaign and accepted a share loss? Might the share loss be made worse by Miller Lite's turning away from its equity?

Perhaps more to the point, were there alternatives to changing the identity? Could Miller have moved the campaign so it was more appealing to a younger audience while still maintaining its essence: the maleness, acceptance, and fun settings? Perhaps a younger group around a volleyball court could have replaced the older ex-athletes in a bar.

American Express (also known as Amex) is another example. The "Membership has its privileges" slogan had defined a strong set of upscale associations and a distinctive brand personality. However, the Amex green card eventually suffered a serious loss in business, in part because its rivals were very aggressive and in part because retailers considered Amex's charges to be excessive. The Amex response was to replace the advertising that supported the historic identity with a campaign from a new agency in which an oversized card was placed in unusual contexts.

Again, this change in strategy (which was ineffective and short-lived) raises questions. Did American Express panic? Should the brand have stuck with building on its equity even if a loss in market share was created by competitive intensity and a changing marketplace? Did the change actually accelerate the sales decline? In this case, we do know that American Express pulled the plug on the new advertising and decided to go back to its prior agency.

Other brands have also somewhat sheepishly returned to slogans and identities that had been long discarded. KFC's "We do chicken right" and Seven-Up's "Uncola" are examples of brand identity concepts and slogans that reappeared after a long absence. These cases and others like them suggest that a core identity and execution are often harder to improve on than is assumed and that there should be a heavy burden of proof placed upon alternatives to the status quo.

THE SEARCH FOR THE FOUNTAIN OF YOUTH

The challenge for many brands is to respond to a changing environment and/or to contemporize a brand identity without walking away from the existing identity, which is usually the key element of brand equity. Updating the brand is a particularly acute challenge for heritage brands such as Campbell's, Kodak, Hallmark, General Electric, John Deere, Hewlett-Packard, Quaker Oats, Chevrolet, Allstate, Jell-O, and AT&T.

Heritage brands (often the oldest brand in their respective categories) have the "Sincerity" characteristics of being honest, authentic, wholesome, trustworthy, friendly, familiar, caring, and unassuming. Consumer brands of this type usually elicit emotional responses from consumers based on their childhood experiences, or perhaps on an idealized childhood that they would have liked to have had. Brands like Hewlett-Packard and GE engender feelings of trust and respect. The identity equity is thus extremely strong and valuable. The problem that these brands all face, though, is that they can also appear stodgy, old-fashioned, and tired. Most need to somehow become more contemporary, fresh, and energized.

There are two variants on the heritage brand problem. The first involves consumer brands, such as Jell-O and Levi's, that need to appeal to the younger generation (kids, teens and early twenties). Being perceived as old-fashioned can be fatal in some of these product categories, as competitors with fewer identity constraints go full speed ahead to reach the MTV generation. The second variant is typically encountered by firms marketing high-tech products or durable goods. These companies, in part simply because they are older, are often viewed as not being on the cutting edge in a context in which being perceived as a technological laggard is a big handicap.

Changing one's identity radically, as Miller Lite attempted, is like tearing down an existing house in order to build a new one. There are no constraints, such firms feel; the perfect house can be designed. A less expensive alternative, however, is to remodel the old house using what is still serviceable. One way to remodel, simply redecorating, corresponds to letting the identity *evolve*. Another way to remodel is to add on to the house, expanding a room or adding another room or wing. This add-on option corresponds to *augmenting* the brand identity.

EVOLVING AN IDENTITY

When a person gradually loses weight or becomes less compulsive about a hobby, it is only over time that the change becomes noticeable. Similarly, a brand can gradually evolve to become more contemporary while still being familiar. Sometimes an evolution can involve only the extended identity, but sometimes the core identity needs to evolve as well. There are a host of ways an identity can evolve to become more contemporary. They include the use of symbols, names, slogans, and new products.

Symbols

A symbol can be the anchor that keeps a brand seemingly stuck in the past unless it is updated. Thus over the years the Pillsbury doughboy has gotten livelier and more active, just as Betty Crocker, Aunt Jemima, the Virginia Slims and Charlie women, and even the Morton Salt girl have all changed to become compatible with current fashions and attributes. The Prudential rock similarly has evolved to a more abstract representation in order to signal a more modern orientation. In all cases, the meaning of the symbol has not changed; indeed, the hope invariably is that the symbol will still represent the heritage of the brand.

Name

An out-of-date brand name may need to be changed in order to better reflect the brand's evolving identity. For example, Federal Express has changed its name to FedEx in part to put less emphasis on "Federal," which suggested stability and reliability when the concept of overnight delivery was new, but which now could seem militaristic and bureaucratic, and could even cause Federal Express to be confused with the U.S. Postal Service's Express mail.[1] The FedEx name is more streamlined and contemporary and, in fact, was already being used by customers as a "nickname" for Federal Express. The accompanying new logo has a larger, bolder, and more contemporary typeface which, together with the new name, fits better with FedEx's current identity as an innovative global leader.

Slogans

The General Electric story illustrates the role that slogans can play in evolving an identity. An effective slogan has the power to capture the essence of a brand identity, yet it can be changed, replaced, or augmented more easily than a brand name. GE replaced *electricity* with *technology* (and later *progress*) in its slogans, in each case giving a slightly more modern perspective on the brand. Finally, the "bring good things to life" slogan, with its emotional element, was introduced. All of these themes were consistent with the central concept that GE as a corporation develops technology-based innovations that help people live better. At the same time, they allowed the corporation to evolve over time from electricity to a broader focus on technology and innovation.

New Products

Quaker Oats used new products and a sense of contemporary trends to update the ultimate in stodgy brands. The company's hot oatmeal, anchored by the Quaker man and the famous blue cylindrical package, had several strengths: an old-fashioned but nurturing personality, an image of being honest and having healthy ingredients, and links to positive childhood experiences. However, it was also perceived as being inconvenient, not too tasty, and even somewhat authoritarian. To become modern without losing its heritage, Quaker introduced products such as single-serving, microwavable Oatmeal cups (with spices and sweeteners to improve the taste) and the new Oat Squares and Quaker Toasted Oatmeal cereals. These new products both corrected deficiencies and added vitality to the brand.

Another new-product story is Jigglers from Jell-O. Nearly one hundred years old, Jell-O has a strong kid/fun association—with Jell-O a kid can make a mess, be creative, and have fun. There is also a mom/family connection (making Jell-O is a special thing moms do with kids). The problem was that by the late 1980s, Jell-O was not considered topical by the MTV generation and it had seen its sales volume cut in half. Jigglers, which allowed users to have a creative experience making an outrageous hand-held dessert, revitalized the Jell-O brand while fitting perfectly with the kids/fun/mom equity. The product was introduced with a promotion (involving little cutouts used to cut Jigglers into interesting shapes) that got more than five million responses.

AUGMENTING THE IDENTITY

A second option is to retain an existing identity but to augment it with additional extended or core identity elements. A limitless variety of dimensions can be added, such as different attributes or personality characteristics, new market segments, new user imagery, product extensions, and new emotional benefits. A few examples will illustrate.

Adding User Imagery

Levi Strauss reached out to the younger generation by using urban, hip user imagery in its TV commercials, event promotions, and endorsements that is very different from its brand personality based on miners and ranchers working with their hands in durable denim jeans. (Recall the discussion of user imagery and brand personality in Chapter 5). As noted in Chapter 5, the problem now facing the brand is to make sure that its heritage associations and core identity do not fade.

After unsuccessfully trying for many years to change its corporate image, DuPont also finally rang the bell by skillfully employing user imagery. The ads showed a basketball player using an artificial limb made with DuPont technology. This association, which communicated innovation in a very personal and emotional way, substantially augmented DuPont's identity.

Product Extension

Putting one's brand in another product class augments the identity by adding not only the product class association but also attributes that may be relevant to that product class. Contadina, for example, was a strong canned-foods brand with an authentic Italian heritage and association. When Nestlé took this brand into fresh refrigerated pastas and sauces, the result was a revitalized identity and such a healthy growth vehicle that Nestlé is now calling Contadina one of its strategic brands.

Adding an Emotional Benefit

Taster's Choice has long been associated with offering convenience and good taste in today's busy world—in early ads, it was the heroic brand that allowed a young wife to fool her husband into thinking that she had freshly brewed the coffee. In 1990, however, a new identity dimension was added through a soap-opera series of advertisements that involved a man and a woman meeting and becoming romantically attracted. Although the couple still personified the core identity of Taster's Choice—a convenient, yet full-flavored coffee for busy young professionals—they did so in a more contemporary way (and with a sexual tension that an audience of previous decades might have found downright racy). The result was an association with the emotions surrounding this emerging relationship, as well as another quality cue. (The quality of Taster's Choice motivated the couple's initial interaction, and provided an excuse for further meetings.) Taster's Choice saw its market share grow more than 3 percent over three years, a rather dramatic success in a stable category.

The Use of Subbrands

Often the augmentation will need a subbrand to help establish the new dimension, especially if it involves a new product class or a distinctively new market. For example, the Canon Rebel endorsed by Andre Agassi provided youth and energy to a rather mature brand. The use of subbrands in this context is discussed in the next chapter.

PROVIDING LINKS TO THE HERITAGE IDENTITY

When a long-standing brand identity is changed dramatically and/or forcefully, there is a risk that the heritage identity may fade or be less influential. The question, then, is how to change while still reinforcing the heritage identity.

Symbols

Coke went to Hollywood's best creative talent to create a diverse set of commercials that broke the "one sight, one sound" mold in which a campaign would use a single creative concept and jingle. The set of twenty-eight new commercials provided a contemporary style for every segment; indeed some ads were indistinguishable from MTV videos. To link this strong new identity statement to the heritage of Coke, the commercials also brought back the Coca-Cola bottle icon. Of course, Coke still had the problem of communicating the icon's meaning to teens unfamiliar with its long history.

In durables, RCA sought to create a sense of innovation and technology. The vehicle was a set of new products—such as a projection-screen home theater—and an advertising campaign with the tag line "Changing entertainment, again." In order to provide links to the brand's heritage, RCA brought back Nipper (the dog listening to a gramophone in the RCA icon dating from the turn of the century) and introduced Chipper, a puppy, to represent the new RCA. In one ad the two dogs are shown watching an entertainment system. These symbols not only link the brand to its past but also provide a key point of differentiation.

The Heritage of Innovation

Collins Radio, an aerospace company, tells an innovation story in the context of the history and tradition of the firm. The story starts with the founder, Al Collins, who, as a teen in 1925, developed the only technology that could communicate with arctic explorers. Eight years later, Admiral Byrd took Collins' radio equipment on his historic expedition to the North Pole. In 1950 Collins Radio pioneered radio navigation systems, and in 1963 the first space trip relied on Collins' communication equipment. In ads, each of these innovations has been couched visually in terms of a commemorative stamp. Emphasizing that the firm has a tradition of being at the cutting edge not only provides a link to the heritage but serves to support an innovative/cutting-edge position.

BUILDING ON EQUITY

The goal for a brand should be to build equity that has value and can be used through time. Existing brand identity equity therefore should be used as a base that can be allowed to evolve or be augmented without giving up or undercutting its underlying value. The value of change always needs to be balanced with the value of consistency and the power of a hard-earned heritage.

QUESTIONS TO CONSIDER

1. Create a history of brand identities, positions and executions for your important brands. What is the legacy/heritage of the brand, as represented by the first positioning efforts? What has changed? What has been common through time? Have the changes been effective? Now do the same for the major competitor brands. Which competitors have the longest-running position, symbols, and visual imagery? Has that paid off for them?
2. Are there biases toward change in the organization? Why? How can these biases be reduced or neutralized?

3. Evaluate the current position and its execution. Are they well conceived? Would you call them great? Effective? Are they still working, or are they tired? Are they contemporary? Are they working for all target markets?
4. How can the current position and execution be energized and updated without affecting their basic thrust? Are there ways to evolve the brand to keep it contemporary?

8

MANAGING BRAND SYSTEMS

The whole is necessarily prior in nature to the part.
—Aristotle

A house of brands is like a family; each needs a role and a relationship to others.
—Jeffrey Sinclair, brand strategist

TOWARD A SYSTEM OF BRANDS

There was a time, not too long ago, when most brands were singular symbols that stood for discrete products or services. Hewlett-Packard (HP) stood for test equipment, Miller stood for a specific beer, Cadillac stood for a certain kind of automobile, and AT&T represented telephone service.

Today the situation is far different. The fragmentation of mass markets has created multiple consumer contexts that often cry for identity modifications: Older consumers are looking for something different in a Lexus, for example, than are younger consumers. Companies sometimes have extended brands into product areas that are not clearly related. And many firms now have a bewildering combination of brands involving complex interrelationships.

As a result, companies often find themselves struggling to manage a number of different brand identities in several different situations and for a variety of audiences. For example, Hewlett-Packard must manage not only the HP mother brand in a host of products and markets, but also a complex set of interrelated brands for printers (for example, LaserJet, DeskJet, and DesignJet), software (HP VidJet Pro), test equipment (TestJet), hardware features (LaserJet's Resolution Enhancement) and many more contexts. Today's Miller beer customers need to sort through brands such as Miller Lite, Miller Genuine Draft, Miller Genuine Draft Lite, and Miller Super Dry. Cadillac has the Seville STS, Eldorado Touring Coupe, Fleetwood Sixty Special, Allante, DeVille and Brougham (to say nothing of branded features like Traction Control, Speed-Sensitive Suspension, Zebrano wood, the Cabriolet Roof, and dozens more). And AT&T has some 1,500 brand names to manage and coordinate.

This proliferation of brands and products within a single organization raises both concerns and challenges. When is a separate brand justifiable? How can a set of brands in overlapping contexts work together to create synergy? How can overlapping brands avoid undermining each other? How can the confusion factor be reduced? Brand complexity also means that a brand will have different roles to play, roles that need to be coordinated. Thus Pillsbury is a product-line brand in one context, an endorsing brand in another, and a corporation in still another. Is that wise? What are the risks? Finally, existing and future brands, subbrands, strategic brands, and so forth all need to be coordinated. This is not an easy job.

BRANDS SYSTEM OBJECTIVES

A key to managing brands in an environment of complexity is to consider them as not only individual performers but members of a system of brands that must work to support one another. A brand system can serve as a launching platform for new products or brands and as a foundation for all brands in the system. But in order for the system to thrive, it must have a reciprocal relationship with each of its brands; they must support the system as much as the system supports them.

Thinking in terms of a brand system also assists with resource allocation, because it makes clear that a brand creates value by helping other brands in addition to generating its own value proposition. Thus, a systems perspective adds the question of whether or not the whole system will benefit from a brand investment.

The goals of the system are qualitatively different from the goals of individual brand identities. The goals of the system include the following:

- *Exploit commonalities to generate synergy*. A set of brands may be related by brand name (Weight Watchers or Kraft) or a partial name (such as the Hewlett-Packard Jet series), yet have different identities because different products or markets are involved. The challenge is to exploit commonalities in order to generate synergy in the form of enhanced brand impact or reduced execution.
- *Reduce brand identity damage*. Differences between brand identities in different contexts and roles have the potential to undercut a brand. The challenge is to manage the system to avoid such undesirable outcomes.
- *Achieve clarity of product offerings*. A system goal should be to reduce confusion and achieve clarity among the product offerings.
- *Facilitate change and adaptation*. All brands need to adapt and change in response to external forces. A system can help manage the process so that needed changes will occur in a timely and effective manner.

- *Allocate resources*. Each brand role requires resources. Too often a brand investment decision is based on an insular analysis of the brand-related business, and therefore neglects the impact a brand can have on the other brands in the system and fails to adequately consider future brand roles.

FIGURE 8–1
Brand Hierarchies

CORPORATE BRAND	General Motors	Nestlé	HP
RANGE BRAND	Chevrolet	Carnation	HP Jet Brand
PRODUCT LINE BRAND	Chevrolet Lumina	Carnation Instant Breakfast	LaserJet IV
SUBBRAND	Chevrolet Lumina Sports Coupe	Carnation Instant Breakfast Swiss Chocolate	LaserJet IV SE
BRANDED FEATURE/ COMPONENT/SERVICE	Mr. Goodwrench Service System	NutraSweet	Resolution Enhancement

BRAND HIERARCHIES

As illustrated in Figure 8–1, brands within a system usually fall into a natural hierarchy. Brands at each level in the hierarchy have a particular role to play in the system, and (as will be explained later in this chapter, as well as in Chapter 9) brands on one level often have important relationships with those on other levels.

At the top of the hierarchy is the *corporate brand*, which identifies the corporation behind the product or service offering. The General Motors corporate brand, for example, represents the organization that makes GM automobiles, including the people, programs, systems, values, and culture. Nestlé and Hewlett-Packard also represent corporations.

A *range brand* is a brand that ranges over several product classes. Thus such corporate brands as GM, Nestlé, and Hewlett-Packard are themselves range brands. In addition, GM's Chevrolet is a brand that ranges over vans, trucks and cars, Nestlé's Carnation brand ranges over instant breakfast, evaporated milk, and infant formula, and HP's

Jet brand name covers such products as DeskJet, LaserJet, OfficeJet, FaxJet, and DesignJet.

Beneath the range brand, if one exists, is the *product line* brand. These are the brands associated with the organization's specific products: for example, Chevrolet Lumina, Carnation Instant Breakfast, and HP LaserJet IV. Basic product brands can be refined through *subbranding*, as with the LaserJet IV SE, Carnation Instant Breakfast Swiss Chocolate, and Chevrolet Lumina Sports Coupe. A second and third level of subbrands can additionally refine the product offering.

Finally, the brand can be further delineated by the branding of product features or of services associated with the product. Thus Chevrolet can offer the Mr. Goodwrench service system, Carnation can use NutraSweet, and LaserJet has Resolution Enhancement.

UNDERSTANDING BRAND ROLES

The first step toward managing a brand system is to inventory each brand in the brand portfolio. Each brand identity should be gauged, a task that can be done using the framework outlined in Chapters 3, 4, 5 and 6. In this chapter and Chapter 9, the focus will turn from individual brands to the relationship among brands in a system and the roles that each brand can play in different contexts. Understanding these roles and relationships is key to understanding how the system is structured and how it can be managed effectively.

Figure 8–2 provides an overview of the roles that brands can play in a system; these roles will be discussed in the balance of this chapter and in Chapter 9, where brand extensions are covered. The chapter will also discuss a key issue in developing brand systems: What is the optimal number of brands? At what point are there so many that the result is confusion, and communication resources are spread too thin? Leveraging the brand name in a variety of ways, including employing horizontal and vertical extensions and using range brands, category brands, and co-brands will be discussed in Chapter 9.

DRIVER ROLES

A driver brand is a brand that drives the purchase decision; its identity represents what the customer primarily expects to receive from

FIGURE 8–2
Brand Roles

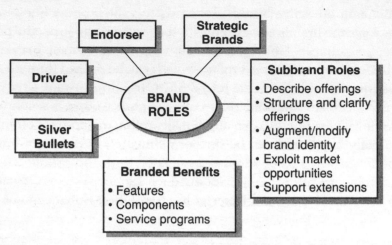

the purchase. The brand that plays the driver role represents the value proposition that is central to the purchase decision and use experience. For example, with the Gillette Sensor razor, customers are primarily buying the technology and performance represented by the Sensor name. As a result, the Sensor is the driver brand, and its name and symbol need to have a strong identity and clear visibility on the package, on the retail rack, and in the mind of the user. For Pillsbury Microwave Popcorn, the corporate name (Pillsbury) is the driver brand because it represents the value proposition offered (Pillsbury provides quality microwave products) while "Microwave Popcorn" is just a generic descriptor. In contrast, for General Mills PopSecret, the "PopSecret" name is the driver brand because it represents the primary value proposition offered by the product (a secret formula that delivers superior performance), while General Mills is just an endorser.

Now consider the BMW 700 series or Lexus 300. For most customers, BMW and Lexus are the driver brands because they are primarily buying the value proposition represented by BMW or Lexus, rather than that offered by a particular model. However, for the Ford Taurus and the Mazda Miata, there may be dual driver brands. The Taurus and Miata names and images might, for example, have more influence on the purchase decision and on defining the use experience than do the Ford and Mazda names but the latter may still play an active role. It may be important to learn the relative influence of each brand in such cases: For example, if the brand strategy was to make Taurus the driver brand but customers were buying the car based on its Ford identity, this would suggest that the Taurus communication program was inefficient.

Dual driver brands can cause conflicts if the brands belong to different companies. In the Intel Inside campaign (mentioned in Chapter 1), Compaq felt that Intel was becoming the driver and thus eclipsing the Compaq name. As a result, Compaq withdrew from the Intel Inside program, even though there were substantial costs and risks in doing so. Compaq wanted to make sure that it was the driver brand with respect to its computers.

The extent to which a brand plays a driver role will influence both the investment that the brand will need and the nature of the brand identity. The identity of a brand that has a primary driver role needs to generate real customer response, or it will not fulfill the key aspect of its role.

THE ENDORSER ROLE

In the endorser role, a brand provides support and credibility to the driver brand's claims. Because the corporate brand usually represents an organization with people, culture, values and programs, it is well suited to support a driver brand, and thus it often plays the endorser role.

For example, General Mills is an endorser for Cheerios, Gillette is an endorser for Sensor razors, and HP is an endorser for the Laser-Jet printer series. The primary role for these endorsers is to reassure the customer that the product will deliver the promised functional benefits because the company behind the brand is a substantial, successful organization that would only be associated with a strong product. The endorser might have special credibility with respect to certain areas of expertise (such as Betty Crocker in food products, or Honda in small engines), or it could have a broad umbrella effect (such as GE).

This reassurance is of particular importance when the product is new and untested. In fact, an endorser brand can sometimes fade after it provides this initial support. By acting as an endorser, for example, Levi's was able to lend credibility with both retailers and customers to the Dockers brand when it was first introduced. While the name Levi's means young, rugged, urban, male, and denim, however, Dockers is aimed at the middle-aged man who requires a different fit and style. There was a real risk that the Levi's user imagery would be diluted by Dockers and that, conversely, the Levi's image would inhibit Dockers from moving into relatively more fashionable clothing. As Dockers got stronger, it made sense to drop the Levi's endorsement.

The endorser, however, can still play a role later in the brand life cycle. Gillette, the endorser of Sensor, provides credibility that comes into play when a competitive move challenges the brand. For customers actively considering whether to stay with Sensor or change brands, this moment of evaluation can pivot on the extra substance provided by the Gillette name. Even so, it is still the driver brand, Sensor, that must play the major role in winning and keeping customers.

For durable and industrial products such as Hewlett-Packard test equipment, an endorser can signal that a substantial company will make sure that the brand is supported with service and parts backup. A customer investing a large amount of money or time in a product will want to know that resources and commitment are behind the brand. An endorser brand sends that signal.

A brand can perform both the endorser and driver roles when it simultaneously represents the value proposition provided by a product and the support of an organization. For example, for test equipment such as the HP Digital Voltmeter, HP (the organization) plays the role of the endorser and HP (the product) plays the role of the driver. For GE jet engines, GE is similarly a driver (as a product) and endorser (as an organization).

Brand-Bridging Strategies

The Levi's Dockers case illustrates *brand bridging*, where an endorser brand is used at the outset but then is allowed to fade from view in favor of the product.[1] Perhaps there is an image mismatch as in the Dockers case or maybe the subbrand would have more potential if not tied to a parent. Cup-A-Soup (Lipton's), Twinkies (Hostess), and Intensive Care (Vaseline) are other examples of products for

THE USE OF ENDORSER BRANDS

Two UK researchers examined the top twenty brands of each of the top twenty suppliers of two major grocery chains in England.[2] They coded the brand strategies of the four hundred brands into one of four categories. The first two categories (48 percent of the cases) involved a driver brand and no endorser brand. The remaining two categories (52 percent of the cases) involved an endorser brand role.

- *Corporate* (or subsidiary or division) *dominant* (driver) brand names constituted 16 percent of the cases. Examples included Shell Oil and Heinz Ketchup.
- *Brand dominant* names, which use only a single brand name, composed 32 percent of the cases. Procter & Gamble and Mars primarily use this strategy.
- *Endorsed brands*, where a driver brand is endorsed by a corporate (or subsidiary or division) name, made up 14 percent of the cases. Unilever and 3M employ this strategy.
- *Dual brands*, in which two names were given equal prominence, existed in 38 percent of the cases. Examples included Cadbury's Dairy Milk Chocolate and Friskies Gourmet A La Carte.

which the endorser brand was withdrawn or de-emphasized when the driver brand became strong enough to stand alone.

STRATEGIC BRANDS

Attempting to support and grow all brands is tempting. Such a policy, however, usually reduces the chances that really strong brands will be created or maintained. Instead, resources often are expended unproductively on problem brands. Thus a strategic imperative is to allocate resources by classifying brands into divestment candidates, milkers, and strategic brands.

A *divestment candidate* is a brand that faces an unattractive market with a weak brand position or that does not fit the future vision of the firm. Its market may be overcrowded, with squeezed margins and a flat or declining sales base, or the brand may lack points of differentiation and may require significant investment in order to create a winning strategy. There may be industry dynamics, such as changes in distribution, that can be expected to make the brand's position even worse. Finally, the brand may not fit the direction the firm wants to take in the future. In such situations, consideration should be given to divesting or killing the brand.

A *milker* is a brand that may be tired but has some real strengths. It may have a core customer base that will support reasonable margins. Because the brand can be maintained with minimal support, it can provide a positive cash flow to fund other brands.

A *strategic brand* is one that is important to the future performance of the organization. There are two reasons why a brand may be considered strategic. First, it may represent a meaningful quantity of sales and profits in the future. Perhaps it already is a large, dominant brand (sometimes termed a megabrand) and is projected to maintain or expand its position, or perhaps it is now a small brand but is projected to become a major one.

Second, the brand could also be a *linchpin* of other businesses or of a future vision of the firm. For example, IBM considers OS/2 a strategic brand not so much because of its sales potential but because it represents the future ability to control the operating platform of IBM computer lines. If another platform (such as Microsoft's Windows 95) becomes the standard, IBM will be much less of a force in the hardware and applications software businesses. For Oldsmobile, the Aurora is strategic in part because it represents the renewal of the Oldsmobile name. Aurora must succeed if Oldsmobile is to prosper. The Marriott Honored Guest Award branded program (which provides incentives for frequent visits) is strategic for Marriott because it represents a key area of differentiation in the hotel industry of the future.

The organization needs to commit whatever resources are required to fulfill a strategic brand's mission. The point of labeling a brand as strategic is so that its support does not get compromised when the sales and profit targets of problem brands are in jeopardy.

SUBBRAND ROLES

A subbrand is a brand that distinguishes a part of the product line within the brand system. For example, Buick uses the subbrand Roadmaster to distinguish a specific model (including its characteristics and its personality) from another model, such as the Riviera. Both are Buicks, and both enjoy the umbrella of the Buick name, but each is a distinct product.

The subbrand can be a driver or a descriptor brand. For example, with General Mills PopSecret, the subbrand has the driver role, while in the case of Pillsbury Microwave Popcorn, the subbrand is a descriptive brand name.

To develop a coherent and effective branding system, it is important to know the roles of a subbrand and determine what roles are involved in each context. A sound subbrand strategy involves several aspects. First, the subbrand should be consistent with and support the parent brand's identity. Second, the subbrand should add value by fulfilling one or more of the following tasks:

- Describe offerings
- Structure and clarify offerings
- Augment or modify the identity
- Exploit market opportunities
- Facilitate a horizontal or vertical extension strategy by qualifying or modifying the parent brand

A subbrand should also be cost justified in that it requires little investment to establish or the subbrand business is large enough to provide resources needed for its own development. The first three subbrand roles above will be discussed in the sections that follow. The last role, supporting horizontal and vertical extensions, will be covered in Chapter 9.

DESCRIBE OFFERINGS

A brand fulfilling the descriptor role communicates the product class, a feature, a target segment, or a function of a brand; for this reason, it usually is not established as a driver brand. In the case of Oral-B Tooth and Gum Care Toothpaste and Oral-B Anti-Plaque Rinse, the descriptive brands ("Tooth and Gum Care Toothpaste" and "Anti-Plaque Rinse") indicate the function of the product. Though the two Oral-B products are different (and will have different associations and value propositions), Oral-B is the driver brand, dominating the purchase decision and defining the use experience for both products.

The advantage of a descriptive brand is that the subbrand does not divert attention from or dilute the driver brand. For example, the "Low Fat" descriptive name in Hidden Valley Low Fat Dressings does not detract from the Hidden Valley brand name. The brand benefits from the advertising and shelf presence of the low fat line. If Hidden Valley were to give the low fat line its own brand name (as it tried to do with the "Take Heart" name that was a casualty of the U.S. Food and Drug Administration's objection to that name's implied health claim), the new name could possibly be used to extend the low fat line into categories other than dressings, but the role of the Hidden Valley name would be reduced to an endorser brand.

Just because a brand is a descriptor, however, does not mean that it cannot become a driver brand. Levi's Loose is a brand that describes its major characteristic and function. But it is also an important brand in its own right and, in particular, has characteristics and user imagery that are different than Levi's. Consequently, it is necessary for Loose to become a driver brand with its own identity.

Consider the following descriptive subbrands:

Purina dog food: Dog Chow, Dog Chow Little Bits, Hi-Pro, Fit & Trim, Puppy Chow, and Puppy Chow Chewy Morsels. The extent to which Purina is a driver or endorser varies; it is more of an endorser for the subbrands Puppy Chow and Dog Chow, but it plays a more significant driver role for Hi-Pro and Fit & Trim. Note that there are two levels of subbrands—for example, Puppy Chow and Puppy Chow Chewy Morsels. Note also that the descriptive subbrands describe user benefits (for example, Fit & Trim) or product attributes (Chewy Morsels).

GE light bulbs: Soft White, 3-way, Reading Lite, Crystal Clear, Long Life, Energy Choice, Party Bulb (colored bulbs), and Bug Lite.

Crest toothpaste: Tartar Control Crest, Tartar Control Crest with Fresh Mint Gel, Crest with Baking Soda, and Sparkle Crest for Kids.

PertPlus shampoo: Tear-free PertPlus for Kids, Dandruff Control PertPlus, PertPlus for permed or colored treated hair. Each product has versions for dry, normal, and oily hair. In this case the subbrand provides a structure; the customer first chooses a subbrand (such as Dandruff Control) and then selects a dry, normal or oily variant.

GE microwave ovens: GE Space Saver (mounts under cabinet), GE DualWave (has two levels inside the microwave), and GE Carousel (has a spinning food carousel). The subbrands describe product features.

Specify Segments

A descriptive subbrand can specify segments by suggesting that the products provide the functional and emotional benefits sought by that segment. A person can then more likely make the appropriate choice. For example, the names of the Microsoft Office and Microsoft Home software packages delineate between the business and personal computing audience segments.

Prefixes and Suffixes

Companies can create a family of descriptive brands by using a common prefix or suffix to relate subbrands. McDonald's is known for subbranding its products by adding the "Mc" prefix, as with McChicken Sandwich, Egg McMuffin, and McLean Deluxe. HP has used the suffix "Jet" in subbranding such products as its LaserJet, DeskJet, and DesignJet printers.

STRUCTURE AND CLARIFY OPTIONS

When companies create new products or services, they often do so either to meet the needs of a poorly served niche within their current market or to reach out to a niche that is as yet unserved by the company. Unfortunately, the more products a company offers, the more confused consumers may become. If the brand is seen in settings that seem inconsistent with its identity, customers will be unclear about what the brand stands for. Further, when the brand is introduced into a new niche to deliver a different set of functional and emotional benefits, it is more likely that a customer's expectations will not be met and dissatisfaction will result.

Subbrands provide a way to offer different products or serve different markets under one brand name while minimizing both consumer confusion and brand dilution. A subbrand presents the customer with a new option, but it also creates a structure that positions the option with respect to the brand. The customer understands that (1) the new product fits within the brand system and possesses at least some aspects of the brand identity, but that (2) the new product is different on key dimensions from other products in the brand system.

Forte Hotels

Consider the case of the Forte Hotels Group in Britain. Over the course of several years, Trusthouse Forte acquired a number of hotels in Britain, which were offered under several overlapping brand names. As a group, the hotels reflected a wide spectrum of accommodation types, ranging from basic to luxury. As a result, customers experiencing Forte in one context formed expectations that were not met in the next context. Some customers were disappointed when expected amenities were absent, and others were shocked when the price was far above what they had expected. The net result was both confusion and dissatisfaction.

In 1989 Forte decided to develop five distinct subbrands, all under the Forte hotel brand:

- Forte Travellodge—Roadside budget hotels that offer simple, modern rooms and are conveniently situated along major routes
- Forte Posthouse—Accessible three-star modern hotels offering comfortable rooms, good restaurants, and meeting facilities at competitive prices
- Forte Crest—High-quality modern business hotels that specialize in personal service and are mostly situated in major city centers throughout Europe
- Forte Heritage—A collection of traditional British inns offering a combination of comfort, personal hospitality, and character
- Forte Grand—A collection of first-class international hotels offering traditional European standards of comfort, style, and service

In addition, the Forte name was subtly affixed to exclusive hotels in the portfolio, such as the Hyde Park in London and the George V in Paris.

This subbranding strategy brought clarity and purpose to a diverse set of products. Each new brand created an identity with meaning and personality attached to it; by comparison, the brands that were replaced were weak and confused. Now expectations, a key element in service business management, could be managed so that customers were less likely to be disappointed or confused.

This strategy has also allowed the development of the Forte brand, which can then support cross-selling and a reservation system, both potentially critical elements in the competitive hotel industry. It may also play an endorser role as customers look for credibility signals and demand consistency in service within the subbrand groupings.

AUGMENT/MODIFY THE IDENTITY BY CHANGING ASSOCIATIONS

A third role for subbranding is to create the associations needed to compete in an attractive new product market. An analysis of a new business area often shows that the development of a new brand would be prohibitively expensive. All too often, though, an existing brand is inadequate for the new context, as its associations fail to provide the needed advantage—indeed, they might even be a liability. Further, stretching the brand into a new context risks diluting the brand's existing product class or attribute associations.

A practical solution to this dilemma is the use of a subbrand. When subbranding works well, it can draw from the parent brand the reassurance of a familiar name plus other intangibles and personality dimensions. The subbrand allows greater latitude in adding associations and reduces the risk of diluting the parent brand. In essence, there is an internally created co-brand or dual brand.

Support a New Concept or Target

Sure antiperspirant has been marketed by Procter & Gamble to a dual-gender audience and is an active competitor in the category. When P&G wanted to use the Sure name to market a deodorant specifically for males, a subbrand—Sure ProStick—was employed. The ProStick name helped to foster male associations with the new product without threatening the gender-neutral associations of the Sure brand. The Sure brand, meanwhile, provided a name that was established in the category.

Strengthen/Protect Existing Associations

Smucker's jams have always meant high quality as well as home-made taste. However, a "100 percent fruit" claim has become a quality cue in this product category, and competitors using this claim have become a threat to Smucker's. In part to retain the high-end position, Smucker's has introduced a series of jams called Smucker's

Simply Fruit, which it describes as "Just about the closest thing to fresh fruit you'll ever taste." Putting out its own 100 percent fruit product subbrand has augmented the Smucker's identity, thereby solidifying the brand's quality position and reducing the ability of competitors to exploit that market niche.

Soften a Strong Association

A strong brand such as Apple, Harley-Davidson, or Saturn usually has a clear, well-articulated identity and personality. Ironically, these strengths can turn into liabilities when the brand wants to extend into new product areas or new markets. A brand like Kleenex, for example, has such a close association with one product class that it has a reduced ability to stretch into other product classes. A subbrand can help a brand break out of this box.

Consider the case of Apple. From the beginning, an Apple computer's greatest assets were its fun personality and its user friendliness. The Apple Macintosh was thought to be for the home or school (where a playful, casual spirit was appropriate), or it was for specialized advertising or design situations (where offbeat people needed to be creative). Even physically, the Macintosh did not look like it would fit into a business environment. As a result, Apple struggled for a decade to be taken seriously in the corporate world, which was at that time more comfortable with the IBM feel and look. A partial solution for Apple was to create the Mac Quadra line of computers, which were designed to look more like business computers. The Mac Quadra associations have softened the strong Apple personality, making it more acceptable to business settings and applications.

Modifier and Modified Concepts

C. W. Park, Sung Youl Jun, and Allan Shocker provide insight into how subbranding is interpreted by comparing brands that are modifiers (Kellogg's is the modifier in Kellogg's Corn Flakes) to brands that are modified (Corn Flakes is modified in Kellogg's Corn Flakes).[3] (See the composite terms in Figure 8–3.) Comparing the brand names Slim-Fast (which connotes low calorie and convenience) and Godiva (which connotes good taste, richness, and luxury) in both the modifier and modified roles, they found that, while characteristics and attitudes toward both the modified and modifier brands affected the composite brand, the characteristics of the modified brand had more influence (in

terms of both perceived attribute importance and attribute performance ratings) than the characteristics of the modifier. (Thus an
"apartment dog" would be perceived first and foremost as a dog, albeit
a type of dog that would fit into an apartment living.) For Slim-Fast
cake mix by Godiva (where Slim-Fast was the modified concept), the
low-calorie attribute was rated higher in importance and in performance than for the Godiva cake mix by Slim-Fast (where Slim-Fast
was the modifier); the reverse was found for the attributes richness
and luxury.

FIGURE 8–3
The Role of the Subbrand as Modifier

COMPOSITE TERM	MODIFIER	MODIFIED CONCEPT
Apartment dog	Apartment	Dog
Pet rock	Pet	Rock
Slim-Fast cake mix by Godiva	Godiva	Slim-Fast cake mix
Godiva cake mix by Slim Fast	Slim Fast	Godiva cake mix
Healthy Choice from Kellogg's	Kellogg's	Healthy Choice

Further, they found that the modified brand was the dominant concept in memory and was affected by the composite more than the
modifier brand. (Thus the concept of pet rocks may affect the way
people think of rocks more than the way they think about pets.) The
Slim-Fast by Godiva composite brand enhanced attitudes toward
Slim-Fast diet products (they rated higher on good taste and luxury),
but not attitudes toward the Godiva modifier. When a less appealing
modifier, Slim-Fast by Chunky, was used, the Chunky modifier was
similarly unaffected by the composite. Thus a modifier—and therefore an endorser—can be expected to risk less and receive less benefit
from a composite brand.

EXPLOIT MARKET OPPORTUNITIES

A subbranding strategy can allow a firm to engage in *strategic opportunism*, a management strategy which emphasizes detecting and

responding quickly to opportunities that emerge in the market.[4] When an emerging niche is detected, a subbrand tailored for that segment can be developed—usually with a minimum of investment. If the segment grows, the subbrand can become the basis for a long-lasting business; if it has a short life, the subbrand can be allowed to die without putting the core brand in jeopardy. Strategic opportunism, supported by a subbranding strategy, provides a way for a firm to be flexible and quick on its feet when coping with a dynamic and uncertain environment.

Firms such as Ralston Purina in pet foods, General Mills in cereals, Ziff Communications in magazines, and Nike in footwear all engage in branding policies that represent strategic opportunism. While other pet-food firms support and build their key brands over time, Ralston looks for trends and gimmicks that will appeal to a niche segment. Thus it has brands like Deli-Cat, Kitt'N Kaboodle, and Mature. In cereal, General Mills has introduced brands like Triangles, Oatmeal Crisp, and Cinnamon Toast in order to appeal to a current taste or trend. In computer magazines, Ziff has exploited apparent opportunities by introducing an on-line edition of its *PC Magazine* as well as two magazines for the home computer market to go with its stable of computer publications.

Nike, a company particularly good at strategic opportunism, introduces hundreds of shoes each year for some thirty sports. By applying its skills in product design and customer research, it identifies segments and develops responsive subbrands. This strategy is supported by the development of strong emotional ties forged by both innovative products and athlete endorsements. The new products tend to be so congruent with the target segment that customers sense that Nike is reaching out to them. The athlete endorsers provide instant credibility and a brand personality. Thus in basketball, for example, Nike has not only Air Jordan (Michael Jordan) but Force (David Robinson and Charles Barkley) and Flight (Scottie Pippen).

SUPPORT VERTICAL AND HORIZONTAL EXTENSIONS

The role of a subbrand in supporting extensions, both horizontal (where the brand is used in a different product class) and vertical (where the brand is extended up or down with respect to quality) will be discussed in Chapter 9, which focuses on leveraging the brand name.

BRANDING BENEFITS

A problem facing many brands is that their identity is difficult to communicate because it lacks distinctiveness, credibility, or memorability. The solution may lie in branding features, components, or service programs that provide customer benefits.

BRANDING A FEATURE

Oral-B has long been at the high end of the toothbrush market as "the brand more dentists use." In the early 1990s, though, its position came under attack from Johnson & Johnson's Reach toothbrush and two new entrants—Colgate's Precision and Procter & Gamble's Crest. A sleepy category quickly became vicious. Oral-B responded with a new product given a descriptive brand name: the Advantage Plaque Remover toothbrush. Two key features of its unique design were themselves branded—the Power Tip bristles at the end of the brush, and the Action Cup shape that conformed to teeth and gum contours. Oral-B had already branded the Indicator bristles which changed color when the brush becomes worn. Figure 8–4 illustrates the role that the branded features play in the Oral-B position.

When designing a new or improved product, there should be one or more design features that enable the brand to excel. The task then usually is to communicate those features. The problem is that, however important these features are to the product designers, there is likely a monumental lack of interest among the target audience. Even when the communication registers, it can sound like typical puffery and thus lack credibility. A name such as Action Cup provides a way to crystallize one of several detailed features, making it easier to understand, accept, and remember.

When AT&T developed improved voice quality, they labeled it "Your True Voice." The act of branding this feature was critical to communicating it successfully. They then leveraged the True term with services such as AT&T True USA Savings (which offers a 20 percent discount if you spend $25 a month on AT&T long distance services)

FIGURE 8–4
Oral-B Branded Features

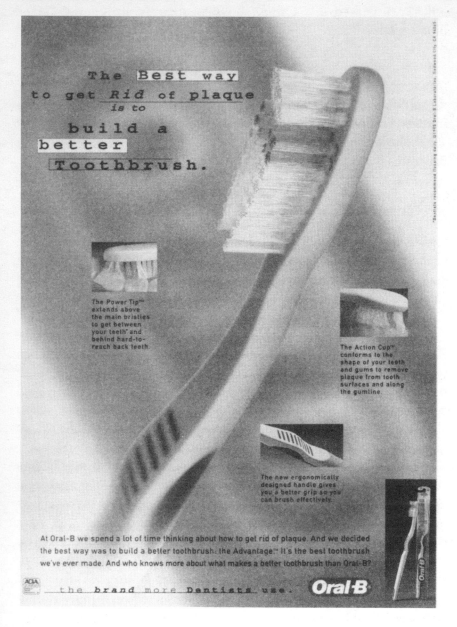

and AT&T TrueWorld Savings (a program that, for a $3 monthly fee, allows customers to call anyone in a selected country at a reduced per minute rate). Both were created in response to MCI programs (Friends and Family and Friends Around the World, respectively). The True USA Savings and related programs are credited with reversing a steady decline in market share for AT&T.

The very act of branding a feature gives it credibility and enhances the ability of that feature to differentiate and add value. A study by Carpenter, Glazier, and Nakamoto found that the inclusion of a branded attribute (such as "Alpine Class" fill for a down jacket, "Authentic Milanese" for pasta, and "Studio Designed" for compact disc players) dramatically affected customer preference toward premium-priced brands.[5] Respondents were able to justify the higher price because of the branded attributes. Remarkably, the effect occurred even when the respondents were given information implying that the attribute was not relevant to their choice.

BRANDING A COMPONENT

An approach similar to branding a new feature is to brand a component or ingredient or, more commonly, to make visible a component or ingredient that has an established brand name. Thus Kellogg's Pop-Tarts saw sales sharply increase when it added Smucker's fruit filling. Other examples include Ben & Jerry's Heath Bar Crunch Ice Cream, Nestlé's Lite Ice Cream Bars with NutraSweet, Pillsbury's Chocolate Deluxe Brownies with Nestlé syrup, Chicken of the Sea's lunch packs with Kraft condiments, and Gateway computers with "Intel Inside." Sunkist and Ocean Spray are also among the brands that have seen widespread use as ingredients.

Component brands are not restricted to food products. Timberland boots, for example, feature a Gore-Tex fabric bootie and Cordura nylon. These branded components bring credibility to the claims by Timberland that their boots are waterproof and lightweight. In contrast, a simple statement by Timberland in its advertising that its boots are waterproof and lightweight because they are made of the finest materials would be much less differentiating and persuasive.

Adding a branded component can provide a point of differentiation because of the associations that consumers already have with the component brand. Thus, when Hershey's chocolate morsels are featured as part of a Betty Crocker cake mix, consumers automatically make the chocolate associations that Hershey's has spent years developing. In addition, if the perceived quality of Hershey's chocolate is relatively high, it has the potential to enhance the perceived quality of Betty Crocker products.

A branded ingredient, however, adds value only when consumers perceive it to be superior to what they already expect. In one study conducted by Research International, branded cookies were evaluated by customers with and without a premium brand chocolate chip ingredient. The branded chocolate chip helped Nabisco and Keebler achieve a higher price (or a higher share at the same price), but it did not help Pepperidge Farm. This was because consumer expectations of the Pepperidge Farm ingredients were already so high that the branded ingredient did not provide added value (although it did not hurt either).

Branding a component also provides some cost benefits for both the core brand and the component brand. Savings are realized for each organization because the costs of manufacturing and advertising are usually shared between the two. As a result, each enjoys the benefits of more exposure at a reduced cost.

BRANDING A SERVICE PROGRAM

Branding a service is an often-overlooked way to build brand strength. Hyatt has branded several services for its business travelers, including the following:

- *Hyatt Business Plan*—Provides work space, a phone, and a fax machine in your hotel room, plus access to copiers, printers, and business supplies right on your floor
- *Hyatt Gold Passport*—Allows customers to earn points redeemable for travel awards
- *Touch and Go*—Automatic check-in via an 800 number
- *Regency Club*—Access to a private floor with special services
- *Meeting Connection*—A team that helps plan meetings

Hyatt has even packed all five programs into a range brand called the *Business Portfolio*, "where we go the extra mile to keep you up to speed." It provides a focus for the relationship between the business customer and Hyatt.

Branding a service can be especially powerful when selling to an organization. Thus Levi-Link brands a set of services which link Levi Strauss to its retail customers. The Levi-Link brand gives this set of services more cohesiveness, visibility and impact.

SILVER BULLETS

A *silver bullet* is a subbrand or branded benefit that is employed as a vehicle for changing or supporting the brand image of a parent brand. The term was first coined by Regis McKenna, who observed that the images of corporate brand names in the high-tech world were influenced by key products. While Regis called products such as these silver bullets, the focus here is on brands.

Silver bullets among brands are not hard to find. The Sony Walkman supports the innovative miniaturization identity that is central to Sony. The Mazda Miata, the Dodge Viper, the Ford Taurus, and the Mercedes 206 all played silver-bullet roles for their parent brands. For example, the Miata created a strong, sporty personality that influenced perceptions of Mazda, and the Taurus showed that Ford could design and build innovative cars. Asahi Dry (mentioned in Chapter 4), a dramatic success in the mature Japanese beer market, transformed Asahi from a tired, faltering also-ran into an exciting, innovative, and successful company.

John Fluke, a big name in hand-held meters, entered a new business when it acquired the oscilloscope line of a major European firm. A resulting branding problem was how to change the Fluke image so that it meant oscilloscopes in addition to hand-held meters. A new product—a hand-held oscilloscope termed the Oscillometer—provided a vehicle to augment the Fluke brand identity. The key for Fluke was to recognize the silver bullet role of the Oscillometer and to adjust its presentation and communication program accordingly.

Because a silver bullet has a role that extends beyond supporting its own business, it deserves extra resource allocation in the form of advertising and/or product development dollars. Firms should beware of the bottom-line trap—the tendency to justify any investment in a sub-

SAN JOSE SHARKS

The city of San Jose is often perceived as a rather nondescript bedroom community with a deteriorating, ill-defined downtown that is very much in the shadow of San Francisco. In reality, however, San Jose has a lot going for it. With the support of a progressive, competent city government, it has revitalized its downtown with a set of hotels, a convention center, and a new arena that would be the envy of any city.

The challenge for the city is to communicate the reality and promise of San Jose to convention planners and to firms that are relocating. Enter the San Jose Sharks, a major-league professional hockey team. The Sharks are doing for San Jose what millions of advertising dollars never could accomplish, changing San Jose into a "major league city." The Sharks thus are San Jose's silver bullet.

The San Jose Sharks sell out all of their games, and there is a waiting list for season tickets, even though the team rarely won a game during its first three years of existence. Further, Sharks memorabilia is sold across North America and outsells the memorabilia of all other hockey teams and of most professional franchises in any sport. This is in part due to a dramatic logo (shown in Figure 8–5, it features a shark biting through a hockey stick) and a spunky, fun personality. The remarkable part of the Sharks' success is its impact in attracting conventions, tourist flow, and even major business operations to San Jose. It has measurably changed the image of the city.

FIGURE 8–5
The San Jose Sharks Logo

Reproduced with permission of the San Jose Sharks.

brand on the basis of its ability to pay off on that subbrand's bottom line. If the role of the Oscillometer is to affect the image of John Fluke, extra resources that do not "pay off" in Oscillometer sales and profits are merited because of its role in the branding system. Identifying silver bullets thus becomes very important.

BRANDED BENEFITS AS SILVER BULLETS

A branded benefit (feature, component or service) can also play a silver-bullet role by supporting the image of the brand to which it is attached. Thus it can do more than help communicate a functional benefit.

The Action Cup and Indicator bristles play a silver-bullet role for Oral-B toothbrushes and the Oral-B brand by reinforcing the technological edge that Oral-B products provide. The True brand for AT&T also reinforces the key innovation image of AT&T. "The Room that Works," a hotel room designed for the business traveler, plays a silver bullet role for Marriott, AT&T, and Steelcase, the co-developers.

A large health maintenance organization (HMO) might use silver bullets to attack an image problem among its members and prospective members, who perceive that the HMO is an impersonal bureaucracy that emphasizes efficiency but lacks human compassion for its patients. The perception is based in part on a semiautomated appointment system (instead of a doctor's secretary) and a system in which same-day services are provided by a team of physicians rather than by a patient's regular doctor.

The image problem could be attacked in part by branding ongoing programs and using them as silver bullets to impact the total brand identity. For example, the HMO's same-day appointment system could be given a brand name (such as Urgent Care) and an identity that emphasizes the responsiveness of the HMO to the need to receive same-day personal contact with a physician ("We are there for you"). The brand might be given a light, colorful symbol (a cartoon owl, for example) and a friendly personality to enhance the ability of the brand to affect the HMO image.

Similarly, a program in which elderly people with heart risk factors meet regularly might be given a brand name (such as HeartClub) and a personality that reflects the care and support this group is receiving. A symbol (such as a pair of cheerful heart-shaped characters) could represent the support and feelings engendered by the program. These brands and perhaps others could be the silver bullets needed to modify the identity of the HMO.

HOW MANY BRANDS?

General Motors has thirty-three brand names, including seven for Buick alone (Roadmaster, Park Avenue, Riviera, Century, Skylark, Regal, and LeSabre). BMW and Mercedes basically each have one; their models are indicated by numbers (such as the BMW 300 series). Does Buick have too many? BMW too few? What is the right number?

Deciding whether to introduce a new brand name involves gauging the trade-off between the value that the brand might create and the cost that it might incur. For some brand roles, such as descriptive or ingredient/feature brands, the brand may require little investment to establish because the name itself communicates adequately. In other cases, the cost and risk is high and a substantial payoff must be expected. The four questions posed below help structure the issues.

1. Is THE Brand Sufficiently Different to Merit a New Name?

A new name is usually worthwhile when there is a need to signal that the product is not just a variant of what went before. Consider two new subbrands of the 1980s: Ford Taurus and Mazda Miata. Both Taurus and Miata were new designs and represented departures from the associations previously established by their respective endorser brands. Saturn (described in Chapter 2) also illustrates how a new product representing a departure from the past will justify a new name.

In contrast, when Oldsmobile wanted to appear new in 1992, it also considered a new brand name—but it lacked a new car. To create a new name without a new product would have been a waste and perhaps a joke. The brand was in a bad situation, but a new name alone was not the answer. Fortunately, in 1994 the Oldsmobile family actually did get a new car with, appropriately, a new name (the Aurora).

2. Will a New Name Really Add Value?

Because some firms do not take full advantage of existing core brands, they end up with too many different brands to support and manage. 3M was one firm that had this problem. Their decentralized, entrepreneurial organization encouraged a proliferation of names. Each new product group wanted a name that was specifically conceived for its product; the result was that a host of brands emerged each year. To place a lid on new names, a high-level committee of top executives began to meet regularly to approve any new names. Their actions reduced the number of new names to a trickle. One key criterion was that the new brand name must really add value over the coupling of an existing 3M brand (such as 3M or Scotch) with a descriptive brand name.

Established brand names, including a corporate name, can often be stretched by using descriptive subbrand names. GE is an example of a firm that follows this practice (such as for GE Jet Engines). Similarly, Hewlett-Packard identifies most of its test equipment line with descriptive subbrands attached to the HP corporate brand name.

3. Will an Existing Brand Be Placed at Risk if It Is Used on a New Product?

This question reflects the second criterion used at 3M. If the use of an existing brand risks damaging or confusing its core identity or perceived quality, then there is an argument for a new brand. Suntory has its name on a host of products, including soft drinks, beers and fine whiskey; the name is further supported by widespread use of event sponsorships and advertising. Nevertheless, Suntory is still protective of its name. When the firm started a major fast-food chain that served fried chicken, hamburgers, and pizza, it decided that the chain was not upscale enough to carry the Suntory name.

4. Will the Business Support a New Brand Name?

A third 3M criterion is that the new business must be large enough to support the necessary brand-building investment. In addition, there must be an expectation that the brand will be around for a long time so that if the name is successfully established, the investment will be worthwhile. The fact is that it is costly to establish and maintain a brand name, and the cost is always underestimated.

TOWARD A BRANDING STRATEGY

In many organizations today there is a proliferation of brands and brand extensions and a bewildering set of overlapping and often inconsistent brand roles. Worse, even if there is a strategy for a brand in one context, there often is no strategy which coordinates other brand contexts and roles (or it is woefully inadequate). There is no concept of how the brands and their roles fit together. Nor is there a plan for the future; each branding decision is made separately, even though the sequence of brand extensions will affect the success and ultimate perceptions of the brands and their relationships. Also lacking is a conceptual structure to help customers deal with the resulting confusion.

Seeing a set of brands as a brand system helps to create an effective and efficient branding strategy. Brands do not exist in isolation, but rather relate to other brands in the system. An important role for a brand is to help support other brands in the system and to avoid creating confusion or using an inconsistent identity. The idea is to create synergy and clarity and to avoid conflicting messages. In the following chapter, a methodology is intro- duced that helps to ensure that the systems perspective is being considered.

QUESTIONS TO CONSIDER

1. Inventory your brands. Sort out the brand hierarchy. For each brand identity, examine the different brand contexts (different products and different markets). In which is the brand a driver brand, and in which is it an endorser? Is there a risk of confusion and inconsistency? What can be done about it? How do the brands relate to each other? Which should be supporting other brands? Which have the potential to confuse?

2. Is there confusion about each brand's offerings? Could subbranding help clarify this? Are there contexts in which the brand identity does not quite fit? Would a subbrand to modify the brand identity be helpful? Could subbrands help the brand be more responsive to emerging marketing opportunities?

3. What are the silver bullets for each brand? Would it be useful to brand a feature, component, or service program? Or to exploit an existing branded feature, component, or service program as a silver bullet?
4. What are the strategic brands—those that are important because of their current or potential size, or because they will affect the future of other important brands?
5. Are there too many brands? Too few? What criteria are in place to decide whether a new brand should be added?

9

LEVERAGING THE BRAND

The great thing in this world is not so much where we are, but in what direction we are moving.

—Oliver Wendell Holmes

Bic has defined its business not as pens but as disposability. Clairol has defined its business to be items that offer a head-care benefit. Sunkist has limited its extension to products which have an orange flavor association.

—Edward Tauber, brand strategist

THE HEALTHY CHOICE STORY

ConAgra is a diversified food company made up of major independent operating companies that market an array of branded products. These companies include Armour-Swift Eckrich, Beatrice Cheese, ConAgra Frozen Foods, ConAgra Poultry Company, Golden Valley Microwave Foods, and Hunt-Wesson. Products encompass shelf-stable and frozen prepared foods, dairy and deli items, processed meats, and poultry and seafood products. Major brands include Hunt's, Wesson, Manwich, Peter Pan, Orville Redenbacher, Act II, Swiss Miss, La Choy, Healthy Choice, Banquet, Morton, Patio, Country Skillet, Chun King, Kid Cuisine, Armour, Swift Premium, Eckrich, Butterball, Country Line, Treasure Cave, Miss Wisconsin, Reddi-Wip, Singleton and Taste'O Sea.[1]

In 1985 ConAgra's president, Mike Harper, had a heart attack and became motivated to change his diet. He was stunned to learn that many processed foods—including those made by ConAgra—were high in fat and sodium and thus were unwise selections for anyone concerned about heart disease. The options in the supermarket for those looking for heart-healthy food were limited. The specialty products that did apply had a justifiable reputation for tasting bad.

Consumers by and large were unconcerned, in part because they were not sensitive to heart risk factors, and in part because the fat and sodium content of brands was communicated only in fine print on packages. Heart risk factors were becoming more widely known, however, and the concerned segment was growing. Unfortunately the processed food industry had yet to get the message.

As a result of Mike Harper's wake-up call, ConAgra changed its mission from "We build on basics" to "Feeding people better," and it made a commitment to market even more nutritious and healthy consumer products. The cornerstone of the strategy was first laid by ConAgra Frozen Foods with its 1987 introduction of Healthy Choice Frozen Dinners. The brand's objective was to minimize fat and control the level of other undesirable components like cholesterol and sodium. However, the products also had to have a taste that was competitive with other national brands. The core identity was great taste and good nutrition.

Purchasers of Weight Watchers and Stouffer's Lean Cuisine products, which were positioned more as weight control brands, represented the target market because heretofore many of the consumers interested in weight control were the same individuals that were attracted to overall health. Healthy Choice appealed to this large and growing subsegment (see Figure 9–1).

The Healthy Choice frozen food line was successful for several reasons. First, its products did not have a taste liability; they were at least comparable to competitors on that key dimension. Second, because

FIGURE 9–1
Healthy Choice ad

Reproduced with permission of ConAgra Frozen Foods.

of its established lines, ConAgra Frozen Foods had access to distribution channels and thus could be sure that major supermarket chains would carry the new products. Third, the timing was just right: Healthy Choice appeared just when the segment interested in health and heart risk factors was growing from a small segment into a large mainstream market. Fourth, Healthy Choice's competitors were committed to a different, more narrow position (weight control) and were slow to respond, in part because of their prior success. Weight Watchers, in particular, was not motivated to undercut its franchise by leading the market into another direction.

Soon after Healthy Choice appeared, competitors did retaliate with subbrands such as Stouffer's Right Course and LeMenu Light Style. Each, however, had positioning problems. The Right Course subbrand was tied to Stouffer's and appealed mainly to Stouffer's users. LeMenu Light Style targeted Weight Watchers and was not well positioned to compete with Healthy Choice; in fact, it later was reintroduced as LeMenu Healthy. In contrast, Healthy Choice was a new brand that could develop a strong position with appeal to a broad market.

Later other subbrands, such as Kraft Budget Gourmet Hearty & Healthy, Tyson Healthy Portion, and (finally, in mid-1992) Weight Watchers Smart Ones, were introduced by competitors. These latecomers had the difficult job of enticing away members of the now-established Healthy Choice segment. Meanwhile, Healthy Choice continued to expand and improve its dinner and entree lines with offerings such as Fiesta Chicken Fajitas, Country Glazed Chicken, and Cheese French Bread Pizza.

The power of a brand to extend itself depends on the breadth of product lines that can be related to the core brand identity in terms of the latter's value proposition and basis of relationship. The Healthy Choice core identity of taste and nutrition was not tied to the frozen food area, but traveled well throughout the store. In this case, the core identity was broad enough to provide the foundation for a powerful range brand.

Thus other ConAgra operating companies started to look for product areas to which they could apply the Healthy Choice brand and identity. Product classes in which no brand featured a strong heart-healthy dimension were prime candidates. Frightened competitors nervously reexamined their brand offerings and product class profile to see if they were vulnerable; the answer was usually yes. A flurry of new products—often using subbrands like Lite, Fresh, Healthy, Right Choice, or Fat Free—attempted to preempt or respond to Healthy Choice. Because of its strong identity and presence in other food categories, however, Healthy Choice was formidable even when others developed a "healthy" subbrand.

In 1995 Healthy Choice had an estimated sales at retail of $1,275 million, up from $858 million in 1993, $471 million in 1991, and $30 million in 1989.[2] The brand appeared on more than three hundred products, including soups (the Healthy Choice soup line was named as product of the year in 1992 by *Progressive Grocer* magazine), ice cream (the best-selling national brand of light ice cream), and cold cuts.

Healthy Choice is an example of a brand identity that adds value over a broad product range. Whereas in the 1980s Weight Watchers was one of the most successful new range brands, Healthy Choice earned that claim in the 1990s.

THE KINGSFORD CHARCOAL STORY

One of Clorox's major brands is Kingsford Charcoal, which dominates the $300 million retail charcoal market with a nearly 60 percent share. Kingsford's core identity is quality charcoal (quality and performance are part of the identity for all Clorox brands), while its extended identity includes barbecues and summer relaxation. The premium brand in the market, Kingsford commands a price that is sometimes double that of private labels. Indeed, having a Kingsford bag is prestigious enough for some users that they will refill the bag with private-label goods—just as others might put department-store jewelry in a Tiffany box. Over time, Kingsford has leveraged its name by engaging in numerous line extensions. In the process, some branding issues have emerged with respect to when Kingsford should be used as an endorser brand and when it should be the driver brand.

In 1980, Clorox introduced Match-Light instant charcoal with Kingsford as an endorser rather than a driver brand. The objective was to provide Kingsford with some distance in case Match-Light did not perform well. Because the Match-Light briquette was pretreated with a controlled amount of lighter fluid, it was easy to light, quick to heat up, and ready to cook in half the normal time. The brand in fact did perform very well, and it seems possible in retrospect that if a descriptive subbrand had been used (such as Kingsford Instant Light), Kingsford would have gained visibility and received more credit in customer's eyes for the Match-Light success. Further, the Kingsford line would have more clarity.

In 1986 Kingsford with Mesquite Briquettes were introduced, followed by Kingsford BBQ Bag Briquettes (a 2.5 pound single-use pretreated bag). Both of these products used Kingsford as the driver brand. Kingsford Charcoal Lighter appeared in 1989, also with Kingsford as the driver rather than an endorser. Interestingly, consumer research found that many thought that they were buying Kingsford Charcoal Lighter even before it was introduced. In 1992 the Kingsford Pro-Charcoal Grill was marketed; the product's short life reflected the fact that Clorox lacked distribution clout in the grill area.

When one of the established barbeque sauce brands (KC Masterpiece, a regional premium brand) was acquired in 1986 by Clorox and taken national, another branding issue arose: Should Kingsford become an endorser to KC Masterpiece, thereby gaining more visibility and reinforcing its position as a quality product for the barbecue experience? Certainly, Kingsford did fit the category and would provide a quality association, and the endorsement would have provided added visibility for the Kingsford name. However, it was perceived that the corporate brand personality of Kingsford could have a negative impact on the strong, folksy KC Masterpiece personality.

Maintaining its focus on its core charcoal business and its quality position, Kingsford has now developed an improved briquette that lights faster and burns even longer than existing products. The improved product has been phased in along with an imprinted K on each briquette. Thus the Kingsford briquette will now be distinguishable from others and will have the élan of having a brand name on it—a powerful signal in itself.

Kingsford is an example of a disciplined brand. While there have been numerous line extensions, the brand has not strayed far from its identity.

LEVERAGING THE BRAND

One recipe for strategic success is to create and leverage assets. With its awareness, perceived quality, associations and customer loyalty, a brand is usually the most powerful asset that a firm owns. A strategic question, then, is how that brand can be leveraged to create larger and stronger business entities.

Figure 9–2 suggests a variety of ways. The simplest is to create line extensions within the existing product class. Leveraging the brand up or down in the existing product class is another option that often is strategically necessary but has significant risks. Brand extensions—that is, extending the brand into other product classes—are the ultimate way to leverage. As Figure 9–2 also suggests, brand extensions can be made on an ad hoc basis or be driven by a strategy to create a range brand. Co-branding is another leverage option.

FIGURE 9–2
Leveraging the Brand

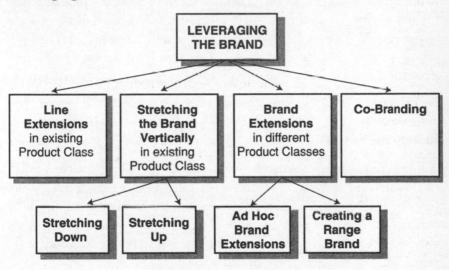

LINE EXTENSIONS

A line extension is a new version of the product within the same product class. New flavors, new packaging options, or new sizes are all line extensions. Line extensions can increase costs without compensating increases in volume and make the brand less focused and more difficult to communicate.[3] However, line extensions can also expand the user base, provide variety, energize the brand, manage innovation, and block or inhibit competitors.

EXPANDING THE USER BASE

Brand-loyal customers may view a brand as serving their particular, unique needs—a basic flavor of Gatorade, for example, may appeal to them. However, customers without these unique needs may feel that the brand is not for them. Thus a strong brand may foster loyalty, but in an exclusionary way. A line extension can overcome this obstacle by expanding the brand's appeal. For example, Cheerios is seen as a health-oriented breakfast staple, but Honey Nut Cheerios reaches out to those who prefer presweetened cereals. A number of food manufacturers have introduced low-fat versions of their products, thus breaking down a use barrier that exists for many health-conscious consumers.

A line can also be extended by adding a functional benefit to a product: for example, a convertible version of a car, a squeeze bottle for margarine, or a conveniently located mini-version of a fast-food restaurant. With these added functional benefits, the brand is in a position to attract new customers. The result of an on-target line extension can be a new but highly loyal segment that is resistant to competitive offerings.

PROVIDING VARIETY

A line extension can also give loyal users a way to enjoy variety without switching brands. For instance, new entrées in the Healthy Choice frozen-dinner line allow customers to change their daily eating routine while remaining loyal to the brand. And a baking-soda version of Crest gave consumers the chance to try a new toothpaste craze without buying a new brand.

ENERGIZING A BRAND

A line extension can energize a brand, making it more relevant, interesting, and visible. In doing so it can create a basis for differentiation, make communication efforts more effective, and stimulate sales. Consider Hidden Valley Honey Dijon Ranch salad dressing, which revitalized a stagnant (though healthy) brand. New and old customers had an additional reason to use Hidden Valley, and its advertising became more effective because there was "news" to report. The Honey Dijon dressing was a big winner and resulted in not only sales but a spark of interest in all Hidden Valley salad dressings. Diet Coke similarly helped to add youth, vitality, and visibility to the Coke image. In general, line extensions—especially if they add products that appeal to consumers—will create an energy that can substantially strengthen brand equity.

MANAGING TRUE INNOVATION

Line extensions provide an explicit channel for product innovations that can be a powerful vehicle for obtaining competitive advantage. Product innovations can create differentiation, enhance a brand's value proposition, expand usage contexts, and block competitors. When there is no clear outlet for innovation within a brand management organization, creative thinking is often stifled. Conversely, when members of a brand management team know that their brand is open to innovative line extensions, then team members are likely to rise to the challenge.

In order to bring new benefits to consumers, the Kimberly Clark feminine-hygiene line introduced the smaller Ultra Trims and the more absorbent Supremes. Glade Air Fresheners began with aerosols and have since added solid forms (for continuous freshening), clip-ons (for the car), and a variety of more cosmetic packages. Without a line extension option, these innovations might not have been created.

BLOCKING OR INHIBITING COMPETITORS

A line extension does not have to be a financial blockbuster in order to provide value for the firm. Especially for leading brands, line extensions can be strategically worthwhile even when they do not achieve high rates of return. Horrific results occurred when General Motors, Xerox, and others permitted Japanese firms to gain a toehold at the low end of their respective markets because the potential returns at that level did not meet the American firms' financial criteria. Line extensions can preempt such competitive moves. With this in mind, the seemingly endless line extensions of Tide and Crest make more sense.

MOVING THE BRAND DOWN

Today's markets, from tires to clothes to computers, are becoming increasingly value centered. More and more buyers are turning from prestige and luxury to lower-cost brands that deliver acceptable quality and features. To combat this trend (or to take advantage of it, if you prefer), firms are offering lesser versions of their traditional brand-product package. What is behind this consumer trend toward value? And how can firms adopt a branding strategy that will accommodate downscale versions without weakening the brand?

DRIVING FORCES

One basic force behind the increased sensitivity to value and price is overcapacity created by the combination of new competitors and fairly static markets. The new competitors come in part from brands being extended from adjacent product classes, brands entering from other markets (notably from other countries), and new or revitalized store brands that are now often competitive in quality. Because they often introduce parity products without innovative, distinctive value propositions, the new entrants, as well as the struggling third- or fourth-place brands, are forced to emphasize price promotions and sales events instead of product. As a result, customers come to believe that the brands are not very different; brand loyalty erodes, and customers focus on features and price. As fewer and fewer customers are willing to pay the historical brand premium, market share starts falling (sometimes dramatically) for those who maintain their price levels.

A second driving force is the retail environment created by new channels that typically have a lower cost structure, engage in aggressive price competition, and freely use private-label goods. New specialty superstores such as Home Depot, Circuit City, and Tower Records leverage their singular buying power for consumers interested in an individual product category. Warehouse clubs such as Price Club are major factors in categories ranging from food to computers. Direct marketing has exploded in the past decade, often providing considerable cost savings to participants. Dell and Gateway, for example, became two of the top five players in the computer market by selling directly through ads placed in computer magazines and catalogs. Customers were supported over the phone by a staff of technicians backed up by third-party service organizations for the rare cases when they were needed. With prices one-third less than IBM and Compaq, they forced these leading firms to change strategies and forever altered the face of computer marketing.

A third driving force is technological change. A new market for a product can be introduced because of new technology; examples might be disposable razors and single-use 35mm cameras. Technological change can also influence the cost structure, as brands emerge that are simpler and cheaper, creating new price points. When this phenomenon happened in food processors, the inability of Cuisinart to keep up led to Black & Decker and others taking over.

These forces represent a major paradigm shift. The old assumptions do not hold any longer, and there is enormous pressure on participants at the low end. For example, John Deere makes a lawn tractor that sells through full-service dealers. Although the price points in that channel have not eroded, a large and growing portion of the market is now being served by volume retailers such as Home Depot. This new channel features products being sold at half the price that John Deere commands. Thus John Deere must either find a way to participate in this new channel or accept a declining share of the market. The problem that John Deere and many others face is how to make this transition without damaging the brand's accumulated brand equity.

MOVING DOWN IS EASY; PROTECTING THE BRAND IS HARD

Mountain bikers discover that going down, while much easier than going up, usually creates a challenge of recapturing the vertical. Like mountain bikers, brands move down easily (if sometimes inadvertently), and they find that there are problems and challenges created by getting to the bottom. The biggest challenge is to avoid harming the brand, particularly in terms of its perceived quality associations.

The problem is that moving down affects perceptions of the brand perhaps more significantly than any other brand management option. Psychologists have documented the fact that people are influenced much more by unfavorable information than by favorable information. Initial negative information about a person, for example, is very resistant to subsequent positive information, whereas an initial good impression is quite likely to be altered by subsequent negative inter-actions. The use of negative political ads is an illustration of this principle at work.

Similar results have been found in more traditional marketing research contexts. For example, Motley and Reddy presented con-sumers with repositioning statements for Saks (a prestigious depart-ment store) and for Kmart (a discount department store).[4] The state-ments described the store as either very upscale, very downscale, or in between. Results indicated that attitudes toward Kmart were not affected by the statements, even when the store was described as very upscale. In contrast, attitudes toward Saks were influenced by both the downscale depiction and the in-between portrayal. In a related study, Arndt found that negative word of mouth had twice as much impact on purchase intentions as did positive word of mouth.[5]

Downward Movement Need Not Be Fatal to the Brand

It should not be assumed that a downward entry is always too risky. If the new product can be made distinct from the parent brand through the use of a subbrand and other devices, the risk can be reduced. Sony's apparent ability to operate at the high end with some products (such as televisions and the Walkman) and at lower price points with others (such as audio products) suggests that consumers can com-partmentalize perceptions. There is further evidence from laboratory studies involving consumer products that people can insulate parent brands from extensions, even when the latter reflect lower quality levels or have quality problems.

For example, Keller and Aaker found that the perceived quality of a brand of potato chips was not affected by its extension to cookies or ice cream, even when the extension was described as poorly accepted because of taste and texture.[6] Similarly, in a study involving the ex-tension of a fruit juice brand into sherbet, Romeo found being exposed to an unfavorable evaluation from *Consumer Reports* of the sherbet did not hurt the fruit juice brand's perceived quality (al-though perceptions were affected by unfavorable reports about a line extension to the fruit juice brand).[7] In another study, Bhat and Zimmer found that extending Sony and Bic to low price/quality points did not affect attitudes toward the parent brand.[8]

The key to reducing the brand risk is to distinguish the new con-text from the original category. Loken and John found that an extension of shampoo to an inferior tissue product did not affect the perceived quality of the shampoo, but only if respondents were first asked if the extension was representative of the brand.[9] The implication is that customers can separate the brand's identity into two product classes, but they may need help doing so. If the extension is far afield (such as Coca-Cola to clothes), the risk of transferring negative quality impressions is reduced; of course, though, there is also the risk that the brand will not contribute anything positive in the new context and may even make customers feel uncomfortable.

A brand should indeed guard its equity and, in particular, its perceived quality. The bottom line, however, is that a brand can take some risks. A strong brand is resilient and can stand some extension difficulties, especially if the extension has some degree of separation. The question then is what is the best amount of separation? What will protect the brand but still work?

The Risk of a Stand-Alone Brand

Although the creation of an entirely new brand will result in the ultimate separation and protection of the core brand, it does not guarantee success. IBM created such a brand, Ambra, with its own separate organization to compete with mail order firms. The brand sourced its products in Asia and was marketed in Europe and the United States. Less than two years after its introduction, though, Ambra was killed. In retrospect, IBM should have found a way to use its own name, one of the strongest brands in the United States and Europe. Creating a new brand at any level with credibility is most difficult, as the Ambra case rather graphically illustrates.

DROPPING THE PRICE AND MAINTAINING QUALITY PERCEPTIONS

Perhaps the most direct approach to moving a brand down is to lower its price. Marlboro, Budweiser, and Pampers are among the brands that have recognized that their equity will not support a large price premium in the face of price-oriented competitors and powerful retailers. Thus they have "value priced" their products to make them competitive. However, although consumers have begun to question higher-priced brands, the reality is that the price point is still a positioning cue. A sharp price reduction can indicate to customers that—as they may have begun to suspect—the brand really is not different from any other brand, and is therefore of average quality.

If the brand has lost all credibility in terms of offering a different or better product, dropping the price is a risk-free strategy. When Schlitz, for example, saw its sales fall to less than 1 million barrels from more than 17 million barrels, it had nothing to lose by being associated with a lower price and occupying a solid position in the price brand category.

Many brands, however, still retain a very worthwhile market segment at the premium end of the market. Further, they offer premium quality or features that prevent them from obtaining cost parity with their new competitors. If these brands wish to move down, it is therefore important that they retain some quality differentiation. The challenge then is to start competing at a new price point *without* repositioning the brand as a lower-quality price brand.

The key to adjusting price while retaining a quality position is to convince retailers and customers that the change does not reflect a different quality level. Procter & Gamble, for example, reduced prices in the context of an everyday-low-price program that it presented as a new way of doing business. The company emphasized that consumer and trade promotions had led to channel inefficiencies for the retailer, as well as confusion and bother for the consumer. By offering an everyday low price, P&G reduced the incentives for retailers to engage in such costly practices as diverting (buying a product on deal, shipping it across the country, and warehousing it for months) and forward buying (buying for inventory to take advantage of a trade deal). The new pricing policy also helped to reduce costs in ordering, warehousing, and logistics systems. As a result, the price reductions were perceived as a part of a larger coherent strategy.

In contrast, consider the move by Marlboro to abruptly drop prices on its flagship brand in the face of falling market share. The move may have been strategically wise, but it was perceived by some retailers and customers (and shareholders) as a panic reaction and thus cast a cloud over the brand's equity. The dramatic price reduction was not supported by the kind of logical strategic reasoning offered by P&G, so consumers and retailers used their own logic to explain the drop. Of course, the Marlboro brand is so established and strong that it is difficult to damage. The fact that the price cut did reverse the fall in market share is an indicator that the brand is strong but had become overpriced.

THE USE OF SUBBRANDS

Subbrands such as Kodak's Funtime film have the potential to permit entry in an emerging low end without threatening the parent brand's equity in the higher ranges of the market. There are two problems, though, with adding subbrand offerings that use the premium brand name at a lower price point. The first is possible cannibalization, in that buyers will shift to the cheaper version; the second is the risk that extending the brand down will taint the brand name.

The job of the subbrand is to reduce these risks by distinguishing the downscale subbrand from the parent brand. In one study, Aaker and Markey explored a toilet paper extension from Kleenex and a low-calorie orange juice from Snapple Fruit Drinks.[10] In each case, an inferior extension (a hard, coarse toilet paper and a watery orange juice) affected attitudes toward the parent brands unless a subbrand was used. The subbrand served to insulate the parent brand from the inferior performance of the extension.

In computers, IBM, Compaq, and even Dell, the premium mail-order house, have used subbrands to provide entry at a lower price point that had become the heart of the market. The Compaq Pro-Linea computers, the IBM ValuePoint line, and the Dell Dimension line are all subbrands that distinguish less expensive lines from the rest of the offerings. Of course, there is still cannibalization; being able to buy a lower-priced computer with the endorser name is attractive and will certainly appeal to some who would have bought the original brand instead. Further, the distinction between the economy lines and the other lines is sometimes fuzzy. The subbrand signals, however, that it does not possess the features and quality of the lines positioned above it. Moreover, those who move from the premium brand to the subbrand might otherwise have been attracted to the value brand of another manufacturer, so that what seems like cannibalization is actually strategic brand protection.

In contrast, Gap stores—a successful retailer of distinctive casual clothing—backed away from a subbrand because of cannibalization and image dilution issues. In 1993, Gap faced competitors who were targeting value-conscious customers by offering Gap-like fashions at prices that were 20 to 30 percent lower. To compete against this threat, Gap tested warehouse-style outlets called Gap Warehouse that sold a broad array of clothing at competitive prices. The problem was that the clothing was too similar to what was sold at the Gap. As a result, a decision was made a year later to change the name to Old Navy Clothing Co., with Gap relegated to a much less prominent endorser role at the outset and scheduled to disappear entirely over time.

The risk to the brand is much lower when the extension is qualitatively different from the parent. For example, Gillette has historically meant quality, innovative razors for men. Believing that a position in the growing disposable razor market was crucial, Gillette launched the Gillette Good News line. The subbrand's younger, lighter personality contrasted with the masculine/macho Gillette persona and played a key role in distinguishing the disposable brand from the rest of the line. The fact that the Gillette Good News disposable was a premium entry in the disposable category also helped to reduce the potential damage to the perceived quality of the Gillette brand.

DESCRIPTIVE SUBBRANDS FOR VALUE POSITIONING

The name and logo of a subbrand can assist in signaling a lower-level product. By containing the word *value*, IBM ValuePoint suggests that it is a low-end addition to the IBM line. Stanley's Professional and Thrifty subbrand names clearly position the two lines. Masterlock has a "Lockers and Bikes" line (of lighter locks) as well as a "Sheds and Gates" lock. Fender makes high-quality electric guitars that sell for $1,500 to $3,000, but they also have a "Starter" electric guitar priced at $199. A brand may also use a series of numbers to denote clearly where in the quality/value spectrum the products fit. For instance, the 100 series may be qualitatively larger and superior to the 90 series and the 70 series.

WILL THE IDENTITY STRETCH?

One concern is whether the brand has an identity that can span the vertical line definition or whether the identity is compromised by new entries at the low end. BMW's 300 series (the smallest and least expensive), 500 series, and 700 series reflect very different sizes and price points. Each of them, however, still have the same identity—

"the ultimate driving machine." A car that is responsive and fun to drive works at all the price points.

In contrast, the identity for Mercedes is based in part on prestige and exclusivity. Thus the Mercedes 190, which costs less than $30,000, presented a problem because of its potential inconsistency with the Mercedes identity of status cars for the affluent. When Mercedes redefined its identity to focus on quality rather than status, the 190 subbrand fit in better and provided a way to extend the Mercedes franchise to a younger group of buyers.

CREATING A DIFFERENT PERSONALITY: THE PARENT–CHILD RELATIONSHIP

Because of the identity problems that can result when a brand moves down, it may be useful to use the subbrand's personality as a way to differentiate the new, lower-priced entry. If it is given a strong personality which is different from that of the original brand, the risks of cannibalization and image tarnishing are reduced.

Because family relationships are so familiar to consumers, they offer a clear and rich opportunity for creating distinct but related subbrand personalities. The subbrand could be a child (either son or daughter) of the original brand (the father or mother), one who cannot yet afford or appreciate the better version. Or it could be the grandparent of the original, one who appreciates good value more than premium quality.

Consider a parent brand with an honest, caring, hardworking, small-town persona—for example, John Deere, Chevrolet, or Kodak. The son of this brand (perhaps named John Deere Jr.) could have many of these same characteristics; after all, he (or it) is a chip off the old block.

The son, though, could also be different in many respects from the father. He would likely be drawn to simpler, less expensive options—perhaps looking to move up as he accumulated money over time. Other characteristics will depend in part on the product class. A son with youth and vigor might be appropriate for a motorcycle or bicycle. A serious, nerdy son might be reassuring for a new line of lawn equipment or trucks. For clothes, it might be better to have the son be spontaneous and fun to be with, perhaps similar to the Jolly Green Giant "Little Sprout" character. For a sports car or mountaineering line, the son might have a reckless, living-on-the-edge element to him. In any case, the personality of the son offers a point of distinction from the parent brand and a way to connect with a target market while still providing a coherent link to the brand's heritage.

DISTINGUISHING THE SUBBRAND

The product itself is one way to separate the subbrand from the parent brand. If the product is clearly different in terms of features, applications, and users, the risk to the core brand is reduced. Courtyard by Marriott, for example, is very different from Marriott itself—it has fewer services and offers a different hotel experience. The Gillette Good News is a very different product than Sensor and the rest of the Gillette line. If a retailer such as Nieman's went downscale, the two types of stores might be separated by color scheme, ambiance, background music, and featured clothing styles as well as the service spectrum.

When the product is more difficult to distinguish because key product characteristics are not visible, the problem is more severe. This is true for Kodak Funtime film, the Kodak Funsaver camera, or the IBM ValuePoint line (as least for many inexperienced computer users). In such cases it becomes important to create different personalities and to manage the symbols associated with the new brand. Even a different logo and color can help to provide the necessary separation.

Aiming at a different market will not only provide a point of distinction but reduce the image-tarnishing risk, because customers of the parent brand will be less likely to be exposed to the new offering. The downscale offering of an upscale health chain, for example, could be for a younger clientele (say, in their twenties or thirties) or could focus on a small-city market, leaving the large cities for the parent brand.

The parent brand can also be managed in a way that accentuates the distinction between it and a subbrand. For example, a line of tools might be upgraded and given a subbrand name (such as the "Pro-Choice") at the same time as a thrifty subbrand (the "HomeMaster") is introduced. In essence, the tactic is to simultaneously move the brand up and down. The downlevel Gillette Good News subbrand works in part because the rest of the razor line is positioned (and thus elevated) by the Gillette Sensor. It is easier to separate Gillette Good News from Gillette Sensor than it is to separate either subbrand from Gillette.

Alternatively, the line of tools for the main brand might remain the same, but a ProChoice line might be created at the same time the lower-level HomeMaster line is introduced. The result is three levels, with any tarnishing effect of a lower subbrand compensated by the "halo" effect of a higher brand.

MOVING A BRAND UP

A brand may be a leader in volume and market share, with the enviable advantages of economies of scale and retail clout. It is on the store shelf, in the pantry, and in the customer's mind. However, its price has been squeezed by retailers and consumers, especially from below by both price brands and store brands.

In this context, an attractive growth segment often emerges at the very high end of the market. This segment enjoys much higher margins, and it also provides interest and even newsworthy developments in what might be a somewhat tired category. Microbreweries (such as Anchor Steam), designer coffees, upscale waters, sporty luxury cars, and specialty magazines all represent target niches that are less price sensitive than the larger market center. How can brands "move up" to take advantage of this growth and vitality and get out from under oppressive margin pressures?

USING A NEW BRAND

When the existing brand name is too much of a drag, the only feasible alternative is likely to be the creation of a stand-alone brand. For example, when Black & Decker created a line of tools for construction professionals, there was a feeling that the target segment would not be attracted to (and even would be uncomfortable with) Black & Decker equipment because of the latter's association with the do-it-yourself homeowner. Thus the DeWalt brand was created. The DeWalt equipment is a cut above Black & Decker in terms of performance, is bright yellow (in contrast to the green of the Black & Decker line), and has no mention of the Black & Decker parent brand.

A similar logic was responsible for Honda's Acura, Toyota's Lexus, and Nissan's Infiniti. In each case, the core brand—which signaled economy and simplicity rather than prestige, handling, and comfort—had the potential of preventing the new product from credibly occupying the upscale position.

However, the option of successfully introducing a new brand is often either too costly or simply not feasible, especially when the task is to become the third or fourth brand in the mind and on the shelf. An alternative is to use a subbrand of an existing brand to create a upscale entry.

THE ROLE OF A SUBBRAND

Using a subbrand, such as Coors Gold or Holiday Inn Crowne Plaza, to penetrate the high end of a market has several advantages. First, it avoids much of the expense of creating visibility and associations for a new brand name. It is potentially easier to associate Holiday Inn with an upscale hotel or Coors with a super-premium beer than to start with a new name. Second, the applicable assets of the brand can help provide a value proposition. Thus customers of Holiday Inn Crowne Plaza know that they can access the Holiday Inn reservation system directly using its 800 number, and Coors Gold customers recognize that their beer is connected to High Priority, the Coors program to fight breast cancer. Third, the subbrands can provide a perceived quality lift to the core brand names, Holiday Inn and Coors.

There are some risks of damaging the core brand when moving up, although much less than when moving down. There is the possibility that the premium version can, by comparison, make the core brand look more ordinary than it was previously perceived to be. For example, Coors is not as appealing when Coors Gold is available—the Coors drinker is less likely to believe that Coors is the best. A much more serious risk, though, is that the core brand will keep the premium brand from achieving its full prestige. For example, the strong image of Holiday Inn as a familiar, unpretentious hotel was a real handicap when the Crowne Plaza subbrand was trying to compete at the very high end of the market. As a result, the parent company decided to drop the Holiday Inn connection and let Crowne Plaza go on its own.

In the worst case, the premium brand becomes an object of ridicule, like someone with a financial windfall who has purchased the trappings of nobility and developed pretensions of grandeur. The

Ernest and Julio Gallo Varietals (an effort to move the Gallo name up into premium wines) may have this impact on some consumers, although why such an entry may still make sense for Gallo will be explained later in this chapter. The key to reducing this risk is to make the subbrand distinct from the rest of the offerings under the brand umbrella.

SEPARATING THE SUBBRAND

The basic problem with using a subbrand to move up is that the brand often lacks credibility at the higher end. How can a believable claim be made that a subbrand under the sponsorship of a middle-tier brand can really meet the standards of a high-end market? One key to making it happen is to have a silver bullet within the higher-end line that demonstrates the subbrand's ability to deliver—a visible flagship Holiday Inn Crowne Plaza in New York or London, for example. Another is to clearly separate the line from that of the core brand.

Black & Decker's Quantum line of equipment, developed for the twenty million or more serious do-it-yourself consumers, is a good example of making an upscale subbrand clearly distinctive from the core brand. Black & Decker accomplished this separation in part through the use of a newsletter (Shop Talk), a telephone advice program (Power Source), and several silver-bullet products (such as a ductless drill using a specially designed vacuum system). Quantum also used a color—silver with yellow printing—that sharply contrasted with the metallic green of the Black & Decker line.

A subbrand that is upscale will often employ a descriptor such as "special edition," "premium," "professional," "gold" (Coors Gold, Kodak Gold, Kodak Royal Gold), or "platinum" (the Platinum card). Wineries use "private reserve" or "library reserve" or "limited edition" names to capture the higher end; airlines have "Connoisseur Class" and the "Red Carpet Club." Such a tactic can clearly signal a move up, but a descriptive name can make it more difficult to develop an independent identity for the subbrand. In gourmet coffees, Euro-Roast from MJB has been more successful than Maxwell House Private Collection and Folgers Gourmet Singles, perhaps because the MJB subbrand has more distance from its parent. EuroRoast, in addition to connoting upscale quality, also has a European association that adds interest and credibility.

WILL THE IDENTITY STRETCH?

A key issue is whether a brand can be stretched upward. Brands whose identities are inconsistent with an upscale entry will find an upward move more difficult. For example, Rice-A-Roni, in a variety of flavors, is used in everyday meals; in fact, it is often the core part of the meal. Thus the effort to move upscale with Rice-A-Roni Savory Classics was not successful—Rice-A-Roni, consumers felt, was just not something you served for a fancy entertaining dinner.

In contrast, the basic Uncle Ben's rice is perceived as a simple, austere product, but one that can participate in fancy recipes. Thus that brand's upscale Uncle Ben's Country Inn rice dishes, which include Rice Alfredo Homestyle pilaf and Herbal rice au gratin, worked. The Country Inn subbrand indicates that the recipes are inspired by the finest inns and may even suggest a relative who is associated with interesting country restaurants. And the Uncle Ben's name, though not upscale itself, is not incompatible with an upscale setting or recipe and thus acts as less of a drag than Rice-A-Roni.

AN UPSCALE ENTRY AS A VEHICLE FOR DOWNSTREAM ENHANCEMENT

Another key motivation for creating an upscale version of the brand is to affect the original brand identity positively. The aid an upscale (or upstream) brand provides by enhancing the core (or downstream) brand's identity is termed *downstream enhancement*. In such cases, the potential profitability of the new brand may be of secondary importance, or even nonexistent. An example of carefully managed downstream enhancement comes from Gallo wine.

The Gallo name was (and is) a dominant force in the wine business. Its biggest volume product was the trademark Gallo "jug wine" line, which was facing competition from brands such as Glen Ellen. These competitors were encroaching on Gallo's huge niche by positioning themselves as just above Gallo in quality. To protect itself, the Gallo elephant needed to move up a small notch, a very formidable task.

Ernest and Julio Gallo Varietals—a line of upscale, corked wines that reflected a much higher quality than that of Gallo's traditional products—was the vehicle used to accomplish this task. Given Gallo's jug-wine reputation, though, why would the company choose to put its name so prominently on a product striving to compete in the high end? Why take the chance that the upscale wine would lose credibility as a result of the Gallo name?

The answer: downstream enhancement. The key target of the extension might not have been consumers at the high end but rather the core Gallo consumer, even if he or she never bought a Gallo Varietal. A high-end product gave the company an opportunity to tell the story of Gallo quality from a different perspective. Over time, and given enough communication support, this new perspective may well have an impact on the overall Gallo quality perception, and the benefits in terms of competing at the lower end might well justify the expenditures required to market a subbrand at the high end. Thanks to substantial advertising support and distribution clout, the upscale product finally did become profitable, but this was likely regarded as a bonus to the real objective of the subbrand.

Another tactic is to develop a new upscale brand, then attach the core brand name in order to help enhance the latter brand's identity. For example, although Coleman is a leading camping equipment brand, it has historically been associated with an image of being "heavy and cumbersome."[11] This association contributed to resistance when Coleman attempted to move up-market to backpacking equipment. Thus Coleman launched the stand-alone Peak 1 brand, which was more successful in part because it did not have the parent brand's associations. When the Coleman name was added to Peak 1 a few years later, the new line's reputation was already established; the Coleman name was no longer a problem and, in fact, could contribute a sense of substance (especially for new buyers). Further, and more important, the Peak 1 association enhanced the identity of Coleman.

BRAND EXTENSION DECISIONS

Another way to leverage a brand with extensions is to use it to enter and create advantage in another product category. The good, bad, and ugly issues involved in making a brand extension decision (as summarized in my previous book, *Managing Brand Equity*) are as follows.

Good. The brand's associations, perceived quality, and awareness/presence help the extension.

More good. The extension reinforces the associations and awareness of the brand.

Bad. The name does not add value to the extension or even has
negative associations.

Ugly. The core brand name is damaged or diluted by the extension,
or the brand franchise is cannibalized.

More ugly. The opportunity to develop another brand name is forgone.

This analysis, though, assumes only an ad hoc decision to extend a
brand to another product class. Another perspective on extending
brands is discussed below.

CREATING RANGE BRANDS

The 1990s has seen the emergence of a brand concept that has caused
some firms to look at their business very differently. A *range brand*
creates an identity that works across product classes. A range brand
can also be conceived as a spanning symbol that assists customers in
seeing relationships between products—relationships that they might
have missed. By thus breaking through consumers' existing catego-
rization structures, range brands can extend a brand in new ways. A
range brand is sometimes called a *megabrand*, but the megabrand
term can also apply to a strong brand with high market share (such as
Budweiser or Coke) that does not span product classes.

RANGE BRANDS VERSUS BRAND EXTENSIONS

The 1980s was the era of brand extension: A strong brand was identified, and there was a search for product classes in which it would fit.
One rationale was to exploit the assets of the firm by applying them to
new business areas; another was to reduce the cost and risk of entering such areas. Extension decisions were thus made incrementally.
How can the brand name be used to save money, to reduce risk and
to expand sales and profits? As Figure 9–3, suggests, the scope was
usually a single product class, and the perspective was short term.

A range brand looks at brand strategy holistically rather than incrementally. The objective is to create a strong brand asset that will be the
basis of a business with a real competitive advantage. The core of a

FIGURE 9–3
Range Brands

	BRAND EXTENSION	RANGE BRANDS
DECISION FOCUS	Incremental	Strategic
DECISION SCOPE	Product class	Product class groupings
TIME FRAME	Short term	Long term

range brand strategy is to develop a vision of the ultimate identity that the brand will possess, and the product lines that the brand will support either as an endorser or as a driver brand. Whereas a brand extension decision will be driven largely by the current brand image, a range brand vision may involve a different future identity for the brand.

The Range Brand Scope

A key decision is to select for inclusion those products that are compatible with the brand's identity or vision as opposed to its current image. Of course, when selecting business areas, a firm needs to assess its ability to make the product, the intensity of competition and price pressures, and market trends. However, with respect to branding, two criteria stand out:

1. The brand identity needs to provide a value proposition or basis for relationship in the product class being considered.
2. The product needs to fit and reinforce the identity.

Product Line Identities

By definition, the range brand will be applied to several product lines. Each of these product lines will have its own product line identity, which will usually be an augmentation of the basic brand identity. To compete in a product class setting will usually require additional associations. Thus, while Healthy Choice has a clear identity based on food that is nutritious, is low in fat and sodium, and tastes good, the Healthy Choice Generous Servings identity includes additional frozen-dinner and portion-size dimensions. The Calvin Klein range brand associates fashion with a New York personality; its product line identities, however, are distinct without being inconsistent. The fragrances emphasize sexuality and rebellion, whereas the suits and eyewear products are more conservative.

A Dynamic Vision

A range brand strategy requires a dynamic brand vision: What is the ultimate brand identity? How should the brand evolve toward that identity? A key part of the plan is to determine in what order the product classes should be entered, as the order can affect the ability of the brand to evolve. For example, Gillette meant razors when it introduced Gillette Foamy—a shaving product, but not a razor. The Foamy shaving cream, a product closely linked to razors, was a bridge to the line of toiletries for men later introduced under the Gillette Series brand. This line would have been more of a stretch for Gillette without the Foamy product to pave the way for a broader image.

The oral care category provides an example of brand identity evolution. Companies in this category have realized that cleaning teeth to prevent cavities is no longer the only mission. Rather, because of the advances in toothpaste and dental treatment, customers now focus on complete oral care, with an emphasis on healthy gums as well as teeth. As a result the major toothpaste companies, Crest and Colgate, have expanded into toothbrushes and other oral health products (such as dental floss), and Oral-B, known for its toothbrushes, has developed a broad line of oral care products. The old brand identities needed to be broadened to provide a value proposition in the new setting; identities that worked for toothpaste and toothbrushes became too narrow to succeed in the oral care category.

WHY RANGE BRANDS?

There are several reasons why range brands can be beneficial. Strategically, the range brand concept can provide coherence and structure to strategy. The essence of a business strategy is to address two questions: (1) What business areas (product-markets) will be included? And (2) what competitive advantage will exist in each of these business areas? Range brands, such as Weight Watchers, Ford, Disney, Oral-B, and American Express, provide answers to both questions.

A second motivation is economic. An economist would observe that a range brand provides classic economies of scope—that is, the fixed cost of maintaining a brand name can be spread across different businesses. A business strategist would see a range brand as providing synergy. A grouping of businesses is greater than the sum of its parts, because an investment in one will help the others. Both perspectives really capture the same potential cost-efficiency. In addition, the awareness and identity of a range brand can reduce the costs and risks of new product efforts.

The reality is that creating or supporting a brand is very expensive in the modern era, especially given high advertising and promotional costs. A stand-alone brand competing with range brands can be at a big disadvantage because of the lack of scale economies (although a well-positioned niche brand, of course, can be a winner).

A third advantage of range brands is that being associated with multiple product classes can add visibility and can reassure consumers that the firm is capable of success in different contexts. Dacin and Smith explored the impact of the number of product classes associated with a brand.[12] The number of product classes in the study was either three (small kitchen appliances, garage door openers, and hand-held garden equipment) or seven (those three plus hair dryers, small power tools, carpet sweepers and telephone answering machines). In evaluating an extension of this brand (into sports watches, or electric irons), a greater number of product classes affiliated with the brand enhanced both the evaluation of the extension and consumer confidence in the evaluation.

RANGE BRANDS AT KRAFT

Examples of range brands at Kraft/General Foods include Philadelphia (Regular, Herb, Salmon, Dip & Sauce, and others), Kraft Slices—regular, flavored and others); and Kraft Mayonnaise—(Real, Yogurt, Mayoliva, and others), and the European brand Miracoli (box dinners, sauces, premium dinners).[13] In each case there is a brand identity—usually drawn in large part from the original product setting—that is carried throughout the line. It involves a value proposition and personality that can affect user choice and satisfaction across product categories. This identity needs to be powerful and relevant, yet flexible enough to work across different contexts.

The core brand identity for Miracoli is authentic Italian taste and a secret combination of herbs and spices. This identity is implemented in all the advertising and packaging in all product lines. For example, the advertising for each line shows the same Italian homemaker, who has a consistent personality and credibility.

The brand identity for Philadelphia is the gold standard of quality—a delicious treat that is expensive, but worth it. Each of the product lines augment this identity. Philadelphia Light, for example, is the fresh and light cream cheese with the famous Philadelphia taste.

HONDA: CREATING MULTIPLE IDENTITIES

Honda is an interesting range brand because its product lines represent a significant stretch. Honda could rely on its reputation for economy, workmanship, and expertise in small motors to extend to products like lawn and garden tools. However, its decision to put the Honda name on automobiles was risky (although successful).

Why was Honda able to stretch its brand? First, there was a common identity involving associations such as competence, efficiency, few defects, and good engines, even across disparate products. Second, its automobiles were excellently made; stretching is a lot easier when superior products are involved. Third, Honda had substantial resources to put behind the automobile brand, and big budgets often paper over problems (witness Coke's ability to recover from "new Coke"). Finally, the product line identities were strong and distinct. In essence, many consumers perceive two Honda brands—one for automobiles and one for small engine products. It does not really matter which product class consumers think of when Honda is mentioned, but it does matter that Honda and the appropriate associations come to mind when either product class is cued.

WHAT PRODUCTS? HOW BROAD?

The key task in developing range brands is to identify the product classes for which a brand can provide leverage, contribute to the value proposition, or enhance the relationship between the brand and the customer. Ed Tauber, a seasoned brand extension researcher, recommends that prospective customers be asked the following questions about any proposed extension concept: How will this brand differ from its competitors? How will it provide value? If customers cannot answer these questions, the odds of success go way down.

The selection of product classes for which the brand will add value will depend on the brand's identity. Attribute associations, for example, will work only in particular contexts. According to a study by Broniarczyk and Alba, Close-Up has a breath-freshening association that would work for mouthwash and breath mints, but that would be much less effective for dental floss and toothbrushes.[14] In contrast, because of its dental protection associations, Crest works with dental floss and toothbrushes, but less so with mouthwash and breath mints. There is more latitude if the perceived quality is high. Aaker and Keller showed that a high level of perceived quality helps a brand travel further.[15]

Stretching a brand beyond its perceived area of expertise can be risky. A study by Park, McCarty, and Milberg found that a hypothetical extension of Timex into garage door openers, smoke detectors, and colognes had a negative impact on Timex, while extensions into nearer categories like batteries, calculators, rings, and bracelets did not.[16] The researchers also found that extending Rolex into functionally oriented products like door openers, batteries, and calculators hurt the brand, but that extensions into prestige products helped it.

When a brand's identity moves beyond product associations to organizational associations, brand personality, and (in general) more abstract associations, it will travel farther. Some bases for identity—such as prestige (Rolex), fashion (Vuarnet), and health (Healthy Choice)—are not associated with a specific product class and will be capable of casting a wider shadow than an attribute that is tied to a specific product.

Consider the Calvin Klein brand, which began with designer clothing but now can be found on not only clothing of all types (including underwear, jeans, and men's suits) but also fragrances and eyewear. Braun is associated with electric shavers, clocks, and a wide range of household appliances including food processors, hand blenders, coffee makers, and curling irons. Disney, which started out making short cartoons, is now also strongly associated with feature-length film production, theme parks, clothing, toy stores, a hockey team and cruise lines.

The extendability of these range brands is particularly remarkable when one considers the limited reach of some of their competitors.

What if suitmaker Brooks Brothers marketed a line of perfume or hosiery? What if the Cuisinart kitchen appliance brand was placed on an electric razor? And what if the Montreal Canadiens hockey team wished to put its name on a theme park or a film company? The ability of some range brands to extend further than many of their competitors is strongly related to the way in which their identity has been developed and allowed to evolve.

A logical brand scope is a product category; a *category brand* is a range brand that represents a product category such as baking mixes. Category brands increasingly have an advantage over orphan brands—that is, brands not supported by category cousins (such as Nestlé Morsels, the only product offering by Nestlé in the baking section). Retailers, exploiting information technology, are managing whole categories rather than individual products. Stocking, pricing, and promotion decisions thus are increasingly being made at the category level. As a result, retailers find it efficient and strategically more coherent to deal with category brands.

CO-BRANDING

A brand can also be leveraged by entering another product class, not by a brand extension, but by co-branding.

INGREDIENT BRANDS

One form of co-branding is to become a branded ingredient in another brand. Hershey's, for example, might have trouble extending into cake or cookie mixes, because such products require different manufacturing processes and because consumers might question Hershey's ability to deliver high quality in those areas. With little risk, however, Hershey's could become a branded ingredient in a Betty Crocker cake mix. The strength of the brand name thus would be exploited without Hershey's becoming involved in a running a new business. Such co-branding provides many of the advantages of an extension with less risk.

Becoming an ingredient co-brand provides another benefit of brand extensions: more visibility for the brand. KC Masterpiece barbecue sauce got a huge lift in visibility and credibility when a major chip firm introduced the KC Masterpiece–flavored potato chip.

Makers of KC Masterpiece were only too glad to do the R&D to make this happen and to provide the flavoring ingredient. Intel, Nutrasweet, and others have gained visibility by getting manufacturers to feature their brand and logo prominently on packaging and in advertisements.

COMPOSITE BRANDS

Another form of co-branding is having a *composite brand*—the bundling of two brands to provide an enhanced consumer benefit or reduced cost. For example, the Yoplait subsidiary of General Mills used the Trix brand to introduce Trix Yoplait yogurt, a product geared for children. No additional television advertising expenditures were applied to the new product beyond the 12 to 15 million dollars already spent on Trix cereal; the company capitalized on the high awareness level of Trix cereal and its identity among children.

In the credit card industry, MasterCard led the charge with aggressive co-branding as a means to segment the market and target desirable niches. The AT&T Universal Card (which combines with the AT&T calling card) and the GM card (which allows the user to earn rebates on GM cars) have been exceptionally successful. A MasterCard co-brand like AT&T gains visibility in addition to providing added value in the form of convenience to their customers. The AT&T and GM cards also provide a relationship link with customers because there are incentives to buy GM cars and to use AT&T as a long distance carrier.

Healthy Choice combined with Kellogg's to create a line of "Healthy Choice from Kellogg's" cereals that have a superior taste and a good position on the health dimension. The cereals, using descriptive subbrands such as "multigrain flakes" and "multigrain squares," contain vitamins (including beta carotene), fiber, light sweetening for taste, and no fat. They use a distinctive green package with the Healthy Choice running logo. The partnership gives Healthy Choice the Kellogg's endorsement and better access to the cereal category. Kellogg's benefits from new products with high sales potential that will add to the brand's clout in the store and to its identity as an innovative cereal supplier. Kellogg's also gets a second chance at a product concept where it had failed without the Healthy Choice name and credibility.

THE BRAND SYSTEMS AUDIT

1.   *Strategic brands*. What are the strategic brands—brands that are strategically important and should receive more than their share of resources? The critical aspect here is to identify those brands that have small sales now but will become more important sales and profit contributors in the future, and those brands (such as branded services) that are important points of leverage even though the business with which they are associated may never be an important profit generator.

2.   *Endorser brands*. What brands are playing endorser roles? In what way do they add value? Is their identity appropriate for that role? Are there cases in which the endorser should recede, or even become disassociated? Are there other contexts in which an endorser should be added or made more pronounced?

3.   *Branded benefits: services/features/ingredients*. What services, features, or ingredients should be branded (or, if already branded, are underexploited)? How would branding them add value?

4.   *Silver bullets*. What brands or branded benefits are playing or could play a silver-bullet role? Are they being exploited properly? Are additional silver bullets needed?

5.   *Range brands*. Identify the range brands. Do their brand identities work in each context? Is there a plan that specifies what prod-

THE SYNERGY OF CO-BRANDING

Co-branding is a classic search for synergy. Two brands together can share brand-building dollars and the risk of a new product launch. Further, they can bring to the party brand associations that, in combination, can create a point of differentiation. The problem is finding the right fit and solving the implementation problems of two organizations, with different systems and cultures, working together.

THE BRAND SYSTEMS AUDIT

Chapters 8 and 9 have presented the brand systems view. The concept is that brands rarely operate in isolation. Rather, a set of brands will form a system. The challenge is to manage the brand system to

ucts the range brands will include in the future? Which should be the firm's range brands of the future? What are the brand identities of these range brands? What is the vision of the range brand in terms of products to be included—for which would the range brand act as an endorser brand?

6.   *Co-brands*. Are there opportunities to partner or co-brand? What types of partners would serve to reduce limitations of our identity? What types would enhance the identity? In each case would it be more appropriate to be a modifier brand or a modified brand?

7.   *Extension options*. Is there a brand that is a good candidate for horizontal extension? Why? What identity elements will provide leverage?

8.   *Vertical extensions*. Identify a brand that should be moved up or down. Develop a strategy. Would a subbrand be useful?

8.   *Clarifying with subbrands*. Identify an instance in which the offerings are confusing and lead to expectation problems. Could subbrands or subsubbrands be used to clarify or manage expectations?

9.   *How many brands*? Are there too many brands? Too few? What criteria should guide the decision to add a brand?

achieve synergy and clarity and to fully develop and exploit the potential of each brand. A place to begin this management process is to conduct a brand systems audit (see insert). The audit provides a way to cycle through the brand systems concepts and relationships that have been discussed.

QUESTIONS TO CONSIDER

1. Should the brand be moved up or down? Why? What are the risks? What are the alternative ways to accomplish the goals?
2. What line extension options exist? What objectives are there for a line extension program?
3. Identify the candidate range brands. What are the pros and cons of each? Identify the firm's range brands of the future. What are

the identities of these range brands? What is the vision of the range brand in terms of products to be included—as an endorser brand and as driving brand? What are the identities of the product line brands under the range brand's umbrella?

4. Are there opportunities to partner or co-brand? What types of partners would reduce limitations of your brand's identity? What types would enhance the identity? In each case would it be more appropriate to be a modifier brand or a modified brand?

10

MEASURING BRAND EQUITY ACROSS PRODUCTS AND MARKETS

Far better an approximate answer to the right question, which is often vague, than an exact answer to the wrong question, which can always be made precise.
—John Tukey, statistician

A brand is a set of differentiating promises that link a product to its customers.
—Stuart Agres, Young & Rubicam.

What brands are really strong not only within a product category but also across product categories? What makes a brand strong anyway? These are very basic questions. Answering them requires an in-depth understanding of brand equity and of individual brands and their context, and addressing them can provide insights as to how to build strong brands and track their strength over time.

Three efforts to measure brand strength across product categories will be discussed below. The focus will be on (1) the measures that are employed and their rationale, and (2) the substantive insights and hypotheses that emerge from the measurement efforts. As will be discussed, brand equity measurement across categories has practical utility for firms operating in several product arenas, but it also provides insights and a starting point to develop a brand-specific tracking system. Drawing on these three measurement efforts (and the concepts of brand equity and brand identity already put forward), a set of ten measures of brand equity, the Brand Equity Ten, which can be used to measure brands across categories will then be proposed.

YOUNG & RUBICAM'S BRAND ASSET VALUATOR

The most ambitious effort to measure brand equity across products, termed the Brand Asset Valuator, is that of Young & Rubicam (Y&R) a major global advertising agency, who measured brand equity for 450 global brands and more than 8,000 local brands in twenty-four countries. Each brand was examined using a thirty-two item questionnaire that included, in addition to a set of brand personality scales, four sets of measures:

1. *Differentiation*—Measures how distinctive the brand is in the marketplace.
2. *Relevance*—Measures whether a brand has personal relevance for the respondent. Is it meaningful to him or her? Is it personally appropriate?
3. *Esteem*—Measures whether a brand is held in high regard and considered the best in its class. Closely related to perceived quality and the extent to which the brand is growing in popularity.
4. *Knowledge*—A measure of understanding as to what a brand stands for.

FIGURE 10–1
Top U.S. Brands for Each Y&R Brand Asset Valuator Dimension

Differentiation	Relevance	Brand Strength	Esteem	Knowledge	Brand Stature
Disney	AT&T	A-1	Band-Aid	Campbell's	Campbell's
Dr Pepper	Band-Aid	CNN	Campbell's	Coca-Cola	Coca-Cola
Ferrari	Campbell's	Disney	Hallmark	Heinz	Crest
Grey Poupon	Hallmark	Dr Pepper	Heinz	Hershey's	Hallmark
Jaguar	Heinz	Grey Poupon	Hershey's	Jell-O	Heinz
Porsche	Kodak	Häagen-Dazs	Kodak	Kellogg's	Hershey's
Rolls-Royce	Kraft	Hallmark	Phil. Cream	Kodak	Jell-O
Sharper Image	Reynold's Wrap	PBS	Reynold's Wrap	McDonald's	Kellogg's
Snapple	U.S. Postal	"60 Minutes"	Rubbermaid	Pepsi-Cola	Kodak
Victoria's Secret	United States	United States	United States	U.S. Postal	Kraft

Note: The brands are listed in alphabetical order.

Note: Brand Strength is Differentiation multiplied by Relevance;
   Brand Stature is Esteem multiplied by Knowledge.

Figure 10–1 identifies some of the brands high on each of these dimensions (as well as two other dimensions which will be discussed shortly), and thus provides some insight into what the constructs are measuring.

Y&R put forth the hypothesis that brands are built sequentially along these four dimensions, as shown in Figure 10–2.

FIGURE 10–2
The Young & Rubicam Model of Brand Dynamics

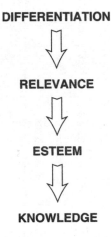

DIFFERENTIATION MULTIPLIED BY RELEVANCE = BRAND STRENGTH

Differentiation comes first in the Y&R model. Brands such as Snapple, Dr Pepper, Grey Poupon, and Ferrari stand apart from their competitors, and that provides one basis for brand strength. If there is no point of difference, a brand's value will be low. The Y&R model hypothesizes that a new brand with ambitions to become strong must start by developing a point of real differentiation. Conversely, a loss in differentiation is usually the first sign that a strong brand is fading. Differentiation leads.

To support the hypothesized role of differentiation in the brand-building process, Y&R explored differentiation differences among two sets of brands. "Up and coming" brands—those gaining in sales and popularity—were, on average, high on differentiation (in the top third of all brands) and lower on the other three dimensions (in the bottom 40 percent). The opposite was found for fading brands. These two results suggest that differentiation indeed drives some key dynamics. Of course, more definitive judgments will require obtaining measures over time, so that changes in differentiation can be observed.

Relevance comes next. Unless a brand is relevant to a significant segment, it will not attract a large customer base. Ferrari and Jaguar are very high in differentiation but extremely low in relevance; few individuals seriously consider buying one because these cars are impractical for daily use or are too expensive. There is a strong association between relevance and household penetration (the percentage of households that buy the brand). Kodak, for example, has high relevance and market penetration, while its competitors Agfa and Fuji have significantly lower relevance and penetration. In general, small brands tend to be low on both relevance and penetration. AT&T, Band-Aid, and Campbell's, the U.S. brands highest on the relevance dimension, all have high penetration.

Brand strength represents differentiation multiplied by relevance. The logic is that a brand must have both characteristics in order to be strong. Further, it is not easy to have high marks in both; few brands high on one dimension are also high on the other. Note how few of the top ten brands on differentiation and relevance made the top ten on brand strength. Growing brands and strong, established brands such as Hallmark and Disney tend to be high on brand strength.

ESTEEM MULTIPLIED BY KNOWLEDGE= BRAND STATURE

Esteem and knowledge complete the hierarchy and combine to form the *brand stature* construct. *Esteem* combines perceived quality with perceptions of a growth or decline in popularity. On average, esteem is largely based on perceived quality. But there are brands for which a decline or growth in popularity affects esteem. Further, there are countries (such as Japan), in which perceived popularity generally accounts for greater variability in esteem than does perceived quality.

Knowledge indicates that the customer not only is aware of the brand but also understands what the brand stands for. Young & Rubicam posits that knowledge—the true understanding of the brand—is the culmination of the brand building effort. Unlike awareness, it is not simply built by exposures; rather, it is generated by a real customer intimacy with the brand.

Comparing Esteem and Knowledge. Comparing a brand's esteem with its knowledge often provides some important insights. For instance, some brands rank higher in esteem than in knowledge. This means that relatively few people understand what the brand stands for, but those who do hold it in high regard. A brand in this situation is likely to have some unrealized potential—which it may or may not be poised to take advantage of—if it can find a way to expand knowledge. Brands with higher esteem than knowledge include Fisher-Price, Crayola, National Geographic, WD-40, and 3M.

Conversely a brand may have high knowledge but low esteem. This means that more people know what the brand stands for, but relatively few hold it in high regard. Exxon, the National Rifle Association, MTV and all rate higher in knowledge than in esteem, and the same is true for most cigarette and alcohol brands. Brands with this profile are usually losing penetration, or they are serving a market that has a polarized opinion about the brand.

Characteristics of Brands with High Stature. The Y&R Brand Valuator follows a previous brand measurement effort by the Y&R sister company Landor Associates that measured brand equity across countries. Although only the stature dimensions (knowledge and esteem) were measured, some observations from this firm's research are instructive.[1] One observation is that the high-stature brands, such as Campbell's, Coke, Hallmark, and Kodak, tended to have considerable longevity and a rich heritage and identity. The Y&R study, however, shows that young brands such Doritos (since 1966) and Sesame Street (since 1969) have also achieved stature (and brand strength) as has Ocean Spray, a brand revitalized by brand extensions.

The Landor studies also showed that the stature of brands varies sharply over countries and segments. In the United States, the high-stature brands tend to be consumer packaged goods, whereas in Europe and Japan car brands have higher stature; in Japan, retailers also get high marks. With respect to segments, McDonald's scores much higher among the 18–29 age group than in other segments. Brands like L'Oréal, New Freedom, and Sure & Natural rate high among women, while brands like Playboy, Motorcraft, and Louisville Slugger are high among men. Toyota is high in stature among import car buyers.

THE POWER GRID

Further diagnostic information can be obtained from a stature-by-strength diagnostic framework termed a *power grid*, as shown in Figure 10–3. Brands that are high on both dimensions (the upper right quadrant) have the greatest equity to protect and exploit. The bottom left quadrant is generally made up of brands that are just getting started; however a brand that stays too long in this quadrant is not likely to be successful in the long run.

FIGURE 10–3

The Y&R Power Grid: Stature Versus Strength

**Brand Stature
(Knowledge & Esteem)**

Low	High	
Dove Chocolates	Disney	
Teddy Grahams	Sesame Street	
Snapple	Doritos	**High**
Swatch	Sony	
Molson	Ocean Spray	**Brand Strength (Differentiation & Relevance)**
QVC	Oldsmobile	
TAG Heuer	Bayer	**Low**
Starbucks	Wesson	
Timberland	Ramada	

According to the Y&R hypothesis, the brands in the upper left quadrant are either strong niche brands or brands with a significant opportunity to grow by increasing their stature (knowledge in particular). The lower right quadrant, in contrast, is largely populated by brands that are tired but still retain some esteem and knowledge. Two-thirds of these brands are lower in esteem than in knowledge, and 90 percent of them have lower ratings for differentiation than for relevance. Because they have lost brand strength, they are sinking.

TOTAL RESEARCH'S EQUITREND

EquiTrend, developed by Total Research, provides a nice contrast to the Y&R Brand Asset Evaluator measures. Much more parsimonious,

EquiTrend is based on a small set of simple yet powerful questions. Although limited in scope compared to the Y&R study, EquiTrend has developed data over time that greatly enhance its ability to make judgments about the dynamics of brand equity and its effects. Its annual survey of 2,000 respondents started with 133 U.S. brands, and by 1995 covered over 700 brands in 100 categories.

EquiTrend is based on measures of three brand equity assets. The first is *salience*, the percentage of respondents who have an opinion about the brand. Thus, like the Y&R knowledge measure, it goes beyond the more conventional concepts of awareness, recognition, and recall by demanding that respondents hold an opinion.

The second, *perceived quality*, is at the heart of EquiTrend—in part because it has been found by Total Research to be highly associated with brand liking, trust, pride, and willingness to recommend. It is essentially the average quality rating among those who had an opinion about the brand. Quality is measured using an 11-point scale that ranges from "outstanding" to "unacceptable."

The third, *user satisfaction*, is the average quality rating a brand receives among consumers who use the brand most often. It provides a look at the strength of brands within their user base: For example, MTV is the 100th-ranked brand in perceived quality (with a rating of 5.2), but is the 2nd-ranked brand among its user group (with a 9.3 rating). Similarly, Toyota is the 62nd-ranked brand in perceived quality (an average rating of 6.7) but fourth in user satisfaction (a rating of 9.19). And Estée Lauder was the fifth brand in user satisfaction (a rating of 9.1) but only the 38th brand in perceived quality (a rating of 7.0). One problem with measuring user satisfaction is that some brands, such as Mercedes, have such a small incidence of usage that a national sample becomes inadequate to estimate user satisfaction.

The three measures are combined into an EquiTrend brand equity score. An examination of the top brands over time (see Figure 10–4) shows some remarkable consistency at the top end: Of course, since the EquiTrend data is limited, many U.S. brands are excluded.

Although it is difficult to generalize, several hypotheses emerge from an examination of the top brands (those listed above, plus such others as AT&T, IBM, Levi's, and Lego). First, drawing upon the EquiTrend brand personality data, many of these brands, such as Kodak, Hallmark, Fisher-Price, AT&T, and Lego, seem to be associated with a wholesome, warm, caring personality. Second, most of these brands have clear identities: Levi's, for example, has a strong

FIGURE 10–4

EquiTrend Consistency of Top Brands

BRAND	RATING AMONG BRANDS SURVEYED					
	1995	1994	1993	1992	1991	1990
Kodak Film	1	3	3	2	2	3
Disney World	2	1	1	1	1	—
Mercedes	3	5	8	8	3	2
Disneyland	4	2	1	1	1	—
Hallmark	5	4	4	4	5	6
Fisher-Price	6	6	5	5	6	5

identity based upon its heritage as a product worn by miners in nineteenth-century California and its contemporary user imagery. Third, an advanced technology and premium price position has likely benefited firms such as Mercedes, IBM, and AT&T.

PERCEIVED QUALITY AND PRICE

Analysis of the EquiTrend data has shown that perceived quality is associated with premium price, confirming the PIMS studies mentioned in Chapter 1.[2] For example, premium-priced brands like Kodak, Mercedes, Levi's and Hallmark have substantial perceived quality advantages over competitors such as Fuji film, Buick automobiles, Lee jeans, and American Greetings cards. This relationship is undoubtedly based upon two-way causal flows: A strong brand commands a price premium, and a price premium is an important quality cue. Raising the price when perceived quality has been (or can be) created not only provides margin dollars but also aids perceptions.

PERCEIVED QUALITY AND USAGE

Perceived quality is also shown to affect usage. An interesting observation from the EquiTrend database is that there is nearly a straight-line relationship between the proportion of consumers using a brand most often and the perceived quality rating of the brand; 39 percent of consumers who rated a brand as a 10 in quality also indicated that they used that brand most often. As Figure 10–5 shows, when the perceived quality rating fell, so did the usage. Of course, the relation-ship is muted for high-ticket markets. For instance, only 2 percent of the consumers who rate Mercedes-Benz as a 10 actually drive one most often (although more than 80 percent of those who drive one rate it this highly.)

BRAND EQUITY AND PRICE ELASTICITIES

The EquiTrend database was juxtaposed with price elasticities based on consumer research (using conjoint analysis) for two packaged-goods product classes.[3] In all contexts, the sales decrease stimulated by a 10 percent price increase was substantially more for a brand con-sidered to have good quality than a brand perceived to have superior quality.

STOCK RETURN

Even more intriguing is the relationship (described in Chapter 1) between the change in brand equity, as measured by EquiTrend, and stock return. Among the thirty-four EquiTrend brands that are associ-ated with a stock return (for example, Kodak, IBM, AT&T, Exxon,

FIGURE 10–5
Equity/Sales Relationship

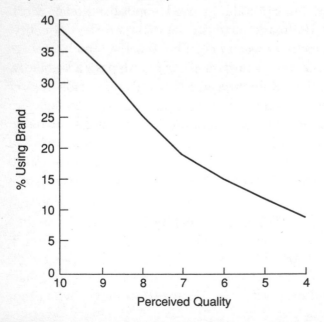

Goodyear, and Coke), brand equity had about the same impact on stock return as did return on investment, the accounting value known to be associated with stock market movement. This relationship was found even after controlling for both advertising expenditures and awareness.

INTERBRAND'S TOP BRANDS

Interbrand, a UK-based branding consulting company, used a very different approach to identify the strongest brands in the world. Its a set of criteria, chosen subjectively, included the business prospects of the brand and the brand's market environment, as well as consumer perceptions. Five hundred brands were evaluated based on seven criteria:

1. *Leadership*. A brand that leads its market sector is more stable and powerful than the second-, third-, and fourth-place brands. This criterion reflects economies of scale for the first-place brand in communication and distribution, as well as the problems that also-rans have in maintaining distribution and avoiding price erosion.
2. *Stability*. Long-lived brands with identities that have become part of the fabric of the market—and even the culture—are particularly powerful and valuable.
3. *Market*. Brands are more valuable when they are in markets with growing or stable sales levels and a price structure in which successful firms can be profitable. Some markets, such as frozen dinners and some areas of consumer electronics, are so rife with debilitating price competition that the prospects of any brand being profitable are dim.
4. *International*. Brands that are international are more valuable than national or regional brands, in part because of economies of scale. More generally, the broader the market scope of a brand, the more valuable it is; a national brand is worth more than a regional brand.
5. *Trend*. The overall long-term trend of the brand in terms of sales can be expected to reflect future prospects. A healthy, growing brand indicates that it remains contemporary and relevant to consumers.

6. *Support*. Brands that have received consistent investment and focused support are regarded as stronger than those that have not. However, the quality of support should be considered along with the level of support.

7. *Protection*. The strength and breadth of a brand's legal trademark protection is critical to the brand's strength.

Based upon these criteria, Interbrand determined that the top ten brands in the world in 1990 were as follows:

1. Coca-Cola
2. Kellogg's
3. McDonald's
4. Kodak
5. Marlboro
6. IBM
7. American Express
8. Sony
9. Mercedes-Benz
10. Nescafé

The business-oriented (versus consumer-oriented) view of the Interbrand criteria is useful in part because it is a step closer to putting a financial value on the brand—in fact, Interbrand uses its brand ratings to determine a multiplier to apply to earnings. The subjectivity of both the criteria and the assessment of the brands, however, makes the dimensions difficult to defend and affects the reliability of the resulting measures.

It is easy to challenge the assumptions reflected in the dimensions. Small niche brands, for instance, may be more profitable than so-called leadership brands. Older brands may lose their brand strength. The ability of a market to create or protect margins is difficult to project. A local brand can have advantages in connecting with customers, and thus it may be more profitable than an international brand that must deal with substantial coordination problems. Growth in brand sales, especially if obtained by sacrificing margins, is not necessarily healthy. Further, the Interbrand system does not consider the potential of the brand to support extensions into other product classes. Brand support may be ineffective; spending money on advertising does necessarily indicate effective brand building. Trademark protection, although necessary, does not of itself create brand value.

WHY MEASURE BRAND EQUITY ACROSS PRODUCTS AND MARKETS?

What is a stronger brand name—Kodak, American Express, Mercedes, Ford, or IBM? Why is a brand strong or weak? How is the brand's strength level changing over time? Why? How do brand strengths vary by country and markets and why?

Such questions are fascinating and also practical. Most businesses, if they measure brand equity at all, restrict their measures to brands in the immediate product class and market of interest. Expanding the perspective to include multiple product classes and markets can have significant practical value for the reasons below.

1. *Benchmarking against the best*. Too often managers believe that their positioning alternatives are restricted to what has always been done in their category. A consideration of brands in other categories, some of which may share some common characteristics and challenges, can suggest new identity options. Further, when one evaluates identity implementation programs, a useful benchmark might be other brands with similar identity goals. Thus, with respect to perceived quality, a leading firm in the financial service industry might find Disney to be a more interesting point of comparison than a competitor would be. Benchmarking is common when undertaking cost improvement programs; why not in branding?

2. *Insights into brand building*. Brand equity measurement over product classes and markets provides an opportunity to generate insights about and basic principles for effective brand building and brand management. The observation that Ford increased its perceived quality, and an analysis of how it did this, might suggest programs for Boeing or Maytag. The identification of brands that follow or depart from patterns can provide guidance to others facing similar contexts. A brand whose perceived quality is falling while its awareness and differentiation remain high can look to see how other brands in the same situation handled the problem. An understanding of how key constructs (such as awareness and brand loyalty) relate to each other, especially through time, can be suggestive.

3. *Tools to manage a brand portfolio*. Many organizations offer a number of brands across a variety of markets and countries. If these brands are managed separately and independently, or on an ad hoc basis, then overall resource allocation among the brands may not be made appropriately. A firm such as Grand Metropolitan, for example, owns a host of worldwide brands, including J&B, Bailey's, Smirnoff, Pillsbury, Green Giant, Häagen-Dazs and

Burger King. If Grand Met did not treat these brands as a cohesive portfolio, then strategic decisions made for the benefit of individual brands might in the end hurt the company's overall performance.

THE BRAND EQUITY TEN

Good management starts with good measurement, and the key to managing a portfolio is a common set of measures. Of course, well-developed and accepted financial measures—such as sales figures, cost analyses, margins, profit and return on assets (ROA)—usually dominate brand objectives and performance measures. The problem is that these measures tend to be short-term, so an attractive investment proposal becomes defined as one that will deliver immediate financial results. The system is self-perpetuating, because businesses and managers that can deliver on these dimensions attract more resources. Unfortunately, the best way to achieve in such a system is to starve the brand by cutting back on brand-building activities that will not pay off in the current time period.

Thus the challenge is to develop credible and sensitive measures of brand strength that supplement financial measures with brand asset measures. When brand objectives and programs are guided by both types of measures, the incentive structure becomes more balanced, and it becomes easier to justify and defend brand-building activities. In addition, the potential of short-term financial strategies to erode brand assets becomes more noticeable.

With the three above efforts to measure equity across product classes as background, a set of general measures based on the equity framework presented in Chapter 1 will be proposed here and termed the Brand Equity Ten. Approaches which combine these into a single brand equity measure will then be discussed, as well as the issue of adapting this structure to the problem of tracking equity for a specific brand. The Brand Equity Ten, whose credibility is based upon empirical evidence and a track record, can provide a starting point.

Measure Criteria

What measures will be most effective in evaluating and tracking brand equity over products and markets? Four criteria provided guidance in shaping the Brand Equity Ten. First, the measures should reflect the construct being measured—namely, brand equity. The conceptualization and structure of brand equity should guide the development of the measure set. One objective should be to tap the full scope of brand equity, including awareness, perceived quality, loyalty, and associations. In particular, measures should reflect the asset value of the brand and should focus on a sustainable advantage not easily duplicated by competitors. They should not be indicators of tactics, such as marketing mix descriptors or advertising expenditure levels. Tactics are easily copied and do not represent assets.

Second, the measures should reflect constructs that truly drive the market. Brand equity managers should be convinced that movement on a measure will eventually move the needle on price levels, sales, and profits.

Third, selected measures should be sensitive: When brand equity changes, the measures should detect that change. For example, if brand equity falls because of a tactical blunder or a competitor's actions, the measures should be responsive. If an element of brand equity is stable, the measure should reflect that stability, and the brand's true value should not be masked by noise.

Finally, measures should be developed that can be applied across brands, product categories, and markets. Such brand equity measures will be more general than those used to manage an individual brand, for which specific measures of functional benefits and brand personality are likely to be more unique. Of course, a set of proven and tested general measures can provide structure and guidance to those developing a set of measures for an individual brand. In fact, the measure selected for an across-product/market context should also be at least potentially able to track individual brands, perhaps with supplemental brand-specific measures.

USING RESEARCH TO REFINE THE MEASURE SET

The Brand Equity Ten will not necessarily represent an optimum set of measures in all contexts. Modifications to fit the context and task at hand will be necessary. For example, the food and drink business of Grand Met may require different measures than the high-tech product line of Hewlett-Packard. Further, one firm may want a more extensive (or more compact) set than another firm, perhaps because the scope of affected decisions will be different.

The logical way to proceed is to start with a comprehensive set such as the one proposed here, perhaps even supplemented by additional measures. Research of two types should guide the selection of a final set. The first type should be quantitative. The measures should be applied to a set of brands over time; statistical models can then be used to determine which measures drive objective variables of interest (such as the perceived price premium associated with brand, attitude toward the brand, or purchase intentions). The strength of the relationship between the brand equity measures and these objective variables will then provide a basis for prioritizing the list of candidate measures.

Allstate is one firm that has engaged in such quantitative research. In a study of which brand equity elements affect the perceived price premium associated with the brand, it asked customers how much of a discount a competitor would have to provide to induce them to switch. Noncustomers were asked how much savings Allstate would have to provide to induce a switch. The researchers then explored subjects related to brand equity, including perceptions of Allstate, its services, its agents, and its brand personality. Statistical analysis was employed to determine which variables influenced the price premium observed. These variables were then prime candidates to measure Allstate's brand equity over time.

A second research approach is to develop extensive case studies that describe large positive and negative changes in the price premium measure. Each case study would attempt to determine the causes of the change in the value of the brand. Convincing case studies can suggest variables that influence brand equity and can provide credibility to both the measures and to the whole process.

THE BRAND EQUITY TEN

The ten measures were chosen on the basis of the four criteria set forth above. In identifying these variables, the measurement efforts of Y&R, Total Research, Interbrand, and others were drawn upon.

The measures nominated are grouped into five categories and summarized in Figure 10–6. The first four categories represent customer perceptions of the brand along the four dimensions of brand equity—loyalty, perceived quality, associations and awareness. The fifth includes two sets of market behavior measures that represent information obtained from market-based information rather than directly from customers.

LOYALTY MEASURES

Loyalty is a core dimension of brand equity. A loyal customer base represents a barrier to entry, a possible price premium, time to respond to competitor innovations, and a bulwark against deleterious price competition. Loyalty is of sufficient relevance to use as a criterion variable—that is, one that can be the basis of evaluating other possible measures. If there are brand equity blunders that go to the

FIGURE 10–6
The Brand Equity Ten

Loyalty Measures

    1. Price Premium

    2. Satisfaction/Loyalty

Perceived Quality/Leadership Measures

    3. Perceived Quality

    4. Leadership/popularity

Associations/Differentiation Measures

    5. Perceived Value

    6. Brand Personality

    7. Organizational Associations

Awareness Measures

    8. Brand Awareness

Market Behavior Measures

    9. Market Share

    10. Market Price and Distribution Coverage

---

heart of the customer relationship, they should affect loyalty. You usually offend your core first because they are connected to the brand and they care.

1. PRICE PREMIUM

A basic indicator of loyalty is the amount a customer will pay for the brand in comparison with another brand offering similar or fewer benefits. For example, a consumer may be willing to pay 10 percent more to shop at Sak's rather than at Bloomingdale's, or may be willing to pay 15 percent more for Coke than for Pepsi. This is called the *price premium* associated with the brand's loyalty, and it may be high or low and positive or negative depending on the two brands involved in the comparison.

If a brand is compared to a high-priced brand, the price premium attached to a brand could be negative. For example, suppose Kmart shoppers expect a 20 percent price advantage over Macy's, and would buy at Macy's if the Kmart price advantage was any smaller. This negative price premium could reflect substantial brand equity for Kmart if its prices were actually 25 percent lower.

In measuring price premium, or any brand equity measure, it is useful to segment the market by loyalty. For example, the market might be divided into loyal buyers of the reference brand, customers who are brand switchers, and noncustomers. Each group, of course, will have a very different perspective on the equity of the reference brand. Aggregating over loyalty groups will provide a less sensitive measurement and will cloud the strategic interpretation of the brand equity profile.

The price premium measure is defined with respect to a competitor or a set competitors, who must be clearly specified. A set of competitors is usually preferred for measurement, because the brand equity of a single competitor can decline while the equity of other competitors remains stable. In such a case, using only the declining competitor as a point of comparison would give an erroneous perspective of the brand's health.

The price premium can be determined by simply asking customers how much more they would be willing to pay for the brand. (This is called a *dollar metric*.) For instance, a customer might be asked, "How much more would you pay to be able to buy a Toyota Camry instead of a Honda Accord?"

A more sensitive and reliable measure of price premium, however, can be obtained using conjoint or trade-off analysis. This well-developed market research approach presents consumers with a series of simple choices, which are then analyzed together in order to determine the importance of different dimensions to consumers. For example, consumers might first be asked, "Would you prefer a Toyota Corolla at $14,000, a Honda Civic at $13,000, a Saturn at $12,500, or a Chrysler Neon at $12,000?" If the Saturn is selected, then the process is repeated, but this time with the Saturn priced at $13,000. If the Civic is then chosen, the next set will include the Civic with a $13,500 price. The value of the brand emerges from such a study.

The Best Single Measure of Brand Equity?

The price premium may be the best single measure of brand equity available, because it directly captures the loyalty of customers in a most relevant way. If they are loyal, they should logically be willing to pay a price premium; if they are not willing to pay more, the loyalty level is shallow. Indeed, as noted above, Allstate's research to identify the key drivers of its brand equity focused on what variables influenced the price premium.

There is a natural desire to obtain an estimate of the financial value of a brand. Knowing the brand's value helps to calibrate brand-building investments, and changes in value can assist in the evaluation of marketing programs. One convenient aspect of the price premium is that it can be the basis for a crude estimate of brand value (the price premium associated with existing customers, multiplied by unit sales).

Of course, distribution channel realities may prevent the price premium from affecting the brand's price in the marketplace. Whereas many customers might be willing to pay a 10 percent premium to obtain Coke, the price-sensitive segment and aggressive retailers may make the realization of this price premium in the supermarket infeasible. Nevertheless, the price-premium-based brand value estimate can be helpful.

Intel is one firm that tracks its price premium. Every week, interviewers are in computer stores asking people how much of a discount would be needed before a customer would feel comfortable buying a personal computer without "Intel Inside." As a result, Intel has a continuous measure of its price premium, which can be used to evaluate marketing programs and to monitor the overall health of the brand.

Problems/Cautions

One problem with the price premium is that it is defined only with respect to a competitor or set of competitors. In a market with many brands, several sets of price premium measures will be needed, and even then an important emerging competitor might be missed. For example, Compaq used IBM as its primary frame of reference when others, such as Dell and Gateway, were making large inroads at a much lower price point. Thus Compaq's price over time reflected an increasingly inflated valuation of its brand equity.

An interpretation problem will exist when a brand has different competitors in different markets. For example, in one region Budweiser may face a strong local brand that has little presence elsewhere, whereas in another region microbreweries may be important. To compare Budweiser's strength in these regions, a composite measure needs to be created in each—defined, for example, by the average of the price premium found with respect to the leading private label, the leading regional brand, and the leading national competitor.

Further, there are markets in which price differences are not very relevant because legal restrictions (for example, the Japanese government has long controlled the price of beer) or market forces make it difficult for such differences to emerge. In such contexts, the price premium concept becomes less meaningful. The key to these markets is the ability to gain customers at the prevailing price, and some measure of buying intentions becomes more relevant.

2. CUSTOMER SATISFACTION/LOYALTY

Satisfaction (or liking) is a direct measure of how willing customers are to stick to a brand. Enormous progress has been made in the past decade in the measurement of satisfaction. In fact, a whole satisfaction measurement industry has developed. A direct measure of satisfaction can be applied to existing customers, perhaps defined as those who used the product or service in the last year. The reference could be the last use experience, or simply the use experience from the customers' view:

- Are you satisfied?
- Are you delighted with your experience with this brand?
- Does the product or service meet expectations?
- Would you buy the brand on the next opportunity?
- Would you recommend the product or service to others?
- Were there problems and inconveniences associated with the use of the product and service?

Satisfaction is an especially powerful measure in service businesses (such as car rental firms, hotels, or banks), where loyalty is often the cumulative result of the use experiences.

Satisfaction can also be measured by asking direct questions about loyalty. Loyalty is a relatively simple, accessible concept; people understand loyalty to family, friends, firms and brands. Direct questions about loyalty (Are you loyal to this brand? Do you buy mostly on price?) allow the market to be segmented into loyal users, price chasers, and those in between (as noted in Chapter 1). Another type of measure would be the level of loyalty in terms of the number of brands, where customers would be asked if they felt loyal to one, two, three, or more brands, or if they see all brands as pretty much the same. The percentage of customers who are loyal to a given brand or include it in a set of two or three preferred brands can be a relevant statistic.

Problems/Cautions

An important limitation of satisfaction measures is that they do not really apply to noncustomers. Thus, there is really no measure of the extent of brand equity beyond the customer base.

Another complication is that satisfaction aggregated over the loyal and switcher groups becomes somewhat insensitive and difficult to interpret. Thus it is often necessary to develop a set of loyalty measures by loyalty segment.

PERCEIVED QUALITY AND LEADERSHIP MEASURES

In this section, the perceived quality measure will be augmented by a related variable termed *leadership*. The role of esteem as a summary of perceived quality and leadership is also reviewed.

3. PERCEIVED QUALITY

Perceived quality is one of the key dimensions of brand equity. As noted in Chapter 1, it has been shown to directly affect both ROI and stock return in studies using statistical models. Further, it is highly associated with other key brand identity measures, including specific functional benefit variables. Thus perceived quality provides a surrogate variable for other, more specific elements of brand identity.

Perceived quality also has the important attribute of being applicable across product classes. High-quality banks may mean something different than high-quality beer, of course, but tracking the relative difference in the scores does have meaning.

Perceived quality can be measured with scales such as the following:

- High quality versus shoddy quality
- Best in category versus worst in category
- Consistent quality versus inconsistent quality
- Finest quality versus average quality versus inferior quality

Problems/Cautions

Perceived quality involves a product frame of reference. It makes a difference, for example, if the customer is comparing all automobiles or only subcompacts (such as Saturn or Dodge Neon). It might be necessary to help the respondent by providing a cue as to the appropriate frame of reference. Doing so, however, will add a layer of complication in the interpretation of the results.

Again, there is also the issue of loyalty segments. The interpretation of the perceived quality for the loyal segment versus the switchers versus those loyal to another brand could be different. For example, perceived quality for the switchers might reflect only whether the brand is acceptable or not. Including switchers in the analysis would make the result less sensitive and informative.

Perceived quality may not be a key driver in some contexts. In particular, it may not be responsive to relevant events. It is this concern that leads to the consideration of the leadership variable.

4. LEADERSHIP AND POPULARITY

The perceived quality measure may especially lack sensitivity to the innovations of competitors. For example, Crest's strong position as the leading dentifrice is based on the brand's long-standing endorsement by the American Dental Association. When competitors such as Arm & Hammer introduced baking powder toothpaste and innovative packaging, however, they made a real dent in Crest's customer base. Even though the perceived quality of Crest may not have changed as a result, its brand equity was damaged. What is needed is a supplement to the perceived quality construct that taps the dynamics of the market.

One such construct can be termed *leadership*. Leadership has three dimensions. First, it reflects in part the "number one" syndrome. The logic is that if enough customers are buying into the brand concept to make it the sales leader, it must have merit. Second, leadership taps the dynamics of customer acceptance, reflecting the fact that people want to be on the bandwagon and are uneasy going against the flow. Is the brand growing more popular? Is it considered an "in" product to use? Are people who use it up-to-date, part of the popular trends? Third, it can also tap innovation within a product class—that is, whether a brand is moving ahead technologically.

Leadership thus can be measured by scales that ask whether a brand is the following:

- A category leader
- Growing more popular
- Respected for innovation

As noted earlier, Y&R used popularity growth as a companion measure to perceived quality to develop its esteem construct. Further, one of the eight dimensions of brand strength in the Interbrand system is termed leadership; in that system, it is measured by the relative size of the sales base. In the Interbrand weighting scheme, leadership receives the most weight (25 points out of 100).

Problems/Cautions

The fact that leadership has the dimensions of market share, popularity, and innovation means that it is not a simple construct. Further, it has not been as well documented and researched as such other dimensions as loyalty, perceived quality, and awareness. Therefore there is little proof that it is important enough to merit attention.

ESTEEM—COMBINING PERCEIVED QUALITY AND LEADERSHIP

Following the Y&R model, it is possible to combine perceived quality and leadership into an esteem dimension. The premise is that the inclusion of leadership creates a construct, namely esteem, that means more than just quality.

ASSOCIATIONS/DIFFERENTIATION MEASURES

The key associations component of brand equity is a problem because many of the involved image dimensions are usually unique to a product class and to a brand. The challenge then is to generate measures that will work across product classes.

Measurement of associations can be structured by using three of the perspectives on brand identity noted in Chapter 3: the brand-as-product (value), the brand-as-person (brand personality) and the brand-as-organization (organizational associations).

5. VALUE

One role of brand identity is to create a value proposition. The value proposition, which usually involves a functional benefit, is basic to brands in most product classes: If the brand does not generate value, it will usually be vulnerable to competitors. The value measure provides a summary indicator of the brand's success at creating that value proposition. By focusing on value rather than functional benefits, a measure is created that can apply across product classes.

Brand value thus can be measured by the following:

- Whether the brand proves good value for the money
- Whether there is a reason to buy this brand over others

Problems/Cautions

This measure, like others, will be sensitive to the brand set that is used as a frame of reference by the customer. The relevant set can be cued by using phrases such as "among comparable brands" or "among brands with which it competes."

A substantial issue in the value dimension is whether it really represents a different construct from perceived quality; after all, value can be considered at least in some contexts as perceived quality divided by price. Some evidence comes from a Total Research study based on their EquiTrend database. Total Research concluded that, on average, perceived quality explained 80 percent of the variation in perceived value. And for most brands, perceived quality is a better predictor of purchase history than is value. Consider the ratings for AT&T and MCI as shown below:

	QUALITY	VALUE
AT&T	8.0	7.5
MCI	5.4	5.5
Difference	2.6	2.0

Quality and value are the same for MCI, while for AT&T there is a modest difference. The bottom line is that the same conclusion (AT&T is rated higher than MCI) would emerge whether perceived quality or perceived value were used as a measure.

Total Research, however, concluded that perceived value is more important than perceived quality for some brands, including the following:

- Southwest and Continental Air, which are positioned on delivering low price
- The Discover Card, which was introduced for the value-smart shopper
- Tylenol, under attack from private labels
- Rubbermaid, which has a very functional appeal

Further, the research of Y&R suggests that value and perceived quality represent very different dimensions of customer forces. Perceived quality and (more generally) esteem relate to the prestige and respect that the brand holds. In contrast, value relates more to functional benefits and the practical utility of buying and using the brand. This logic supports the inclusion of value as a separate dimension, although there are certainly cases in which it could be combined with perceived quality.

6. BRAND PERSONALITY

A second element of associations/differentiation is brand personality. For some brands, the brand personality provides links to the brand's emotional and self-expressive benefits as well as a basis for brand–

328 BUILDING STRONG BRANDS

customer relationships and differentiation. This is especially the case for brands that have only minor physical differences and are consumed in a social setting where the brand can make a visible statement about the consumer. For example, only a small percentage of consumers can distinguish between the top four leading brandies, and virtually no taster can distinguish among them when they are mixed in coffee (an important application in Europe). However, brandies have personalities, are served in a social setting, and do make a statement about those who serve and drink the brandy. In that context, the brand personality can be vital.

A brand personality will involve a set of specific dimensions unique to the brand. For a Charlie fragrance, for example, an excitement dimension may be important, while a cowboy personality may have no relevance. Thus some level of detail will be worthwhile with respect to the excitement dimension, while the rugged dimensions may be neglected.

When considering brand personality across products, one option would be to measure a personality spectrum such as the Big Five (discussed in Chapter 5). For tracking purposes, however, the Brand Equity Ten—each with several items—is already unwieldy. What are needed are some measures that will reflect the existence of a strong personality but are not product specific. Candidate scales might include the following:

- Does this brand have a personality?
- Is this brand interesting?
- I have a clear image of the type of person who would use the brand.
- This brand has a rich history.

The last two items reflect user imagery and the brand heritage, two drivers of brand personality that are often relevant dimensions of brand identity.

Problems/Cautions

Not all brands are personality brands, of course. Using personality as a general indicator of brand strength will be a distortion for some brands, particularly those who position themselves primarily with respect to functional advantages and value. The need is thus to use the Brand Equity Ten judiciously and to avoid including dimensions that are irrelevant to a context.

There is a question as to whether brand personality and its measures will be sensitive to changes in brand equity. A brand personality may be excessively stable and thus not reflect the dynamics of the market.

7. Organizational Associations

Another dimension of brand identity is the brand-as-organization, which also can be a driver of differentiation. It is particularly likely to be a factor when brands are similar with respect to attributes, when the organization is visible (as in a durable goods or a service business), or when a corporate brand is involved.

To tap the brand-as-organization, scales such as these could be considered:

- This brand is made by an organization I would trust.
- I admire the brand X organization.
- I would be proud (or pleased) to do business with the brand X organization.

Problems/Cautions

Again, the brand-as-organization, like the brand-as-person, is not relevant for all brands, and an irrelevant measure can be misinterpreted. Measurement of organizational associations also suffer from a lack of sensitivity, because changing the organizational image is difficult.

Differentiation: A Summary Measure of Brand Associations

The three sets of measures of brand associations all tap various dimensions of how the brand can be differentiated from its competitors. Differentiation is a bottom-line characteristic of a brand. If a brand is not perceived as being different, then it will have a difficult time supporting a price premium or maintaining a price that will support an attractive margin. Thus an option would be to replace or supplement the three brand association measures with a single set of indicators of the brand's ability to achieve differentiation.

Measures could include the following:

- This brand is different from other brands.
- This brand is basically the same as the other brands.

AWARENESS MEASURES

8. BRAND AWARENESS

Awareness reflects the presence of the brand in the mind of customers. It can be a driver in some categories, and it usually has a key role to play in brand equity. Awareness measures can reflect in part the scope of the brand's reach in terms of segments. Increasing awareness is one mechanism to expand the market reach of the brand. Awareness, as the discussion in Chapter 1 noted, can also affect perceptions and attitudes.

Brand awareness reflects both the knowledge and the salience of the brand in the customer's mind. Awareness can be measured on different levels including the following:

- Recognition ("Have you heard of the Buick Roadmaster?")
- Recall ("What brands of cars can you recall?")
- Graveyard statistic (recall level of those who recognize the brand)
- Top of mind (the first-named brand in a recall task)
- Brand dominance (the only brand recalled)
- Brand familiarity (the brand is familiar)
- Brand knowledge or salience (you have an opinion about the brand)

The graveyard statistic (the recall level of those who recognize the brand) is based on the graveyard concept introduced in Chapter 1. It is designed to distinguish between the strong niche brand (which has high recognition and recall, but only within the niche segment) and a tired brand (which has slipped into oblivion but still has high recognition). A strong niche brand would do well on the graveyard statistic, and "graveyard" brands with high recognition but low recall would be identified. The dynamics of the graveyard statistic can be predictive of future market trends.

Problems/Cautions

There are a variety of awareness levels, and the appropriate one to use will differ across brands and product classes, making comparison difficult. For some brands (in the software industry, for example), recognition will be important, whereas in other categories (such as automobiles) recognition measures will be high for all but the newest brands. Some brands (like A1, Dixie Cups, or Kleenex) will be so preeminent in their category that they will need to use the dominance measure to generate any sensitivity.

Recall is often inconvenient to measure, as it can complicate and add costs to a structured survey that otherwise would employ scales. The graveyard statistic, of course, is based in part on recall, as are several other measures that are potentially relevant in some contexts. One approach to gaining more sensitivity without employing recall is the use of brand knowledge and salience variables. This approach is used by the Y&R and Total Research efforts, in part to avoid recall questions.

Being aware of a brand name by itself may not be as important as being aware of the name attached to a symbol or visual image. For many brands (like Wells Fargo Bank, Pillsbury and Transamerica), name awareness cannot be separated from familiarity with the brand's symbols and visual imagery. In fact, the awareness levels can be affected dramatically by cueing such symbols and imagery, and in general, the task of creating awareness will usually intimately involve them.

It might therefore be useful to move beyond measuring brand name awareness to measuring awareness of symbols and visual imagery. The measure could be based on an open-ended question about what, if anything, comes to mind when the brand is mentioned. Another tack is to expose respondents to a set of visual images and ask them which ones they recognize. Of course, both the open-ended question and the stimulus exposure is a bit messy in the context of an otherwise straightforward survey instrument.

MARKET BEHAVIOR MEASURES

The first eight sets of Brand Equity Ten measures all require a customer survey that can be expensive, inconvenient, time-consuming, and hard to implement and interpret. A possible exception might be brand loyalty, which can also be measured by repeat-purchase data from scanner panel sources. It is useful to be able to track the brand using other sources of data, including those discussed below.

9. MARKET SHARE

The performance of the brand as measured by market share (and/or sales) often provides a valid and sensitive reflection of the brand's standing with customers. When the brand has a relative advantage in the minds of customers, market share should increase or at least not decrease. In contrast, when competitors improve their brand equity, their share should respond. In this sense, market share is a good summary measure of brand equity.

Market share (and/or sales) data have the advantage of being both available and accurate. Information on submarkets is often also part of the databases. Firms usually track these figures as a matter of course; a customer survey (with the associated costs, interpretation difficulties, and delays) is not required.

Problems/Cautions

There are, however, measurement problems with market share. The product class and competitor set need to be defined, and sometimes this is not easy to do. Should store brands be included? What about brands at a different price point? Is the relevant competitor set compact cars, non-luxury cars, import cars, or all cars? Should Miller Lite be compared to all beers, all premium beers, or all light beers? Further, the relevant competitor set can change, creating interpretation problems.

The biggest problem is that market share indicators are responsive to the short-term strategies that often undermine brand equity. Market share can be obtained by enticing price switchers with promotions and price deals which compromise the long-term value of the brand. Market share can also respond positively even if a brand cuts its brand-building activities or generates ineffective or negative brand-building efforts.

These problems are minimized when market share is only one of a set of brand equity measures which also includes measures of market price levels and distribution coverage.

10. MARKET PRICE AND DISTRIBUTION COVERAGE

Market share can be a particularly deceptive brand equity measure when it increases as a result of reduced prices or price promotions. Thus it is important to measure the relative market price at which the brand is being sold. To do so, the prices of various varieties of the brand weighted by their relative sales volume need to be obtained. The relative market price could be defined as the average price at which the brand was sold during the month, divided by the average price at which all brands were sold.

Market share or sales data are also extremely sensitive to distribution coverage. The gain or loss of a major outlet, or a move into another geographic region, may dramatically affect sales. Therefore, it is important to distinguish the brand equity based on a change in distribution coverage from that created by strengthening the brand's perceived quality or identity. Another measure of brand strength, then, is distribution coverage, which could be measured by either of the following:

- The percentage of stores carrying the brand
- The percentage of people who have access to the brand.

Problems/Cautions

Creating price-level statistics is difficult in a messy market with different channels, different variants of brand offerings, and a complex set of competitors. A standard market basket is not so easy to conceptualize. Further, there are duties, taxes, and retail policies that cloud the issue for products such as beer or wine.

Distribution coverage will have similar data-gathering and interpretation problems. Most brands have a host of sizes and varieties, and sometimes many product classes; distribution coverage measures will need to sort out such complications. Further, if wholesalers are used, the retail distribution data may be expensive to obtain.

TOWARD A SINGLE VALUE OF BRAND EQUITY

Clearly, tapping the Brand Equity Ten can require dozens of measures (see Figure 10–7). Although each potentially has diagnostic value, the use of so many measures is unwieldy. For reporting and tracking purposes it would be useful and convenient to have a single summary measure, or at most a set of four measures. Given that many brands are each being monitored in dozens of markets, there is a need for a summary measure to signal whether the underlying measures should be examined.

Generating one or more summary measures involves four issues.

First, what constructs will be the bases of the brand equity measurement system, and how should they be measured? In Figure 10–6,

FIGURE 10–7
Measuring Brand Equity Across Products/Markets

LOYALTY

1. Price Premium
   - For a 17-ounce package of chocolate chip cookies, Nabisco is priced at $2.16. How much extra would you be willing to pay to obtain Pepperidge Farm instead of Nabisco?
   - Brand Y would have to cost ___ percent less than Brand X before I would switch brands.
   - For a 16-ounce package of chocolate chip cookies, would you prefer Nabisco at $2.16 or Pepperidge Farm at $2.29?

2. Satisfaction/Loyalty (among those who have used the brand)
   - Considering my recent use experience, I would say I was (dissatisfied, satisfied, delighted).
   - The brand met my expectations during the last use experience.
   - Would you buy the brand on the next opportunity?
   - Would you recommend the product or service to others?
   - The brand is (the only, one of two, one of three, one of more than three) brands that I buy and use.

PERCEIVED QUALITY/LEADERSHIP

3. Perceived Quality

   In comparison with alternative brands, this brand is
   - Very high quality
   - Consistently high quality
   - (The best, one of the best, one of the worst, the worst)

4. Leadership/Popularity

   In comparison with alternative brands, this brand is
   - Growing in popularity
   - A leading brand in the category
   - Respected for innovation

Esteem

   In comparison with alternative brands, I
   - Hold this brand in high esteem
   - Highly respect this brand

5. Perceived Value
    • The brand is good value for the money.

    • There is a reason to buy this brand over others.

6. Personality
    • This brand has a personality.

    • This brand is interesting.

    • I have a clear image of the type of person who would use the brand.

    • This brand has a rich history.

7. Organization
    • This is a brand I would trust.

    • I admire the Brand X organization.

    • I would be proud to do business with the Brand X organization.

Differentiation

    • This brand is different from other brands.

    • This brand is basically the same as the other brands.

AWARENESS

8. Brand Awareness
    • Name the brands in this product class.

    • Have you heard of this brand?

    • Do you have an opinion about this brand?

    • Are you familiar with this brand?

MARKET BEHAVIOR

9. Market Share
    • Market share based on market surveys of usage or syndicated data

10. Price and Distribution Indices
    • Relative market-price—the average price at which the brand was sold during the month, divided by the average price at which all brands were sold

    • The percentage of stores carrying the brand

    • The percentage of people who have access to the brand

eight measurement constructs based on buyer perceptions are set forth organized under the four dimensions of brand equity: loyalty, perceived quality, identity, and awareness. A judgment needs to be made as to how many of these constructs should be in the core measure set. Should it be four, or eight, or something in between? Further, for each of the constructs, how should the underlying indicators be combined? Also, should market behavior measures be included?

Second, what weights should be placed on the constructs in order to develop a single summary measure of brand equity? What is the relative importance of the various dimensions of brand equity? As a practical matter, the weights are not as critical as one might expect, because the final number is rarely sensitive to changes in weighting schemes. Thus weighting all dimensions equally is a good default decision. Also, the underlying measures will be available for diagnostics.

Third, how should the constructs be combined? Should a simple weighted average or a more complex formula be employed? Total Research uses awareness multiplied by perceived quality as one component, arguing that the absence of either is fatal.

Fourth, what competitors will form the comparison set? A small but growing competitor can be significant, but it may be overlooked in a standardized analysis. Different markets, particularly if they involve different countries, may have different competitor sets. How will the comparison with competitors be reported? A ratio may be easy to interpret, but it can be very sensitive to movements in the denominator value.

In essence, a model of brand equity needs to be created that is most relevant to the brand or brand set involved. There are two approaches that can be employed. First, a group of relevant managers could engage in a series of exercises addressing the four issues. Second, data on brand equity dimensions could be used to determine what elements are drivers of key objectives such as price premium, market share, or profitability. The Allstate effort to do this used price premium as the target objective.

CREATING MEASURES OVER MARKETS

Another issue is whether the survey instrument needs to be identical over markets (countries, for example). Each market may already have its own tested instrument which has a history that helps facilitate interpretation. It might be extremely costly both in terms of money and "buy-in" (among the country management teams) to add another instrument that is partially redundant and seems to be off target.

One solution would be to charge the management team for each market to create or adapt a measure for the major constructs—namely, loyalty, perceived quality/leadership, association/differentiation, awareness, and market behavior. For each measure, a score would be reported that could be compared to both a relevant competitor set and to the past. In comparing scores across markets, the focus would be on changes from the past and the relative performance with respect to a competitor set. The fact that the exact instruments differ may not be crucial, especially given that any instrument would need to be adapted to a market in any case.

ADAPTING THE MEASURES TO A BRAND'S CONTEXT

When a tracking effort is needed within a brand context, the set of ten measures summarized in Figure 10–6 will provide a good point of departure. However, the measurement set should be adapted to include brand-specific information such as the following:

1. The relative importance to the brand of the different brand equity components.
2. The brand identity, the value proposition, and the brand position.

An analysis of the brand equity structure will be pivotal. What is important to brand equity within each of the four dimensions? Is it recognition, recall, or top-of-mind awareness that is most relevant? What is the relative importance of brand loyalty? If the task is to gain new customers, brand loyalty may be less important. Under the loyalty construct, indicators of the habitual user might be important to manage one segment, while the intensity of involvement might be relevant for another.

The brand identity, value proposition, and brand position will usually also be central. If clear and operational, the brand position will indicate what is central to the communication program, particularly areas in which improvement should be sought. The brand identity and value proposition will suggest dimensions in which declines are to be avoided.

There will usually be a trade-off between completeness and cost plus feasibility. A forty- or fifty-item inventory may provide useful diagnostics. Even a few judiciously chosen questions, however, can provide helpful indicators of the brand's health.

QUESTIONS TO CONSIDER

1. Evaluate the strengths and weaknesses of the three efforts to measure brand equity described at the outset of this chapter.
2. Which of the Brand Equity Ten would be most relevant to an effort to measure brand equity for your brand? Which would help most in identifying brands to benchmark against? What brands excel in some aspect of brand equity?
3. How would you weight the dimensions of brand equity in the context of your brand and industry? What other brands would you use to compare against? How would you report the relative performance of your brand? If you operate in different countries (or markets), will it be desirable/feasible to use the same instruments and brand comparison set in each market? If not, what would you propose?
4. Develop a brand equity measurement instrument for your brand.

11

ORGANIZING FOR BRAND BUILDING

We have met the enemy and he is us.
> —Pogo

Long-term brand equity and growth depends on our ability to successfully integrate and implement all elements of a comprehensive marketing program.
> —Timm F. Crull, Chairman & CEO of Nestlé, Retired

BRAND-BUILDING IMPERATIVES

Building brands involves strategic and tactical imperatives that create significant organizational challenges. Yesterday's organizational charts will need to be modified or changed; the successful brand-building companies in the coming decade will find new structures and systems.

This chapter discusses the organizational imperatives facing brand strategists,(see Figure 11–1) how the organization can be adapted to address these imperatives, and the roles of the advertising agency in the process.

FIGURE 11–1
Managing the Brand

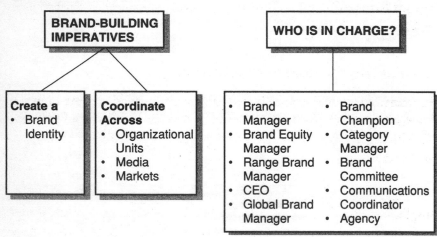

THE STRATEGIC IMPERATIVE: HAVING A BRAND IDENTITY

A basic imperative is to have a brand identity in place to guide the development and coordination of the tactical programs. This identity should have a well-defined core and generate a value proposition and/or a basis for a brand relationship. Too often there is little effort to specify a brand identity, in part because no one is charged with that task. One goal of the brand-building organization is to make sure that someone is in charge and that an identity gets created.

The brand identity needs to be sufficiently rich and defined to help distinguish between on-target, supportive communications and those that are inconsistent and nonsupportive. If the identity is fuzzy or incomplete, it will not provide real guidance—virtually any communication program will appear to be consistent.

Also needed is a vision of the brand's future identity and roles (for example, endorser, descriptor, or driver). Unfortunately, most organizations are product driven rather than brand driven. This means that the brand's future is dictated by the past actions of product developers. At General Mills, for example, the R&D area may produce a new product that takes advantage of novel food-processing techniques. After the product is developed, a brand name is needed; the immediate temptation is to apply an established General Mills name (such as Betty Crocker, the Big G, or Bisquick). If there is no brand vision to guide this type of decision, an identity will drift over time, pushed into uncharted waters by incremental decisions. The result can be a brand that is diffused and meaningless, or one that has drifted away from its core business.

COORDINATION ACROSS THE ORGANIZATION

In many firms, a brand is shared by several businesses. At Hewlett-Packard, for example, the HP brand and subbrands like the Jet series (DeskJet, LaserJet and so on) are shared by very different businesses, each with its own strategy, customer set, and objectives. A host of divisions share the General Electric, Suntory, and Goodyear brands. In such cases, an organizational imperative is to create a mechanism for implementing a common, coordinated brand strategy across all businesses. If no such mechanism is in place, the brand identity is likely to be inconsistently implemented. The result will be customer confusion and lost opportunities for building synergy.

COORDINATING ACROSS MEDIA

Another imperative is to create mechanisms to coordinate brand building across diverse media options which include event sponsorships, clubs and usage programs, direct response marketing, public relations, publicity, promotions, event stores, packaging, and design. At one time, brand building was primarily done through media advertising, and the coordination problem was small or nonexistent. The advertising agency was often the dominant player. Today, effective brand building needs to involve many organizations staffed by individuals who specialize in particular types of media or modes of communication. Each of these people and organizations will have a unique perspective and set of objectives. Making them all march to the same brand identity—indeed, getting them all to even understand the identity—is a formidable task whether the "captain" resides in an agency or with the client firm.

Furthermore, not all media programs will be consistent with the brand's identity. The challenge will be to have measurement systems in place to identify inconsistencies, even if this measurement involves both expense and inconvenience. In addition, the organization must empower an individual who has the will and the ability to discontinue inconsistent programs, even if these programs seem to be helping the brand on other measures.

COORDINATING ACROSS MARKETS

When a brand is active in multiple markets (defined by products or segments), a final imperative is to coordinate strategy and tactics across those markets in order to build synergy and economies of scale while remaining flexible enough to adjust to each market's unique characteristics. The task is usually complicated by the many functional areas that influence brand building (such as advertising, sales, and market research, among others).

ADAPTING THE ORGANIZATION FOR BRAND BUILDING

There are a host of demands on organizations in this era of restructuring, flattening, total quality management, total cost control, customer focus, innovation thrusts, and on and on. In the face of these demands, one challenge for the organization is to get brand building on the list of priorities. Another is to adapt the organization to deal with the brand-building imperatives.

THE ORGANIZATIONAL CULTURE

Firms that are good at developing strong brands usually have a strong brand-building culture, including clearly defined values, norms, and organizational symbols. Brand building is accepted in these firms: Top management visibly supports the brands, and actions that put brands at risk are questioned as a matter of course.

The culture of an organization, more than procedures or structures, is ultimately what drives the attainment of sustainable advantage. Unless brand building becomes an organizational priority, it will be difficult for the organization to address difficult branding problems.

At some organizations, there is a tendency to give lip service to building brands. If one listens carefully, though, one finds the assumption that brand building will occur only after the business "makes the numbers." When sales and profit goals are threatened, brand investment is cut back to compensate. Such organizations talk the talk of brand building, but they fail to walk the walk. A key is to have measurement and reward systems that make it feasible to maintain and enhance brand equity even when the brand is not "making the numbers."

WHO IS IN CHARGE OF THE BRAND?

In too many organizations, the answer to this question is no one. Or there are many people in charge, but each has different objectives. Hewlett-Packard, for example, has hundreds of managers, each with responsibility for the HP brand in a particular business area. Further, marketing products in different countries adds another layer of complexity and additional caretakers of the HP brand.

When a single person is in charge of the business associated with a brand, there will be an incentive to protect and nurture that brand. Suppose, however, that another business unit borrows the brand name, as, for example, the Sara Lee brand name (attached to the Sara Lee Corporation as well as the bakery line) has been borrowed by Sara Lee Packaged Meats (which also has such brands as Hillshire Farm and Ballpark Franks) to use on some top-end deli meats.[1] The borrower (in this case, the Packaged Meats line) has an opportunity to exploit the brand, while the risk of damage to the brand is shouldered by another organizational unit (in this case, Sara Lee Bakery). If the brand is mishandled, it is unfortunate for the Packaged Meats line, but not a disaster. A borrower thus would have less incentive to protect the brand name.

Someone, or some group, needs to be in charge of designing the brand identity and position in today's market, of seeing to it that identity/position implementation is effective and efficient; of ensuring that the identity/position is not compromised; and of designing crisis management plans to handle possible disasters. Several models that have proven successful for different companies are outlined below.

The Brand Manager

Brand managers have traditionally had strategic and tactical responsibility for their brand, including having responsibility for the brand's identity and position, maintaining that identity by securing needed investments, and making sure that all media efforts are consistent with the identity. The brand manager role, first developed by Procter & Gamble in the mid-1930s for brands representing distinct businesses of manageable size, is now being applied in more complex organizations.

One problem is that the brand manager is charged with tactical programs that require day-to-day fire fighting. It is difficult to focus on strategy issues when there is always a crisis to be dealt with. Further, the brand manager is inevitably rewarded on the basis of short-term measures such as sales and profits. He or she thus lacks the motivation to engage in programs that build brands, or to stop programs that risk brand equity. Successful managers are often rewarded with a promotion that takes them away from the brand—a practice that also reduces the incentive to do long-term brand building.

To make sure that strategic, long-term brand building takes place, strategic objectives and a clear brand identity need to supplement the short-term sales and profit goals. Strategic brand objectives should include brand equity dimensions such as loyalty, brand image, and brand awareness, and they should be sufficiently operational so that they can truly guide programs and tactics and be used as a basis for performance appraisal and compensation.

The Brand Equity Manager

Some firms have separated brand strategy from the implementation of the marketing program. A brand equity manager (sometimes labeled as a brand manager) is in charge of creating and maintaining the brand identity and coordinating it over products and markets. Freed from the tactical management of the brand, this manager is responsible for strategic brand research and brand equity measurement. Implementation of the brand strategy is then conducted by tactically-focused managers or (in the case of some large organizations such as Marriott, General Motors, and Hallmark) functional organizational units. The the brand equity manager monitors, reviews, and perhaps approves the tactics from a brand strategy perspective.

The Range Brand Manager

Firms with range brands are naturally organized by products. As a result, the brand is usually managed by different people in different contexts and with different objectives. A solution is the range brand manager—one person who looks after the strategic interests of the brand across the different businesses. The range brand manager supports the brand by making sure that there is an overall brand strategy accepted by everyone and that managers are sensitive to both the need to support the brand identity and the need to avoid inconsistencies. This task involves developing communication vehicles that maximize brand identity synergies across the organization.

The Global Brand Manager

IDV, the spirits business of Grand Metropolitan, has extended the brand equity manager concept to a global operation. Each country has a complement of national brand managers, each of whom is charged with marketing his or her respective Grand Met spirit brand in that country. However, the major IDV brands also have a global brand manager (in the case of Smirnoff, this person is president of the Pierre Smirnoff Company) who is charged with developing a brand identity worldwide, ensuring that the companies in each country are faithful to the brand strategy, communicating and facilitating best practices, and encouraging consistency and synergy across countries. This concept has been extended to Grand Met's Pillsbury operations for brands such as Green Giant and Häagen-Dazs.

The fact that the global brand manager and the national operations have different perspectives and objectives creates a tension that Grand Met considers to be healthy. For many decisions (for example, the selection of an ad agency for a country), the two organizations must reach a consensus. For other decisions, the country management is given some leeway but within clear guidelines. Thus the Smirnoff "Pure Thrill" advertising campaign featuring scenes as seen through a Smirnoff bottle (as discussed in Chapter 7) plays all over the world, but it is adapted to each individual country by using locally meaningful scenes or characters.

The CEO

In some firms the CEO is in charge of the brand, and all decisions that put the brand at risk need to be approved at the top. The CEO, of course, has the authority to cross business units to prevent risky programs or to provide resources when and where they are needed. Further, at least theoretically, he or she should have a long-term perspective. Unfortunately, the CEO also has a host of objectives involving operational measures (such as sales, costs, profits, and new products), many of which conflict with brand building. Moreover, the CEO must answer to a variety of constituencies (including shareholders, employees, customers, and retailers) while running a complex business. These multiple responsibilities make it difficult for a CEO to have single-minded concentration on building and protecting the brand.

The Brand Champion

In practice, brand stewardship is often housed at the highest level of the organization in some variant of the "CEO in charge" model. Typically the brand manager will put forth proposals and programs, and a senior management team will review them. This team is usually the de facto guardian of the brand, resisting efforts that may risk the brand franchise and encouraging programs that will enhance it. Despite their strategic perspective, though, such teams usually are spread thin over many brands and thus lack in-depth understanding of the current brand context. As a result, their oversight can be somewhat ad hoc.

One solution, used by Nestlé, is to create brand champions—senior executives who look after a single brand. Their responsibilities are similar to those of brand equity managers, except the brand champion is at the highest level of the organization. Further, because a top executive is involved, it is natural and appropriate for the scope of oversight to include all of the brand's business areas in all of the countries where the brand is active.

The Category Manager

The category manager role was created in response to the need for companies to think more broadly about efficiencies in distribution and logistics. When a brand identity is tied to a category (such as oral hygiene products), the category manager is in a good position to manage the brand strategically by developing strategies and programs among subbrands and across products within the category. Coordinating with one or two other category managers will be simpler than working with a dozen brand managers.

Even when a category manager is responsible for multiple brands, his or her overview perspective can still be useful in coordinating adjacent and related brands. Gillette toiletries, for example, include Right Guard, a Gillette Series (for men), White Rain, Dry Idea, and Gillette Foamy; Procter & Gamble has seven soaps and several detergents. Individual brand managers, without a category-level perspective, may not necessarily manage their brands optimally in relation to others in the category. The result may be cannibalization problems among too-similar brands.

The problem is that the category manager is often under even more pressure (from retailers and others) than managers of individual products to deliver efficiency and low prices. Brand building will not automatically be a priority.

SmithKline Beecham—the maker of Tums antacid, Contac cold medication and oral care products such as Aquafresh—has established a global category management structure.[2] Each category management team has research, brand, and market groups that report to a category management director at the vice-presidential level. The category management team is charged with developing ways to expand existing brands and offering new concepts for brand groups around the world.

The Brand Committee

Coordination across businesses can be addressed by a committee that spans the organization. Hewlett-Packard, for example, has a brand equity committee of communication executives representing the divisions that use the HP name. The role of these executives is to develop an identity position for HP, to make sure it is communicated, and to facilitate coordination and synergy in the brand-building activities.

The Communications Coordinator

To reduce the coordination problem and to increase opportunities for synergy, a firm can centralize the various communications functions under a single manager. Clorox, Coca-Cola, General Foods, and others have taken this route, placing a senior manager over such functional areas as advertising, media, consumer promotions, marketing research, marketing information services, and consumer response/promotion services. The problem with this approach is that line management is not involved, and staff functions often lack clout, especially when overall budgets are squeezed.

Another problem is that centralized efforts often run counter to the current management imperative to flatten the organization. Tom Peters, in *Liberation Management*, is one of many current gurus who preach that the modern organization must remove bureaucracy and flatten the organization dramatically by putting managers on the front lines, removing layers of management, decentralizing, and empowering.[3] Such an approach is appealing because it promises to improve productivity, responsiveness, and energy; however, it can make coordination of brand strategies more difficult. In that context, a brand equity manager or brand champion might be needed.

THE ROLE OF THE AGENCY

A brand strategy needs a single architect, someone who will implement and coordinate a cohesive brand strategy across multiple media and markets. The advertising agency is often a strong candidate for this role.

In fact, the best brand strategists may be agency personnel. Agencies attract employees who are interested in brand strategy, and these employees often develop brand strategy toolkits and gain insight and experience because of their exposure to different brands and brand contexts. Further, when brand managers change frequently, the agency—with its understanding of the brand and its heritage—is often by default the keeper of the brand equity.

Agencies also inherently provide a strong link between strategy and execution, because both functions are housed under the same roof. Strategy development in an agency thus is more likely to include issues of implementation. Even when they reside on the account side, agency brand strategists will have a good feel for execution. They are more likely to realize that most strategies will be ineffective unless an outstanding execution is generated.

Global brands can benefit from contributions of global agencies with strong country organizations in place. Most global agencies have experience in achieving consistency and synergy across countries. Even agency skeptics believe that agencies are well-positioned to adapt a brand identity from one nation to another.

The advertising agency, as a student of new communication forms and as a communication practitioner, is also in a good position to lead efforts to coordinate across media. Most major agencies have designed R&D programs that explore the use of emerging communication forms. Ogilvy & Mather, for example, has been experimenting with interactive advertising since the early 1980s. Many advertising agencies, however, still have a bias toward media advertising at a time when such advertising is becoming less important. When all you have is a hammer, as the saying goes, everything looks like a nail. Further, an agency's experience at managing alternative media (such as event sponsorship or direct marketing) may be limited.

The challenge for agencies is to be able to develop an integrated communications effort that will access and employ a wide range of communication vehicles. Several of the approaches used to create this ability are discussed below.

THE CONGLOMERATE COMMUNICATIONS COMPANY

The initial approach toward "solving" the integrated communications problem was to create agency conglomerates by acquiring other communications companies with complementary capabilities. The usual mix would include companies specializing in promotions, corporate design, package design, direct marketing, marketing research, trade shows, public relations, and perhaps event marketing. The hope was that internal synergy would result from cross-referrals and clients would receive one-stop coordinated communications efforts.

The general consensus, however is that the conglomerate approach did not work. The disparate organizations that made up the conglomerate had unique cultures and perspectives that did not blend well. Each unit tended to address communication problems as it always had, and the coordination breakthroughs rarely materialized. Further, it was difficult to convince clients that the best talent for each communications task resided within the conglomerate; thus, even if the coordination rationale was persuasive, it was not easy to convince clients to sign on. Somewhat ironically, even referrals within the conglomerate were avoided, since some units lacked confidence in their sister companies and considered them rivals for the client's communication budget.

THE IN-HOUSE GENERALIST AGENCY

Another option is to expand the agency's capabilities to include such other media as promotions, brochures, and public relations. Brand teams spanning communication vehicles can then deal with the coordination issue. A good example of this approach is the set of promotional programs designed for Saturn by Hal Riney & Partners (described in Chapter 2). Riney was named the guardian of the Saturn brand, and the agency created brochures, developed promotions, designed a Saturn site on the Internet, and even got involved in designing the retail concept.

Leo Burnett has deliberately avoided the conglomerate approach in favor of developing and integrating capabilities in direct marketing, promotions, public relations and new media into the firm. The agency's nonadvertising specialists are not allowed to work for non-Burnett clients.[4]

Technology can help an agency deliver efficiency and integrated communication across a variety of media. San Francisco's CKS Group uses technology to span advertising, trade shows, packaging, brochures, corporate design, virtual stores, and (for the Apple Newton) even an interactive kiosk. The heart of the CKS system is computer-stored and -processed imagery that can be shared across applications. A proposed logo or design can be seen on everything from brochures to signage to packaging; an image that works in an ad can be employed in a trade show banner, in a brochure, and on in-store merchandising. The work-in-progress and the final result are available to all members of the team at CKS and to their clients. CKS regards technology (including e-mail and the World Wide Web, as well as shared imagery) as the key to integrated communication.

This in-house generalist approach can work as long as the agency has the talent to handle the new services or the funds to hire new staff members. Agencies, however, do not always have the clients or the revenues to support such a diverse staff. Thus it is not clear that extending an agency broadly is always wise or feasible.

NEW AGENCY ORGANIZATIONAL FORMS: THE SERVICE CLUSTER

Keith Reinhard of DDB Needham Worldwide envisions a future advertising agency—which he terms Agency 2000—based on a dynamic service-cluster team concept.[5] A service-cluster team is a cluster of people drawn from all of the agency affiliate organizations (or perhaps from outside companies aligned with the agency). Strategically, the cluster has one purpose—to serve the client—and it has the flexibility to change with client needs. Thus if promotions are relatively important to the brand strategy for a client, the team will be weighted toward people from the promotions company. Although the promotion team members will still have the support, critical mass, and infrastructure of their promotion firm, the focus and thrust of the team will be the client and its needs.

This multifunctional, service-cluster team can actually form its own organization, as DDB Needham showed when it created a multifunctional agency for a single client, GTE. This agency, called Focus GTE, is composed of people drawn from the various DDB Needham affiliates, representing capabilities including sales promotion, direct marketing, and database marketing. The expectation is that drawing people from different organizations into one place may be the catalyst needed to get over the coordination barrier. In essence, this is an application of the virtual corporation—a fluid grouping of people or organizations in order to optimally address the task at hand.

The service-cluster team can be centrally located, but such a move is expensive and reduces the adaptability that service clusters were conceived to provide. An alternative is to use electronically based communication to link the service-cluster team members. Using computers and video links, all members of the team can share not only data, but ideas and executions as well. A London agency, Electronic Studio, is a leader in using computers and scanners to speed the ad creation process; its system even includes on-line connections to clients. This operating concept, perhaps augmented by video confer-encing, could be extended beyond advertising to include other communication vehicles. The hope is that the technology will link the team members while maintaining the adaptability that a large agency can provide.

A key characteristic of a service-cluster team is that it will focus on creating ideas rather than advertisements. A prime agency differ-ential advantage is its ability to hire, train, and support strategic and tactical creative talent. The concept is to channel this creativity into generating ideas that can drive a brand. These "brand ideas" (a term used by J. Walter Thompson) will then be implemented by whatever media are most appropriate—the implementation will not be re-stricted to advertising. The Black Gold story (below) illustrates.

THE BLACK GOLD STORY

The Danish beer Black Gold was sucessfully launched with a com-munications campaign in which conventional media advertising played a small role. Their agency, DDB Needham, developed an idea for the brand identity first and then located the best vehicles to implement the ideas. The approach differed, therefore, from that of an agency creating an ad campaign.

The identity was to be avant garde to the extreme, mysterious, sensual, and intellectual. The centerpiece of the identity creation effort was an eerie, dramatic, black-and-white six-minute Black Gold trailer that was shown in movie houses. This powerful short piece created an emotional, distinctive platform for the brand. The appearance of the trailer was advertised in advance so that people in the theater would be waiting for it. Four evocative scenes from the trailer were turned into postcards and posters (see Figure 11-2) which provided additional exposure and also a more intimate involvement when they were used. A relevant idea was thus the basis for the campaign. The idea drove the execution.

A radical change in thinking inside agencies is required for them to accept that a brand idea, rather than a great ad concept, can drive a communication program. The underlying premise is that advertising need not be the principal force behind brand communications. A

A Black Gold Visual

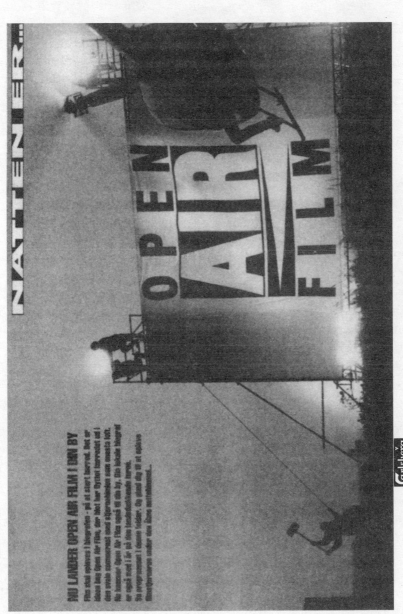

FIGURE 11-2
A Black Gold Visual (Continued)

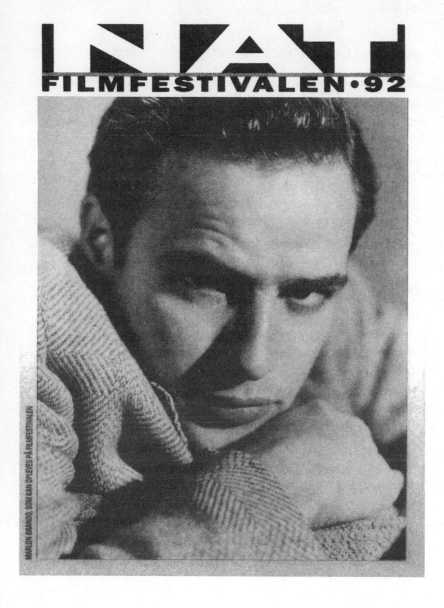

Reproduced with permission from DDB Needham Worldwide A/S.

sponsorship (like the WordPerfect bike racing team, or the José Cuervo volleyball sponsorship) might instead play the central role in communicating the brand identity.

THE AGENCY AS A COMMUNICATION INTEGRATOR

One of the problems of the service-cluster approach is that it assumes that the best talent is available within the agency umbrella. In this era of specialization and fragmentation, that supposition is unlikely. Another approach is to redefine the agency as an integrator of communication services drawn from sources outside the agency. The agency as an integrator and coordinator draws upon its potential to be:

- a good brand strategist
- creative in proposing communication solutions
- well versed in alternative media
- excellent in execution, particularly in developing themes and visual imagery
- an objective voice in client politics

Note that these are *potential* strengths; they will emerge only at the best agencies when they are operating well.

General Motors is one firm moving toward expanding the role of the agency to that of a "general contractor." The agency is expected to manage GM brands while turning to specialists, such as event sponsorship firms and external boutiques, to implement specific initiatives. The agency role is to create ideas, select who will implement those ideas inside or outside the agency, and manage the process to ensure that an integrated communications effort results.[6]

THE CLIENT APPROACH

For many clients, the solution is not to rely on an agency, but rather, to bring the brand strategy in-house. There are often sound arguments for this approach. First, agencies may be good at creating ads, but brand strategy may be better planned by the brand management team. In fact, developing such a strategy should be a top priority for the brand team. If outside help is needed, an agency may not be the best source, particularly if it has have limited research capabilities.

TEN GUIDELINES FOR BUILDING STRONG BRANDS

1.   *Brand identity*. Have an identity for each brand. Consider the perspectives of the brand-as-person, brand-as-organization, and brand-as-symbol, as well as the brand-as-product. Identify the core identity. Modify the identity as needed for different market segments and products. Remember that an image is how you are perceived, and an identity is how you aspire to be perceived.

2.   *Value proposition*. Know the value proposition for each brand that has a driver role. Consider emotional and self-expressive benefits as well as functional benefits. Know how endorser brands will provide credibility. Understand the brand–customer relationship.

3.   *Brand position*. For each brand, have a brand position that will provide clear guidance to those implementing a communication program. Recall that a position is the part of the identity and value proposition that is to be actively communicated.

4.   *Execution*. Execute the communication program so that it not only is on target with the identity and position but achieves brilliance and durability. Generate alternatives and consider options beyond media advertising.

5.   *Consistency over time*. Have as a goal a consistent identity, position, and execution over time. Maintain symbols, imagery, and metaphors that work. Understand and resist organizational biases toward changing the identity, position, and execution.

One client firm found only 13 percent of agency compensation went toward creative effort. Stripping the agency of other responsibilities (including media buying and market research) and adjusting the compensation accordingly saved a substantial sum.

Second, in this era of market fragmentation and media specialization, it may be necessary to employ a team of specialized communication firms that are each the best at what they do. An ad agency might be a team member when advertisements are needed; however, when interactive media or event sponsorships are needed, agencies may not be the best choice.

Third, a client can develop specialized expertise—including research, media buying, and strategy consulting—when needed.

6. *Brand system*. Make sure the brands in the portfolio are consistent and synergistic. Know their roles. Have or develop silver bullets to help support brand identities and positions. Exploit branded features and services. Use subbrands to clarify and modify. Know the strategic brands.

7. *Brand leverage*. Extend brands and develop co-branding programs only if the brand identity will be both used and reinforced. Identify range brands and, for each, develop an identity and specify how that identity will be different in disparate product contexts. If a brand is moved up or down, take care to manage the integrity of the resulting brand identities.

8. *Tracking brand equity*. Track brand equity over time, including awareness, perceived quality, brand loyalty, and especially brand associations. Have specific communication objectives. Especially note areas where the brand identity and position are not reflected in the brand image.

9. *Brand responsibility*. Have someone in charge of the brand who will create the identity and position and coordinate the execution over organizational units, media, and markets. Beware when a brand is being used in a business in which it is not the cornerstone.

10. *Invest in brands*. Continue investing in brands even when the financial goals are not being met.

Campbell's Soup even produced its own Lifetime cable TV special on the key role teachers play in educating children as part of its Labels for Education, cookbook publishing, and point-of-sale programs.[7]

A PARTING WORD

In summary, building strong brands—those that will create customer interest and loyalty by providing a value proposition and a basis for a relationship—requires a clear, effective specification of the brand identity and position. To guide the marketing program most effectively, the identity needs to include, in addition to the core identity, an extended identity and identity symbols. A common pitfall when creating brand identities is to focus on brand attributes. Firms must break out of the brand-as-product box by considering emotional and self-expressive benefits as well as functional benefits and by considering the brand-as-person, the brand-as-organization, and the brand-as-symbol perspectives.

A key to strong brands is to have consistency over time. A firm can maintain consistency by creating an identity and position that will endure, supporting it with brilliant execution, and resisting the powerful biases toward change.

The brand system concept adds a new dimension to the management of brands. A brand system, consisting of intertwined and overlapping brands and subbrands, can generate confusion and inconsistency; the challenge is to manage it effectively so it instead generates impact and efficiency. The key is to understand the roles each brand plays and to manage those brands in the context of their roles.

A brand-nurturing organization is the base on which successful brands are built. The organization needs to be structured so that someone is clearly in charge of creating an identity/position and coordinating the implementation across organizational units, media, and markets.

Brands are the basis for sustainable advantage for most organizations. However, strong brands do not just happen. Rather, they result from the creation of winning brand strategies and brilliant executions from committed, disciplined organizations. This book has attempted to provide concepts, tools, and models to help strategists with that management challenge.

QUESTIONS TO CONSIDER

1. How is your firm now organized? Who is in charge of the major brands? Do they have incentives to build those brands for the future? Does their perspective have a broad enough scope with respect to media, markets, and products?
2. What coordination problems exist across the organization, brands, or markets? What coordination problems exist across media? Are organizational talents and incentives in place which will access the most effective media vehicles to implement brand strategies?

NOTES

Chapter 1. What is a Strong Brand?

1. Drawn in part from Douglas Collins, *The Story of Kodak*, New York: Harry N. Abrams, Inc., 1990.
2. Wayne D. Hoyer and Steven P. Brown, "Effects of Brand Awareness on Choice for a Common, Repeat Purchase Product," *Journal of Consumer Research*, September, 1990, pp. 141–148.
3. Kodak Annual Report, 1993.
4. Robert Jacobson and David A. Aaker, "The Strategic Role of Product Quality," *Journal of Marketing*, October 1987, pp. 31–44.
5. Eugene W. Anderson, Claes Fornell, and Donald R. Lehmann, "Customer Satisfaction, Market Share and Profitability: Findings from Sweden," *Journal of Marketing*, July 1994.
6. David A. Aaker and Robert Jacobson, "The Financial Information Content of Perceived Quality," *Journal of Marketing Research*, May 1994, pp. 191–201.
7. David A. Aaker, "Managing Assets and Skills: The Key to a Sustainable Competitive Advantage," *California Management Review*, Winter 1989, pp. 91–106.
8. The Schlitz story is described in *Managing Brand Equity*, Chapter 4.
9. For example, my colleague Kevin Lane Keller defines consumer-based brand equity in terms of brand knowledge and unique brand associations. Kevin Lane Keller, "Conceptualizing, Measuring, and Managing Customer-Based Brand Equity," *Journal of Marketing*, January 1992, pp. 1–22.
10. Frederick F. Reichheld, "Loyalty-Based Management," *Harvard Business Review*, March-April 1993.

11. Ibid.

12. Christopher W. L. Hart, James L. Heskett, and W. Earl Sasser, Jr., "The Profitable Art of Service Recovery," *Harvard Business Review*, July-August 1990.

13. Frederick F. Reichheld, and W. Earl Sasser, Jr., "Zero Defections: Quality Comes to Services," *Harvard Business Review*, September-October 1990.

14. An example of an event store would be a Nike store in which music and graphic make the store visit an event where people can experience the Nike identity.

15. Dertouzos, Michael L., Richard K. Lester, and Robert M. Solow, *Made in America: Regaining the Productive Edge*, Cambridge: MIT Press, 1988.

Chapter 2. The Saturn Story

1. This chapter is adapted from the article "Building a Brand: The Saturn Story," by David A. Aaker, which appeared in the *California Management Review* in Winter 1994 and received the Pacific Telesis Foundation award for the article published in Volume 36 of that journal that made the most important contribution to improving the practice of management. The use of material from the article is by permission of the *California Management Review*, which owns the copyright. Thanks are due to Bob Ellis of Hal Riney, Tom Shaver (formerly Saturn's advertising manager) and Roberto Alvarez, all of whom made helpful comments on earlier drafts. The material for the article was drawn in part from discussions with Saturn executives, retailers, and agency people and from secondary sources such as Richard LeFauve, "One More Chance," *MIT Management*, Spring 1992, pp. 2–7; David Woodruff, "Saturn," *Business Week*, August 17, 1992, pp. 85–91; Richard G. Lefauve and Arnoldo C. Hax, "Managerial and Technological Innovations at Saturn Corporation," *MIT Management*, Spring, 1992, pp. 8–19; Raymond Serafin, "The Saturn Story," *Advertising Age*, November 16, 1992, pp. 1, 13; Alice Z. Cuneo and Raymond Serafin, "With Saturn, Riney Rings Up a Winner," *Advertising Age*, April 14, 1993, pp. 2–3; T. W. Shaver, remarks to San Diego Advertising Club, November 6, 1991; Don Hudler, address to the Adcraft Club of Detroit, January 17, 1992; 1991 brochure introducing the Saturn.

2. The 1994 Saturn brochure is the source of all of these quotations.

3. Roger B. Smith, statement at the Saturn news conference, January 8, 1985.

4. Richard G. Lefauve and Arnoldo C. Hax, "Managerial and Technological Innovations at Saturn Corporation," *MIT Management*, Spring 1992, pp. 8–19.

5. One by the NADA (National Automobile Dealers Association) and the other by the J. D. Power Company. See Hudler, op cit.

6. Lefauve and Hax, op. cit.

7. 1993 Kelly Blue Book Official Price Guide, Western Edition, September–October 1993.

8. Hudler, op cit.
9. Hudler, private communication, June 1995.
10. Charles J. Murray, "Engineer on a Mission," *Design News*, February 22, 1993, pp. 102–111.
11. T. W. Shaver, op. cit.
12. Don Hudler, op. cit., 1992.

Chapter 3. The Brand Identity System

1. This chapter benefited from long discussions with Scott Talgo of the St. James Group. His experience and insight permeate the chapter.
2. From the cartoon strip "Non Sequitur" by Wiley, *San Francisco Examiner*, February 12, 1995.
3. Credit for this insight, as for many others in this book, is due to Scott Talgo of the St. James group.
4. Erdener Kaynak and S. Tamer Cavusgil, "Consumer Attitudes Towards Products of Foreign Origin: Do They Vary Across Product Classes," *International Journal of Advertising*, 1983, pp. 147–157.
5. C. Min Han and Van Terpstra, "Country-of-Origin Effects for Uni-National and Bi-National Products," *Journal of International Business Studies*, Summer 1988, pp. 235–256.
6. Items drawn in part from the annual reports of McDonald's from 1990 to 1994.
7. Items drawn in part from Nike annual reports from 1991 to 1993 and from Geraldine E. Willigan, "High-Performance Marketing: An Interview with Nike's Phil Knight," *Harvard Business Review*, July-August 1992, pp. 91–101.
8. Figure 3–10 is adapted from Jerome Kagan, Ernest Havemann and Julius Segal, *Psychology: An Introduction*, 5th edition (New York: Harcourt Brace Jovanovich, 1984), p. 25.
9. Duane Knapp, a branding consultant, is an advocate of using value propositions to help guide brand strategies.
10. Stuart Agres, "Emotion in Advertising: An Agency's View," in Stuart J. Agres, Julie A. Edell, and Tony M. Dubitsky, *Emotion in Advertising* (New York: Quorum, 1990), pp. 1–18.
11. Russell W. Belk, "Possessions and the Extended Self," *Journal of Consumer Research*, September 1988, p. 139.

Chapter 4. Organizational Associations

1. This material in part has been drawn from Bo Burlingham, "This Woman Has Changed Business Forever," *Inc.*, June, 1990, pp. 34–44; interview with Anita Roddick, *Business Ethics*, September/October 1992, pp. 27–30; Anita

Roddick, *Body and Soul* New York: Crown Trade Paperbacks, 1992. Thanks to Lorilei Beer of The Body Shop for helpful suggestions.

2. The material in this section is drawn in part from personal discussions with Japanese executives.

3. "Good Citizenship Is Good Business," *Fortune*, March 21, 1994, pp. 15–16.

4. Judann Dagnoli, "Consciously Green," *Advertising Age*, September 16, 1991, p. 14.

5. Lawrence E. Joseph, "The Greening of American Business," *Vis a Vis*, May 1991, p. 32.

6. Bradley Johnson, "Nestlé Unifies Image," *Advertising Age*, C 26, 1992, p. 3

7. Marvin E. Goldberg and Jon Hartwick, "The Effects of Advertiser Reputation and Extremity of Advertising Claim on Advertising Effectiveness," *Journal of Consumer Research*, September 1990, pp. 172–179.

8. Jennifer Aaker, "The Effect of Country-of-Origin Information on Product Evaluation," working paper, Stanford University, 1994.

9. C. Min Han and Van Terpstra, "Country-of-Origin Effects for Uni-National and Bi-National Products," *Journal of International Business Studies*, Summer 1988, pp. 235–256.

10. Kevin Lane Keller, my research colleague and a professor at the University of North Carolina, convinced me over the course of many conversations that corporate brands work in large part by providing credibility.

11. Kevin Lane Keller and David A. Aaker, "Managing the Corporate Brand: The Effects of Corporate Images and Corporate Brand Extensions," working paper, 1995.

Chapter 5. Brand Personality

1. This chapter benefited from the involvement of Jennifer Aaker. The first three sections, in particular, draw heavily on her conceptualizations and research. In addition, she made many substantive comments and suggestions throughout.

2. John W. Schouten and James H. McAlexander, "Subcultures of Consumption: An Ethnography of the New Bikers," *Journal of Consumer Research*, June 1995, pp. 43–61.

3. Ibid.

4. "The Marketing 100," *Advertising Age*, July 5, 1993, p. S30.

5. Jennifer L. Aaker, "Conceptualizing and Measuring Brand Personality: A Brand Personality Scale," working paper, Stanford University, December 1995.

6. Joseph T. Plummer, "How Personality Makes a Difference," *Journal of Advertising Research* 24 (December/January 1984), pp. 27–31.

NOTES 363

7. David Mick and Susan Fournier, "Process and Meaning in Consumer Satisfaction: A Multimethod Inquiry on Technological Products," working paper, Harvard University, 1994.
8. Jennifer Aaker, op. cit. A 42-item BPS used to measure brand personality consists of selected items from each of the 15 facets shown in Figure 5–2.
9. Raymond Serafin, "Chevy Claims 'Genuine Icon Status,'" *Advertising Age*, March 21, 1994, p. 1, 44.
10. Grant McCracken, "Culture and Consumption: A Theoretical Account of the Structure and Movement of the Cultural Meaning of Consumer Goods," *Journal of Consumer Research*, June 1986, pp. 71–84; Grant McCracken, "Who Is the Celebrity Endorser? Cultural Foundations of the Endorsement Process," *Journal of Consumer Research*, December 1989, pp. 310–321.
11. David A. Aaker and Douglas Stayman, "Implementing the Concept of Transformational Advertising," *Psychology and Marketing*, May-June 1992, pp. 237–253.
12. Russell W. Belk, "Possessions and the Extended Self," *Journal of Consumer Research*, September 1988, pp. 139–166.
13. Joel B. Cohen, "An Over-Extended Self?" *Journal of Consumer Research*, June 1989, pp. 125–127.
14. Margaret Mead was one of the first modern social scientists to suggest that today's world requires multiple social selves; see Margaret Mead, *Mind, Self and Society* (Chicago: University of Chicago Press, 1934). For an excellent commentary, see Hazel Markus and Elissa Wurf, "The Dynamic Self Concept: A Social Psychological Perspective," *Annual Review of Psychology* 38, 1987, pp. 299–337.
15. Jennifer Aaker, "The Moderating Effect of Context on the Impact of Brand Personality on Brand Choice," Working Paper, UCLA School of Management, 1995.
16. Fred Posner, "You Have to Have a Brand Become a Friend," speech given to the Advertising and Promotion Workshop, February 1, 1993.
17. Raymond Serafin and Leah Rickard, "Lighting Up Neon," *Advertising Age*, February 7, 1994, p. 16.
18. Max Blackston, "Beyond Brand Personality: Building Brand Relationships," in David A. Aaker and Alexander Biel, *Brand Equity and Advertising* (Hillsdale, NJ: Lawrence Erlbaum Associates, 1993), pp. 113–134.
19. Blackston, op. cit.
20. Susan Fournier, "A Consumer-Brand Relationship Framework for Strategic Brand Management," Ph.D. dissertation, University of Florida, 1994.
21. David M. Buss and Kenneth H. Craik, "The Act Frequency Approach to Personality," *Psychological Review* 90, 1983, pp. 105–126.

22. Fournier, op. cit.
23. France Leclerc, Bernd H. Schmitt, and Laurette Dube, "Foreign Branding and Its Effects on Product Perceptions and Attitudes," *Journal of Marketing Research*, May 1994, pp. 263–270.
24. Jennifer Aaker, "User Imagery Versus Brand Personality," working paper, UCLA, 1994.

Chapter 6. Identity Implementation

1. Paul Feldwick, *BMP Works*, Henley-on-Thames: NTC Publications Limited, 1992.
2. Adrian J. Slywotzky and Benson P. Shapiro, "Leveraging to Beat the Odds: The New Marketing Mind-Set," *Harvard Business Review*, September-October, 1993, pp. 97–107.
3. For an introduction to strategy concepts and supporting analysis approaches, see my book *Developing Business Strategies*, 4th edition, New York: John Wiley, 1995.
4. Kenton Low, "Revitalizing Brand Image Can Often Be More Effective and Less Risky Than Introducing a New Product," address to the 1993 Brand Marketing Forum, Chicago.
5. Kathleen Deveny, "For Coffee's Big Three, A Gourmet-Brew Boom Proves Embarrassing Bust," *Wall Street Journal*, November 4, 1993, p. B1.
6. Susan Caminti, "A Star is Born," *Fortune*, Autumn/Winter 1993, pp. 45–47.
7. This was stimulated by Lynn Upshaw, *Building Brand Identity*, New York: John Wiley & Sons, 1995.

Chapter 7. Brand Strategies over Time

1. Elaine Underwood, "Proper I.D.," *Brandweek*, August 8, 1994, pp. 25–30.

Chapter 8. Managing Brand Systems

1. Peter H. Farquhar, Julia Y. Han, Paul M. Herr, and Yuji Ijiri, "Strategies for Leveraging Master Brands," *Marketing Research*, September 1992, pp. 32–39.
2. Sylvie LaForet and John Saunders, "Managing Brand Portfolios: How the Leaders Do It," *Journal of Advertising Research*, September-October 1994, pp. 64–76.
3. C. Whan Park, Sung Youl Jun, and Allan D. Shocker, "Composite Brand Extension: Its Process, Outcomes, and Promise," working paper, University of Pittsburgh, April 1994.
4. For a more complete description of strategic opportunism and an alternative, strategic visions, see David A. Aaker, *Developing Business Strategies*, 4th edition, New York: John Wiley, 1995.

5. Gregory S. Carpenter, Rashi Glazer, and Kent Nakamoto, "Meaningful Brands from Meaningless Differentiation: The Dependence on Irrelevant Attributes," *Journal of Marketing Research*, August 1994, pp. 339–350.

Chapter 9. Leveraging the Brand

1. All ConAgra brands listed are registered trademarks.
2. ConAgra internal records.
3. John A. Quelch and David Kenny, "Extend Profits, Not Product Lines," *Harvard Business Review*, September-October 1994.
4. Carol M. Motley and Srinivas K. Reddy, "Moving Up or Moving Down: An Investigation of Repositioning Strategies," Working Paper 93-363, College of Business Administration, University of Georgia, 1993.
5. Johan Arndt, "Role of Product Related Conversation in the Diffusion of a New Product," *Journal of Marketing Research* 3 (August), pp. 291–295.
6. Kevin Lane Keller and David A. Aaker, "The Effects of Sequential Introduction of Brand Extensions," *Journal of Marketing Research*, February 1992, pp. 35–50.
7. Jean B. Romeo "The Effect of Negative Information on the Evaluations of Brand Extensions and the Family Brand," in *Advances in Consumer Research*, Rebecca H. Holman and Michael R. Solomon, eds., Association for Consumer Research,1991, pp. 399–406.
8. Subodh Bhat and Mary R. Zimmer, "The Effect of a Brand Extension's Fit and Quality on Attitude toward the Extension and Attitude Toward the Parent Brand," working paper, San Francisco State University, 1994.
9. Barbara Loken and Deborah Roedder John, "Diluting Brand Beliefs: When Do Brand Extension Have a Negative Impact?," *Journal of Marketing*, July 1993, pp. 71–84.
10. David A. Aaker and Stephen Markey, "The Effects of Subbrand Names on the Core Brand," working paper, University of California, Berkeley, 1994.
11. Peter H. Farquhar, Julia Y. Han, Paul M. Herr, and Yuji Ijiri, "Strategies for Leveraging Master Brands," *Marketing Research*, September 1992, pp. 32–39.
12. Peter A. Dacin and Daniel C. Smith, "The Effect of Brand Portfolio Characteristics on Consumer Evaluations of Brand Extensions," *Journal of Marketing Research*, May 1994, pp. 229–242.
13. J. Walter Thompson presentation at the Philip Morris workshop "Growing the Business Via Brands and People," October 1992.
14. Susan M. Broniarczyk and Joseph W. Alba, "The Importance of the Brand in Brand Extension," *Journal of Marketing Research*, May 1994, pp. 214–228.
15. David A. Aaker and Kevin Lane Keller, "Consumer Evaluations of Brand Extensions," *Journal of Marketing*, January 1990, pp. 27–41; and Keller and Aaker, op. cit.

16. C. Whan Park, Michael S. McCarty, and Sandra J. Milberg, "An Examination of the Negative Reciprocity Effects Associated with Direct and Sub-Branding Extension Strategies," working paper, University of Pittsburgh, 1994..

Chapter 10. Measuring Brand Equity Across Products and Markets

1. Stewart Owen, "The Landor ImagePower Survey: A Global Assessment of Brand Strength," in David A. Aaker and Alexander L. Biel, *Brand Equity and Advertising*, Hillsdale, NJ: Lawrence Erlbaum Associates, 1993, pp. 11–30.
2. Robert Jacobson and David A. Aaker, "The Strategic Role of Product Quality," *Journal of Marketing*, October 1987, pp. 31–44.
3. John Morton, "Improved Quality = Less Price Elasticity," Total Research, in-house publication 1993.

Chapter 11. Organizing for Brand Building

1. Sara Lee Corporation, Annual Report, 1994.
2. Patricia Winters, "SmithKline Realigns by Category," *Advertising Age*, March 8, 1993, p. 17.
3. Tom Peters, *Liberation Management*, New York: Alfred A. Knopf, 1992.
4. Julie Liesse, "Fully Integrating Marketing Equation," *Advertising Age*, September 12, 1994, p. S2.
5. Pat Sloan, "DDB Needham Clusters for the Future," *Advertising Age*, May 31, 1993, p. 4.
6. Michael McCarthy, "GM to Redefine Agency Roles, Fees," *Brandweek*, October 17, 1994, p. 3.
7. See *Advertising Age*, January 25, 1993, for comments contrasting agency and client views.

INDEX

367

as reflection of current perceptions, 180
Branding benefits, 257–64
Brand managers, 344–48
Brand name
  dominance, 15–16
  in updating brand identity, 232
Brand name awareness
  as asset in brand equity, 8
  creating brand awareness,
    16–17
  measures of Brand Equity Ten,
    318–19, 330–31
  relative strength of brand,
    10–16
  Saturn creation of brand awareness, 41
  strategic awareness, 17
Brand Personality Scale,
    143–44
Brand position
  advantage over competitors,
    182–83
  attainability, 185
  defined, 71, 176
  identity trap, 71–72
  power of, 201–5
  as reflection of desired perceptions, 180–82
  role of, 176–85
Brand positioning statement,
    183–85
Brand relationship quality (BRQ),
    166–67
Brands
  creating upscale version, 287–91
  as descriptor, 249–51
  distinct from product, 72–73
  expression of personality with,
    155–57
  idea of relationship with person,
    159–67

management with complexity,
    241–42
moving toward high end,
    287–91
moving toward low end, 278–86
as organization, 130–31
as person, 83–84
as personal statement, 156
presence and success, 127–28
roles in brand system, 243–47
strategic analysis of, 189–201
as symbol, 84–85
top brands (Interbrand), 313–14
See also Brand building; Co-
    brands; Corporate brand;
    Driver brand; Identity, brand;
    Leveraging the brand; Loyalty,
    brand; Personality,
    brand; Strategic brands
Brands, strong
  building, 26–36, 356–57
  factors conflicting with
    building, 26
Brand strategy
  complexity and relationships, 27,
    31–32
  in Japan, 110–14
Brand strength
  brand dynamics model, 307
  Interbrand criteria, 313–14
  Saturn, 38–39
Brand system
  audit, 300–301
  benefits of branding features of,
    257–61
  goals of, 241–42
  hierarchies in, 242–43
  managing, 241–42
  role of subbrand in, 248–57
  See also Identity, brand
Brand system audit, 300–301
Bronizrczyk, Susan M., 297

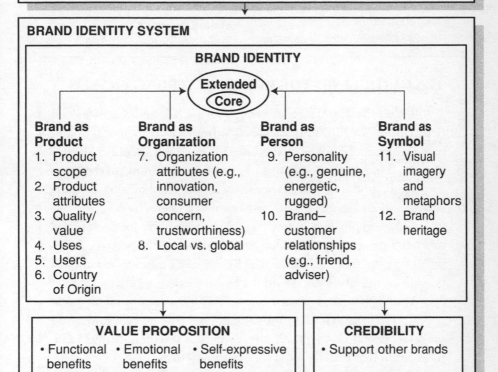

STRATEGIC BRAND ANALYSIS

Customer Analysis
- Trends
- Motivation
- Unmet needs
- Segmentation

Competitor Analysis
- Brand image/identity
- Strengths, strategies
- Vulnerabilities

Self-Analysis
- Existing brand image
- Brand heritage
- Strengths/capabilities
- Organization values

BRAND IDENTITY SYSTEM

BRAND IDENTITY

Extended

Core

Brand as Product
1. Product scope
2. Product attributes
3. Quality/value
4. Uses
5. Users
6. Country of Origin

Brand as Organization
7. Organization attributes (e.g., innovation, consumer concern, trustworthiness)
8. Local vs. global

Brand as Person
9. Personality (e.g., genuine, energetic, rugged)
10. Brand–customer relationships (e.g., friend, adviser)

Brand as Symbol
11. Visual imagery and metaphors
12. Brand heritage

VALUE PROPOSITION
- Functional benefits
- Emotional benefits
- Self-expressive benefits

CREDIBILITY
- Support other brands

BRAND–CUSTOMER RELATIONSHIP

BRAND IDENTITY IMPLEMENTATION SYSTEM

BRAND POSITION
- Subset of the brand identity and value proposition
- At a target audience
- To be actively communicated
- Providing competitive advantage

EXECUTION
- Generate alternatives
- Symbols and metaphors
- Testing

TRACKING

TEN GUIDELINES FOR BUILDING STRONG BRANDS

1.   *Brand identity*. Have an identity for each brand. Consider the perspectives of the brand-as-person, brand-as-organization, and brand-as-symbol, as well as the brand-as-product. Identify the core identity. Modify the identity as needed for different market segments and products. Remember that an image is how you are perceived, and an identity is how you aspire to be perceived.

2.   *Value proposition*. Know the value proposition for each brand that has a driver role. Consider emotional and self-expressive benefits as well as functional benefits. Know how endorser brands will provide credibility. Understand the brand–customer relationship.

3.   *Brand position*. For each brand, have a brand position that will provide clear guidance to those implementing a communication program. Recall that a position is the part of the identity and value proposition that is to be actively communicated.

4.   *Execution*. Execute the communication program so that it not only is on target with the identity and position but achieves brilliance and durability. Generate alternatives and consider options beyond media advertising.

5.   *Consistency over time*. Have as a goal a consistent identity, position, and execution over time. Maintain symbols, imagery, and metaphors that work. Understand and resist organizational biases toward changing the identity, position, and execution.

6.   *Brand system*. Make sure the brands in the portfolio are consistent and synergistic. Know their roles. Have or develop silver bullets to help support brand identities and positions. Exploit branded features and services. Use subbrands to clarify and modify. Know the strategic brands.

7.   *Brand leverage*. Extend brands and develop co-branding programs only if the brand identity will be both used and reinforced. Identify range brands and, for each, develop an identity and specify how that identity will be different in disparate product contexts. If a brand is moved up or down, take care to manage the integrity of the resulting brand identities.

8.   *Tracking brand equity*. Track brand equity over time, including awareness, perceived quality, brand loyalty, and especially brand associations. Have specific communication objectives. Especially note areas where the brand identity and position are not reflected in the brand image.

9.   *Brand responsibility*. Have someone in charge of the brand who will create the identity and position and coordinate the execution over organizational units, media, and markets. Beware when a brand is being used in a business in which it is not the cornerstone.

10.   *Invest in brands*. Continue investing in brands even when the financial goals are not being met.

ABOUT THE AUTHOR

David A. Aaker, the E.T. Grether Professor of Marketing Strategy at the University of California at Berkeley, is the author of ten books and more than eighty articles on branding, advertising, and business strategy. One of the most cited and quoted authors in the field of marketing, Professor Aaker consults and lectures extensively throughout the world on brand strategy problems and issues. He lives in Orinda, California.